Surveillance Countermeasures

The Professional's Guide
to Countering Hostile Surveillance Threats

by Aden C. Magee

DORRANCE PUBLISHING CO
EST. 1920
PITTSBURGH, PENNSYLVANIA 15238

Dorrance Publishing Co
585 Alpha Drive
Suite 103
Pittsburgh, PA 15238
Visit our website at www.dorrancebookstore.com

ISBN: 978-1- 4809-8746- 3
eISBN: 978-1- 4809-8861- 3

Table of Contents

Observation Of Dress
Observation Of Disguise

Countersurveillance Planning
The Countersurveillance Operation

Observation At Night
Vehicular Surveillance Detection And Antisurveillance At Night
Foot Surveillance Detection And Antisurveillance At Night

PREFACE:

Important Up-front Perspectives from the Author

It is an honor to provide *the authoritative work on the topic of surveillance countermeasures* to the ever-challenged field of security professionals and the scores of individuals who endeavor to pursue the highest degree of personal security possible. Surveillance countermeasures are actions taken by an individual or security detail to identify the presence of surveillance, and if necessary, to elude or evade the individual or group conducting the surveillance. In today's prolific hostile threat environment, surveillance countermeasures expertise is a necessary, fundamental basis of security knowledge. This manual now supersedes the previous professional standards as the most authoritative source of surveillance countermeasures knowledge.

This new age "instant classic" for security professionals and individuals concerned with personal security is based on the time-validated techniques as chronicled in the two all-time classics and best sellers in the genre (*Surveillance Countermeasures*, in publication (two editions) from 1994 – 2017), and (*Countering Hostile Surveillance*, in publication from 2006 – 2017). As the originating dates of these two classics suggest, they both draw from a legacy of experience and incorporate techniques that have proven effective in countering the objectives of hostile, covert elements threatening the security of individuals throughout the years. However, as will be addressed, the dates of publication should not be interpreted to suggest that the material is in any way dated or less relevant today; rather, the popular longevity of these publications is a testament to the enduring relevance of the information as it applies to the practice of surveillance countermeasures today and into the future. Therefore, this is a logical departure point at which to retire these two classics and reshape the knowledge therein to the benefit of future generations.

The two books that formed the basis for this updated edition have been overwhelmingly regarded as masterstrokes in the security field. *Surveillance Countermeasures* was a landmark book that established the first-ever methodical approach for surveillance countermeasures practices based on real-world experiences operating against the world's most sophisticated surveillance elements, and based on observations and lessons learned conducting surveillance operations against covert elements trained in and executing the most advanced surveillance countermeasures tactics, techniques, and procedures. The follow-on companion-piece, *Countering Hostile Surveillance*, is an unprecedented and still unparalleled work that provided the next logical progression into advanced concepts and procedures; rising to the Master's level in surveillance countermeasures that could only be recounted and compiled by highly experienced covert warriors who have actually stalked the streets and stood in the shadows. This work now represents the full-spectrum amalgam of surveillance countermeasures methodologies ranging from the foundational baseline of tactics and techniques to the most advanced concepts and procedures.

In addition to a timely and comprehensive resource that the bad guys must hate to see, this updated compilation benefits greatly from the feedback and dialogue with community professionals, resulting from the wide popularity of the two classic works it encompasses and builds upon. Due to years of reader reviews and professional engagements, the author has the benefit of inputs from a wide range of consumers. Although many of the contributors to this base of knowledge were bona fide security experts, many were obviously relative novices who may have lacked full perspective regarding the tradecraft and threat environment, and probably did not maximize the informational value at hand. Therefore, this preface provides the unique opportunity to pre-emptively address a few of the common biases, false assumptions, and general misconceptions that may prejudice readers and detract from their appreciation of the wealth of knowledge this work provides.

The *first key misconception* is a general perception among some that the human-centric applications that should serve as the foundational basis for any effective surveillance countermeasures effort are dated and less relevant given the rapid development of hostile surveillance-enabling *technical capabilities*. In current practice, however, this is a gross misconception as the "non-technical" techniques to ensure personal security/protection have always been (and continue to be) the primary methods employed by professionals who understand the full-spectrum operational environment. To address this issue and dispel any misconceptions the reader may have in this regard, this work dedicates an entire Appendix titled "Technical Surveillance Countermeasures and the Limitations of Technical Surveillance" (Appendix 1) to this topic — so jump to that Appendix anytime to understand the professionals' perspective on this issue. As a teaser, and as is detailed in this Appendix, the overriding irony of the technology myth is that the time-proven techniques developed to ensure absolute security from adversarial elements have actually been developed to be *technologically agnostic* — meaning they were intended to apply across the continuum of operations regardless of how sophisticated opposing technical capabilities may become. Those who have actually walked the mean streets understand that hitching one's wagon to the "pop culture" tech train is a dangerous and potentially lethal risk.

Another common comment (misconception) throughout the years is that a comprehensive work such as this, that provides techniques and processes to counter the world's most sophisticated surveillance threats, is "overkill" in cases wherein the most likely threat to many of the readers (or their clients) may be the lone "gumshoe" or stalker, or at worst case a resource-constrained surveillance effort that is limited to two or three individuals/vehicles. In response to these concerns, readers are encouraged to educate themselves at the "master's" level of understanding, and then scale this understanding to the specific case-by-case circumstances of any given surveillance countermeasures effort. Not to disparage any other authors' experience-base or credibility, but this work is not based on one or a few antidotal and parochial experiences; rather, it draws on real-world observations and the best practices employed by the world's elite shadow warriors. Given this basis, this manual details surveillance countermeasures concepts, techniques, and procedures that are proven effective against the spectrum of surveillance capabilities ranging from the very basic to the world's most sophisticated. Rather than instructing to the "lowest common denominator," as most tactics-focused publications do, this manual takes the opposite approach. The practitioner who can apply techniques and procedures that can defeat the most capable adversaries can certainly tailor their surveillance countermeasures plans/efforts to defeat any lesser threats.

Some ***final related comments*** that are likely as applicable to this work as the two previous ones it builds upon, could be that it is written in a very technical (and in some cases "dry") style, that it might benefit from photographs like other books in the genre, and that it would also benefit from case studies. As it applies to each of these three critiques — *this work is written and scoped with the intent to inform, and not to entertain*. Although photographs may be aesthetically pleasing to some readers, the number of photographs that would be necessary to augment each of the points made in this work would be space-prohibitive, and to incorporate token photographs to meet this need would add negligible benefit (if any) to the overall information value. Although case studies do add value in the sense that they help to emphasize key points, the tactics, techniques, and procedures detailed in this work are all based on the real-world execution or observation of these applications, and are therefore all based on "case studies." In addition, although the generic techniques can be readily disclosed in this work, many of the "case studies" that validated them as operationally effective are classified national security investigations/operations, and are therefore unavailable for use as practical examples. In summary, there is no need for "fluff" such as flowery prose, visually impressive photographs, or real-world antidotes to prove isolated points, because this work contains end-to-end information that is presented as clearly and thoroughly as possible.

1. INTRODUCTION TO SURVEILLANCE COUNTERMEASURES

In today's dangerous environment, security professionals must understand the threat and be able to advise clients regarding the appropriate countermeasures to protect against a hostile surveillance effort. Even the average citizen has security concerns and can benefit from an understanding of the concepts of *surveillance countermeasures* that enhance personal protection. Surveillance countermeasures are actions taken by an individual or security detail to identify the presence of surveillance, and if necessary, to elude or evade the individual or group conducting the surveillance. In basic terms, surveillance countermeasures are actions taken to identify or evade a surveillance effort. Surveillance countermeasures consist of *surveillance detection* and *antisurveillance*. Although there are many methods of surveillance, this instructional manual focuses specifically on the detection and evasion of *physical surveillance*, which involves an individual or group of individuals moving by foot or vehicle to observe and monitor the movement of a target individual.

This manual is unique in scope, as it is certainly not another basic reference on surveillance countermeasures. Books and manuals abound with various tried-and-true methods and tactics to detect and evade hostile surveillance efforts. What is not as readily available or intuitive to the security professional, however, is a reference on the art, science, and theory behind this key aspect of personal protection, given the wide range of potential threats. In fact, it is almost alarming that many security professionals and individuals who regard themselves as security experts are really masters only of the tactics, and not of the theory behind the tactics. The application of surveillance detection and antisurveillance measures is only marginally effective when the individual or security detail does not understand the

1

concept, cause, and effect on which the measures are based. In fact, there are many various surveillance detection and antisurveillance maneuvers, but it is the underlying conceptual basis that makes them effective. The mere application of such techniques is amateurish by design if not planned and executed within the context of how surveillance countermeasures theory applies to surveillance practices. Unfortunately, in many cases, the rote practice of textbook methods without the full appreciation of the "art" and "science" of surveillance detection and antisurveillance measures can lead to costly — and even lethal — consequences.

The new reality of the contemporary environment is characterized by a wide range of unconstrained threats that reflect the ever-growing and pervasive underworld of dangerous actors. The plethora of acute threats to the personal privacy and security of average citizens consist of common criminals and stalkers, private and corporate investigators, government-sponsored espionage and other covert agencies, and international crime and terrorist organizations. In fact, the criminal enterprises that traffic in everything from drugs to humans, and the terrorist organizations that recognize no bounds of conscience, epitomize the contemporary threats that do not acknowledge innocent bystanders and from whom no one is immune.

Another factor that portends an enhanced threat across the spectrum is that the surveillance capabilities that were traditionally associated only with government-sponsored intelligence and security agencies have proliferated widely. Organizations such as criminal, terrorist, and corporate-sponsored elements now have the resources to conduct sophisticated surveillance operations that were previously associated with only the most capable governments. The fact that these elements have training facilities and doctrinal manuals reflects a degree of sophistication that presents significant challenges to the community of security professionals.

Even methods of international espionage have become much more aggressive toward nonmilitary and nongovernment targets. To a large degree, the intelligence services of foreign countries, both friend and foe, are competing in a global war based on economics. With relatively less emphasis on military advantage and more on economic strength, the number of individuals who are vulnerable to espionage due to their business affiliations is vastly increased. This expanding threat is further compounded by the ever-increasing practice of industrial/economic espionage conducted between competing businesses.

In virtually all cases, the elements that threaten individual, corporate, or national security conduct surveillance operations to further their objectives, or as the primary means to an end. In today's hazardous environment, security professionals must understand the threat and be able to advise clients regarding the appropriate countermeasures to protect against a hostile surveillance effort. The average citizen, too, has a vested interest in understanding the concepts of surveillance countermeasures that can enhance personal security. At the most basic level, criminals "case" potential targets to develop information to maximize their probability of success in committing a crime. Sophisticated criminal organizations conduct more extensive surveillance efforts to develop information on individuals they intend to intimidate, exploit, or terminate. Terrorist organizations conduct comprehensive preoperational surveillance to maximize the probability of successful attacks. In preparation for criminal or terrorist acts, surveillance is employed to determine when and where the target is most vulnerable. Ironically, this process of determining potential vulnerabilities of a target is when the threat element is also most exposed to detection and vulnerable to compromise. For example, three of the seven stages of a terrorist operation (intelligence gathering and surveillance, pre-attack surveillance and planning, and operation rehearsal) involve the collection/development of information on the intended target, and require that the threat element conduct surveillance by placing operators in the proximity of the potential target, making them most vulnerable to detection during these stages.

The duration of a surveillance operation depends largely on the sophistication and objectives of the surveillance effort. A surveillance effort to develop information on a target for purposes such as blackmail or coercion is normally conducted in a more deliberate manner and generally requires more extensive coverage. A surveillance effort to determine when and where a target will be most vulnerable to attack takes relatively less time, because the surveillance effort will focus on key/isolated weaknesses rather than on the development of detailed evidence. And in the extreme, a very hasty surveillance effort may be conducted to find and fix the target just prior to an attack. Regardless of circumstances, the potential target cannot assume that there will be multiple opportunities to detect or evade surveillance, and should in turn exercise diligence at all times.

The objectives and importance of surveillance countermeasures are based on an understanding that hostile elements conduct surveillance of a target individual to do that individual harm. Although the existence of a surveillance effort always implies some degree of harmful intent, it is the threat of physical harm that most vividly highlights the importance of surveillance countermeasures. Even a random or spontaneous act of crime is preceded by detectable indications. Surveillance countermeasures are most effective in facilitating the detection of preoperational surveillance which can prove critical when hostile elements are actually in the act of a crime or attack. The effective identification of these indications could provide the time and opportunity to react in an evasive manner under life-or-death circumstances.

In the case of the more deliberate and sophisticated physical threats such as terrorism, kidnapping, or assassination, the perpetrators invariably conduct surveillance of the intended victim. This is the point when operators must expose themselves and are consequently most vulnerable to detection. Proficiency in the techniques of observation and surveillance countermeasures is an effective means to prevent the act or enable individuals to avoid the threat when in harm's way. In most cases, the surveillance efforts in preparation for these attacks can be readily detected, and in fact, post-event investigations of actual attacks regularly determined that there were detectable signs that the victims overlooked or disregarded due to a lack of security awareness. This manual addresses the principles that have developed into time-proven methods of countering the most sophisticated surveillance techniques.

Understanding how the surveillance threat thinks and reacts is the basis of effective surveillance countermeasures. For this reason, this manual sets the stage with a detailed review of surveillance principles, methods, and tactics as a basis for surveillance countermeasures applications. In fact, the surveillance operations overview and the practical applications addressed in this manual provide a more comprehensive understanding of surveillance operations than is found in other resources nominally (and entirely) dedicated to the subject of surveillance.

The techniques and procedures presented in this manual represent concise applications of the most effective surveillance countermeasures based on a comprehensive analysis of hostile surveillance threats. Understanding how a surveillance effort will perceive and react to these countermeasures is vital to the effective application of specific surveillance countermeasures techniques. This manual presents a process approach that enables systematic, discreet, and comprehensive applications for surveillance countermeasures methodologies.

Surveillance countermeasures techniques must be conducted with an appreciation that the surveillance effort they are directed against has a strategy, is proficient, and can react and adapt based on the situation. This key concept dictates that actions without perspective are tantamount to those of a chess player who jumps on the opportunity to take a knight with a pawn, without consideration of his opponent's strategy, intentions, and second- and third-order reactions. Against an able opponent, it is likely that by opting for the immediate tactical success in seizing the knight, the player has contributed to a chain of events that will eventually lead to his demise in checkmate. This chess analogy is fitting because the "mean streets" are not sterile environments, and even the most effective surveillance countermeasures tactics may be counterproductive if executed without a clear "checkmate" endgame strategy that is based on a well-grounded appreciation of how a surveillance effort plans, thinks, and reacts to precise circumstances.

This manual details surveillance countermeasures concepts, techniques, and procedures that are proven effective against the spectrum of surveillance capabilities ranging from the very basic to the world's most sophisticated. Rather than instructing to the "lowest common denominator," as most tactics-focused publications do, this manual takes the opposite approach. The practitioner who can apply techniques and procedures that can defeat the most capable adversaries can certainly defeat the lesser threats. The execution of *techniques* as components of methodical *procedures* to effectively manipulate and exploit a hostile surveillance effort is representative of a security professional operating at the master's level of surveillance countermeasures tradecraft.

The specific examples of surveillance detection and antisurveillance techniques applicable to full-spectrum surveillance operations are limited only by the knowledge of fundamental concepts and the resourcefulness of the practitioner. This manual provides a wealth of specific surveillance countermeasures tactics that can be employed to meet situational objectives, but the specific tactical applications are relatively limitless to the practitioner whose expertise is grounded in the "art" and "science" of the process. And while the application of specific techniques is key to surveillance countermeasures, the true mastery of the art is most reliant on a foundational understanding of how a surveillance effort operates, thinks, and reacts; fundamental surveillance countermeasures planning concepts such as the exploitation of *restrictive terrain*; advanced planning concepts such as *target pattern analysis*; and advanced concepts and procedures such as the *Chaos Theory of Surveillance* and the methodical *break in contact* surveillance detection and antisurveillance procedures.

Spanning the range of theory, science, and art, this manual strikes an optimum balance between the concepts which drive the application of effective surveillance countermeasures, and the specific tactical examples to provide perspective. This methodology establishes a baseline upon which a knowledgeable practitioner can expound to develop an arsenal of purpose-built surveillance countermeasures techniques and procedures, and enable the practitioner to leverage these sophisticated threat-based perspectives.

The reader may find that there is some redundancy in the discussion of key concepts as they apply to surveillance, surveillance detection, and antisurveillance throughout this manual. Although this serves an important purpose in reinforcing these main points, the primary intent is to make the individual chapters stand alone to a certain degree. While this manual builds upon concepts and applications in a logical and compounding manner that warrants at least one complete read to appreciate the overall process, the manual provides a resource for a more focused review of specific topics based on more practical and near-term activities. For example, if an individual or security detail has a short-notice requirement to conduct a specific surveillance countermeasures activity, the applicable chapter in this manual is written in sufficient detail to provide a quick and concise preparation resource.

This manual includes figures to illustrate and add context to key points. This legend provides the standard icons for reference in the figures throughout.

 Principal Vehicle

 Surveillance Vehicle

 Neutral Vehicle

 Principal Traveling by Foot

 Foot Surveillance Operator

 "Eye" Icon Depicts Associated Asset with Primary Responsibility For Observation; or an Associated Asset's Primary Line of Observation

2. SURVEILLANCE COUNTERMEASURES TERMINOLOGY AND METHODS

This manual provides a comprehensive explanation of surveillance countermeasures principles and tactics based on the developmental detailing of the concepts and their applications. Many of the issues discussed in this overview are addressed in detail in subsequent chapters, but it is necessary to begin with a basic understanding of how the individual principles and tactics built upon in this manual apply to the overall surveillance countermeasures effort.

SURVEILLANCE COUNTERMEASURES TERMINOLOGY

The premise of surveillance countermeasures is that an individual is constantly vulnerable to the threat of surveillance. In fact, such countermeasures are the means by which someone who is under surveillance minimizes or negates the specific threat. All surveillance operations have a primary target or focus about whom their purpose is to develop information. Throughout this manual, the target of the surveillance is referred to as the *Principal*. (In this context it is always capitalized to distinguish it from other uses of the word.) The vehicle in which the Principal is traveling, either as the driver or a passenger, is referred to as the *Principal vehicle* (although when the tactics being addressed are centered around a vehicular surveillance, the vehicle may also be referred to as simply the Principal for brevity).

Surveillance operations are primarily conducted to develop exploitable information on a Principal. This purpose can be further dissected into two broad categories of objectives. The first objective involves terrorists and other criminal elements that conduct surveillance of a Principal to determine when and where he will be vulnerable to attack, hostage taking, or other types of hostile efforts. The other primary objective category is to develop information regarding the Principal that he would not freely provide or that he would not want known about himself. To this end, a surveillance operation may be conducted or commissioned to develop information for leverage in a range of possible activities to include business negotiations, legal negotiations, legal prosecution, or blackmail. When the objective of a surveillance operation is to develop information of this or a related nature, activities that are conducted by the Principal which support this objective, if observed, are obviously not in his best interests. Any Principal (or security detail thereof) that employs surveillance countermeasures has performed the analysis and understands what information his likely adversaries would be interested in. Therefore, anytime the Principal conducts activities that would likely meet the objective of the surveillance effort if observed, those activities are referred to as *protected activities*. A primary purpose of antisurveillance is to evade a potential surveillance effort ("clean off") prior to conducting any activity the Principal would want protected.

A surveillance capability (team) is commonly employed as a part of a larger operation. In addition to a surveillance arm, a larger operation may include an investigative team, Human Intelligence (HUMINT) collection agents, administration support (supplies and finances), and an action element that executes the culminating event of the operation, which may be an actual attack in the case of elements such as terrorist organizations. The element that incorporates the surveillance team into a larger, coordinated operation is referred to as the *adversarial element*.

As this manual addresses surveillance tactics that are employed in a total surveillance team effort, the effort is referred to as a *surveillance team* throughout. An optimally effective physical surveillance team normally consists of 12 individuals and six vehicles. This may increase in some cases and be unnecessary in others; even single-person surveillances are not uncommon under certain circumstances. A surveillance team and all-encompassing capabilities is referred to in some contexts as the *surveillance effort*.

A surveillance team consists of surveillants traveling by foot, vehicle, or a combination of both. Throughout this manual, a vehicle the surveillance team uses in an operation is referred to as a *surveillance vehicle*. Individual team members are referred to as *surveillance operators*, or simply *operators*. They are further identified as *foot operators* when engaged specifically in foot surveillance. The term *surveillance asset* can apply generically to a surveillance vehicle or operator.

When a surveillance operator observes the Principal, he is said to have *command* (of the Principal). In a vehicular surveillance operation, the vehicle in command of the Principal is referred to as the *command vehicle*. A foot operator in command of the Principal is referred to as the *command operator*. The term *command* may also be interchanged with *contact*, *control*, or *observation* of the Principal.

Surveillance Principals come in all shapes, sizes, and sexes. A well-rounded surveillance team consists of a good mix of male and female operators. Throughout this manual, however, the Principal and surveillance operators are referred to as *he* for brevity, although this is intended to be a gender-neutral pronoun.

Surveillance Principals generally fall into three categories or target-types: soft, hard, and overt. The *soft* target is one who, based on status and background, is not expected to suspect surveillance coverage. This assumes he has no training in countermeasures and is not likely to employ them as a standard practice. A soft target is not involved in any illegal or clandestine activity, and therefore, should have no reason to suspect surveillance coverage. The *hard* target is one who can be expected to be surveillance conscious, based on status and background. A hard target represents a more sophisticated challenge to a surveillance team because he is expected to have had formal countermeasures training and might employ them during his travels as standard practice. Common examples of hard targets are espionage agents and terrorist operatives, both of which are more often thoroughly trained in surveillance countermeasures tactics and employ them constantly to survive. Reading this manual qualifies the Principal as a hard target. In most cases, such a target's training consists of countermeasures tactics that can be employed in a natural, inconspicuous manner. This is important to the sophisticated target (Principal), because if a surveillance team observes him employing countermeasures, it will assume he has something to hide and intensify the efforts against him. An *overt* target is one who, based solely on present status, is expected to be surveillance conscious and employ countermeasures as standard practice. The overt target represents the greatest challenge to the surveillance team because he is a hard target that can also be expected to be more aggressive or overt in his actions. The most common example of an overt target is an espionage control officer (agent handler) operating under official diplomatic status out of an official embassy or mission. Such targets constantly assume that surveillance coverage is present and conduct a thorough regimen of surveillance detection and antisurveillance maneuvers prior to conducting any operational (protected) activity.

SURVEILLANCE COUNTERMEASURES METHODS

Surveillance countermeasures consist of *surveillance detection* and *antisurveillance*, both of which are further specialized based on their method of application and the form of surveillance they are intended to defeat. And while surveillance detection and antisurveillance have two different objectives, many principles and concepts apply equally to both. For the purposes of this manual, the term *surveillance countermeasures* is used when the concepts and applications being addressed apply to both surveillance detection and antisurveillance.

SURVEILLANCE DETECTION OVERVIEW

Surveillance detection consists of the Principal's efforts to identify the presence of surveillance. Such measures consist of actions taken by the Principal (or a security detail escorting the Principal) to identify indications of, or to confirm the presence of, a surveillance effort. It is conducted by one of three methods, or any combination thereof: passive detection, active detection, or countersurveillance. Effective observation and retention skills are essential to surveillance detection; observation practices are detailed in Appendix 2.

PASSIVE SURVEILLANCE DETECTION

Passive surveillance detection consists of the Principal (or a security detail escorting the Principal) observing the surroundings to identify indications or instances of surveillance without taking any active measures. A general understanding of surveillance principles and tactics facilitates the effective application of passive physical surveillance detection. Passive surveillance detection is conducted during the course of normal activities and is primarily based on an understanding of how a surveillance effort operates in order to identify activities or tactics that are indicative of surveillance. Passive detection is conducted in a manner that does not provide the surveillance effort, if present, any indication that the Principal is observing for a surveillance presence.

Passive surveillance detection is most feasible when the risk of violent activity against the Principal is low, making the identification and neutralization of the surveillance threat, if present, less urgent. Although passive surveillance detection is not usually effective in quickly identifying surveillance, it should always be employed to identify indications of surveillance that may justify the employment of more aggressive (active) surveillance detection techniques. In fact, personal security details continuously practice passive surveillance detection as a minimum baseline procedure.

ACTIVE SURVEILLANCE DETECTION

Active surveillance detection involves specific, usually preplanned maneuvers to isolate a surveillance asset and/or elicit a conspicuous and detectable reaction from a surveillance effort, if one is present. As with passive detection, active surveillance detection is based on an understanding of how a surveillance effort operates. Such an understanding enables the Principal to employ active measures to stimulate compromising actions by the surveillance effort. In fact, active surveillance detection maneuvers are specifically designed to force surveillance assets to react in a manner that isolates them for detection. By orchestrating an unanticipated situation to which the surveillance effort must react, the Principal isolates one or more surveillance assets for detection. Active surveillance detection is employed when the Principal has identified specific indications of surveillance, or as a standard security practice prior to conducting private or protected activities.

COUNTERSURVEILLANCE

Countersurveillance is a more sophisticated and resource-intensive method of active surveillance detection. This method differs significantly from other methods of surveillance detection in that it consists of actions taken by a third party (other than the Principal) to detect the presence of surveillance on the

Principal. Countersurveillance allows the Principal to travel in a more natural manner, since he — or his security detail — does not have to concentrate on observing for surveillance coverage. Countersurveillance can be conducted by the Principal's security detail, but is not conducted by the security personnel who are escorting the Principal. Among the other key advantages is that countersurveillance assets are able to position themselves in locations that provide a field of observation that the Principal would not be able to achieve himself.

Although the focus of this manual is appropriately first-person surveillance countermeasures, countersurveillance is the most sophisticated and effective method of surveillance detection, and is practiced by many professional security, intelligence, and law enforcement agencies. In fact, intelligence operatives use countersurveillance to ensure that their agents are not compromised, and law enforcement agencies employ it to ensure the safety of their undercover operatives during dangerous operations. Personal and executive security elements can employ the principles of countersurveillance to provide a layer of protection that is equal to that of the most elite agencies. The practice of sending a security detail ahead of the Principal to conduct forward route reconnaissance can be considered a form of countersurveillance, but this practice is most commonly conducted for the purposes of physical threat identification or neutralization. This manual focuses primarily on surveillance detection measures that are employed by the Principal (or a security detail escorting the Principal). However, countersurveillance is a sophisticated component of surveillance detection which is detailed in Appendix 3.

ANTISURVEILLANCE OVERVIEW

Antisurveillance consists of actions taken to elude or evade an identified, suspected, or possible hostile surveillance effort. All antisurveillance measures are considered active, in that the Principal executes an active measure to elude or evade a surveillance effort.

Antisurveillance is employed as a standard security practice prior to conducting private or protected activities, or when the Principal has identified specific indications of surveillance and there is an immediate need to elude or evade. Since surveillance is always possible, antisurveillance can be employed even when there is no specific indication that surveillance is present. In fact, professionals in covert activities, such as espionage agents, invariably employ antisurveillance activities as a standard practice, due to their extreme need to ensure that their operational (protected) activities remain unobserved and undetected.

As it applies to hostile threats, there is a distinction between antisurveillance and *anti-pursuit*. This manual addresses the techniques as they apply to the measures taken to elude a surveillance effort, or even to evade an aggressive effort that attempts to maintain contact despite active surveillance countermeasures. However, if and when a surveillance effort transitions into the attack phase of an operation, the Principal's efforts should transition as well from an antisurveillance to an anti-pursuit effort. This manual addresses the spectrum of antisurveillance techniques to include aggressive measures to evade determined surveillance efforts. However, as they apply to the reaction to the threat of physical attack, anti-pursuit measures such as defensive and evasive driving techniques are beyond the scope of this manual.

COVERT AND OVERT ACTIVE SURVEILLANCE COUNTERMEASURES

Active surveillance detection or antisurveillance can be conducted either covertly (discreetly) or overtly. *Covert surveillance countermeasures* attempt to detect or elude a surveillance effort in a manner that would give the surveillance effort, if present, little or no indication that the Principal is, in fact, practicing countermeasures. Approaching the opposite extreme of the spectrum, *overt surveillance countermeasures* are conducted with the primary objective of detecting or eluding surveillance, with little regard for the fact that the surveillance effort will perceive that the Principal is practicing countermeasures tactics. One example is when the Principal runs a red traffic light to elude a possible surveillance. Any surveillance effort observing this overt/aggressive action will become highly suspicious that the Principal is practicing antisurveillance. Throughout this manual the terms *covert* and *discreet* are used interchangeably. Consideration of the covert-overt spectrum is a vital component of surveillance countermeasures planning and execution, and is further addressed in detail in Chapter 5.

3. SURVEILLANCE OPERATIONS PRINCIPLES AND TACTICS

A professional and effective surveillance effort is orchestrated in a systematic manner, employing tactics and techniques that best ensure discreet coverage of the Principal. These time-tested procedures are based largely on an understanding of how the average person observes his surroundings while walking or driving.

The effectiveness of surveillance countermeasures is based on a keen understanding of the surveillance techniques employed by a sophisticated and determined surveillance effort. Surveillance countermeasures are based directly on the surveillance tactics, techniques, and procedures they are used to detect or defeat, and thus a broad understanding of the opposition's operating processes is essential to their effective execution.

This chapter details how the surveillance threat operates. It is by no means a comprehensive tutorial on surveillance; rather, it is designed as an overview to be used as the basis for understanding the surveillance countermeasures principles and tactics addressed in subsequent chapters.

SURVEILLANCE OPERATIONS OVERVIEW

Surveillance is the systematic, discreet observation of an individual to develop information regarding his activities. Physical surveillance is the only means by which a Principal can be observed constantly over an extended period of time. A surveillance operation can only be effective if it goes undetected by the Principal or anyone else (third parties), such as neighbors, associates, employees, passersby, or law enforcement officials.

Communications equipment is critical to the surveillance team consisting of multiple operators and vehicles. The ability of the surveillance assets to communicate allows them to rely on the information provided by the command vehicle or operator to guide their activities. This enables team members to maneuver effectively without having to rely on their visual observations of the Principal or other surveillance assets. Cellular mobile devises readily enable all surveillance assets with communications devices that facilitate hands-free communications. However, unless the surveillance team has a broadcast communications capability — meaning that communications go out simultaneously to all assets — then operational effectiveness is significantly degraded. Therefore, most sophisticated surveillance efforts use radio communications equipment and employ cell phones as a back-up or long-range communications method. In addition, it is generally known that cellular transmissions can be readily collected and retained, and even used as evidence in legal or other similar cases. For this reason, many surveillance teams will not risk the use of cell phones as a primary means of communications due to the risk of compromise or leaving an evidence trail.

A surveillance operation normally begins with limited information regarding the Principal's activities. It may begin by developing information to identify those times or activities on which to focus the surveillance effort. As information is developed over the course of an operation, the surveillance effort develops a pattern of the Principal's standard practices and routines that it uses to plan and conduct subsequent phases of the surveillance operation in a more secure and efficient manner. This process, referred to as *target pattern analysis*, is conducted to determine standard patterns of activity that can serve to effectively focus the surveillance effort. A surveillance effort generally becomes more efficient and effective against a Principal after observing his actions over time and becoming more familiar with his activities. Target pattern analysis enables the surveillance effort to concentrate efforts on the times and events with the highest potential payoff, while limiting the amount of time that it is exposed to the Principal, risking potential detection or compromise. As information is developed, *target pattern analysis* is conducted to determine which patterns the surveillance team can exploit to anticipate the Principal's actions more effectively, and to determine the times and activities that are likely to satisfy the objectives of the surveillance, as opposed to those that are routine and insignificant. The concept of target pattern analysis is also a foundational aspect of surveillance countermeasures.

Target pattern analysis also supports the surveillance effort's assessment of how *soft* (or *hard*) of a target the Principal may be. Generally, a surveillance effort adjusts its coverage based on how surveillance conscious the Principal is observed or perceived to be. If the surveillance effort assumes that the Principal is not surveillance conscious based on target pattern analysis and other information and observations, it will likely be less diligent in the employment of its tactics and the exposure of its assets. Conversely, if the surveillance effort suspects that the Principal may be surveillance conscious, it will exercise greater operational security and provide the Principal fewer opportunities for observation and detection.

As with surveillance targets (Principals), a surveillance effort can range from covert to overt. Sophisticated surveillance efforts primarily operate in a covert manner that is intended to ensure that the Principal observes no indications of surveillance presence. However, there are circumstances when overt surveillance methods are employed. In some cases, this serves as a form of intimidation, or as a "show of force" as may be the case when a foreign diplomat is overtly followed during periods of increased political tensions between countries. A suspected foreign agent may be placed under overt surveillance to make it known that he is under scrutiny and to discourage any nefarious activity. At the extreme, terrorists and other attackers may resort to overt surveillance when they are approaching the attack phase and want to ensure that the Principal is not allowed to escape. At some point in this situation, the hostile activity likely transitions from an overt surveillance to a pursuit. Although overt surveillance is a possibility, the most prolific surveillance threats employ covert (discreet) methods, consistent with the focus of this manual.

A professional and effective surveillance effort is orchestrated in a systematic manner, employing tactics and techniques that minimize the exposure of surveillance assets and potential of compromise to the Principal, while ensuring the observation of the Principal to meet the objectives of the surveillance operation. In addition to techniques and procedures which enhance operational security, surveillance assets employ principles of *cover and concealment* to minimize exposure to the Principal. *Concealment* refers to any aspect of the surrounding environment that a surveillance asset (vehicle or operator) can leverage to obstruct the Principal's view and ability to observe the surveillance asset over the course of a surveillance operation. A surveillance vehicle provides a degree of concealment, as do structures such as buildings. Another example of concealment might be the positioning of a surveillance operator inside a building to observe the Principal through the structure's windows. Darkness is another form of concealment. *Cover* and *cover for action* are concepts that are extremely critical to the effectiveness and security of any surveillance operation. *Cover* is a broad term that generally applies to anything a surveillance operator or vehicle uses to appear natural when observation by the Principal, countersurveillance, or any other third parties is possible. During a foot surveillance operation, cover consists primarily of pedestrians in the area. Similarly, during a vehicular surveillance operation, cover consists primarily of vehicular traffic on the roads. In both situations, the surrounding traffic enables the surveillance operator or vehicle to blend in and appear as any other pedestrian or vehicle. *Cover for action* is a more specific term that refers to actions the surveillance asset takes to establish a plausible reason for being in a given location or undertaking specific activities. Applications of concealment, cover, and cover for action are addressed throughout this manual, as they apply to surveillance countermeasures.

A driving principle of surveillance is that most surveillance efforts will routinely break contact with a Principal rather than accept a high risk of exposure. Most surveillance efforts make operational security their highest priority, because if the Principal becomes aware of coverage, the surveillance effort is severely hindered or rendered completely ineffective. When an operator or asset becomes over exposed to the Principal ("burned") during an operation, they will be replaced. Long-term operations normally require that both operators and vehicles be replaced throughout to maintain security.

SURVEILLANCE OPERATIONS METHODS

There are two primary types of surveillance: physical and technical. This manual appropriately focuses almost exclusively on physical surveillance, which involves an individual or group of individuals observing and monitoring the Principal's activities. The limitations of technical surveillance methods and the primary implications for surveillance countermeasures are addressed in Appendix 1.

There are two primary types of physical surveillance: fixed and mobile.

Fixed surveillance operations are very limited in scope and are addressed in Appendix 4. This manual focuses on *mobile surveillance* wherein the surveillance team observes the Principal's activities while he is traveling. Of course, this requires that surveillance operators and vehicles move with him. Mobile surveillance operations are conducted either on foot, by vehicle, or a combination of both. Many general surveillance tactics and principles apply equally to vehicular and foot surveillance. Alternatively, as will be addressed, there are many that are nuanced to one or the other. This manual addresses comprehensive mobile surveillance operations that are reflective of the world's most sophisticated surveillance elements. There are less complex variations of mobile surveillance which do not meet the criteria of this manual for detailed instruction, such as *progressive surveillance*, which is addressed in Appendix 4 for perspective. Although this manual does not focus heavily on fixed surveillance as an operation in and of itself, mobile surveillance operations are normally initiated by a *stakeout* phase, which is a fixed surveillance activity intended to initially establish *command* of the Principal. Fixed observation posts are frequently employed to support mobile surveillance operations, and are detailed in Appendix 5.

PHASES OF A MOBILE SURVEILLANCE OPERATION

A mobile surveillance operation is a fluid sequence of tactical maneuvers that are dictated primarily by the actions of the Principal. In order to effectively cover the Principal, the team must maintain synchronization through a phased operation with a unity of tactical discipline and purpose.

A comprehensive surveillance operation is conducted in three phases: (1) the stakeout and pick-up, (2) the follow, and (3) the box. An operation progresses through these phases based on the Principal's actions. Ideally, an operation progresses through these three phases and then shifts the order in which they are implemented in reaction to the Principal's activities.

THE STAKEOUT AND PICK-UP PHASE

The *stakeout* is the fixed surveillance phase of a mobile surveillance operation which involves positioning surveillance vehicles or operators based on how the team intends to establish initial *command* of the Principal. This consists of positioning surveillance assets to begin the follow when the Principal emerges from a fixed location such a residence or workplace. This consists of the logical coverage of a specified area to ensure that when the Principal appears, the team is able to make a smooth and effective transition from static positions to a mobile surveillance follow. This is accomplished primarily by employing a *boxing method* intended to cover all routes of travel into and out of the specified area. The employment of an observation post to facilitate the stakeout is addressed in Appendix 5.

In many cases, the stakeout is centered around a location referred to as a *denied area* or *denied location* — such as the Principal's residence and likely his workplace — which is a location that the surveillance team would not have free access to and could only access surreptitiously.

The *pick-up* occurs when the surveillance team establishes initial command of the Principal. It is the result of a successful stakeout or surveillance box, and is the transition to the follow phase.

The Follow Phase

The *follow* begins immediately after a pick-up. Once the Principal begins to travel, the surveillance effort transitions to the follow phase, which involves the transition from static positions in the stakeout to a mobile surveillance follow and continues throughout the mobile surveillance of the Principal while traveling by foot or vehicle. Most of a standard surveillance operation's time and effort is spent during the actual follow phase. For this reason, it is during this phase that the Principal has the opportunity to employ the widest range of surveillance countermeasures. The follow phase of a surveillance operation can be conducted either by vehicle or by foot. Obviously, the Principal's mode of travel largely dictates the surveillance asset employed.

Regardless of how many surveillance assets are employed in an operation, at any given time there is always at least one asset that maintains observation (command) of the Principal. Intermittent losses of contact based on anticipating the Principal's actions, temporary blind spots, and exchanges between assets are normal. However, a surveillance effort will avoid letting the Principal go unobserved through options that would allow the Principal multiple alternative routes of travel, unless the effort is confident of the Principal's destination based on *target pattern analysis* or other means.

The most basic method employed by a surveillance effort with multiple assets to reduce prolonged asset exposure and to reduce the signature of *mirroring* the Principal's movements is to *hand-off* command of the Principal at a turn. (The concept of mirroring is addressed in detail in Chapter 4). During a follow, the members of a surveillance effort with multiple assets *hand-off* command of the Principal among each other. The most basic example of this *hand-off* process is when the Principal is traveling along a route and then takes a turn onto another road. In this case, the surveillance asset traveling most closely behind the Principal continues straight at the intersection, while another surveillance asset that is further out of observation range takes the turn and establishes command (observation) of the Principal. The standard surveillance follow consists of a succession of hand-offs to minimize the amount of time that a single asset is exposed to the Principal for observation and detection. This is also an effective method of disguising the fact that the surveillance effort is mirroring the Principal's movements. In virtually all cases, however, there is a varying degree of time — normally seconds — when no asset has command of the Principal as the hand-off is executed. Chapter 7 (Figures 4 and 5) and Chapter 11 (Figures 17 and 18) provide additional detail as it applies to the surveillance team hand-offs and applicable surveillance detection methods.

The *floating box* is a surveillance method that is characteristic of a more sophisticated surveillance effort, as it generally requires multiple assets and a dynamic broadcast voice communications capability between assets. This method requires a minimum of three assets but is most effectively employed with four or more. Just as the term implies, the floating box involves surveillance assets supporting the following command asset by moving at a pace with the Principal while traveling along parallel routes for a more secure and effective reaction to a turn in either direction. Chapter 10 provides additional detail (with supporting figures) as it applies to the floating box and applicable surveillance detection methods.

Whether surveillance assets travel by foot or vehicle, the terrain and traffic patterns dictate their following distance. In open terrain, the surveillance effort generally increases following distance due to the greater range of observation for both the surveillance effort and the Principal. In denser traffic, the surveillance effort normally follows more closely to maintain observation and be in the appropriate position at critical points along the surveillance route — primarily at traffic options.

Any sophisticated surveillance effort operates based on an understanding of the principles of observation and will conform to what should be perceived as the norm with respect to the surrounding environment. A surveillance effort must use *cover* and *concealment* to protect its activities from observation by the Principal. Generally, in a surveillance operation the primary method of *cover* and *concealment* for surveillance vehicles is other vehicles, and the primary method for surveillance operators on foot is the surrounding pedestrian traffic.

THE BOX PHASE

The *box phase* begins as the Principal stops during a surveillance follow, such as when the Principal returns home or makes a temporary stop such as to visit a friend, gas up the car, or go grocery shopping. As with the stakeout box, a standard surveillance box is a logical positioning of surveillance vehicles or operators to cover all routes of travel out of a specified area. Chapter 7 (Passive Vehicular Surveillance Detection) provides further discussion and figures regarding surveillance box techniques. The primary difference between the stakeout and box phase, is that with the box phase box, there is a normally a higher degree of command over the Principal because the surveillance team likely has the Principal under observation.

A standard surveillance operation consists of a succession of transitions between the box and follow phases until the operation is terminated. A given stage of a comprehensive surveillance operation normally terminates when the Principal reaches a terminal long-term stay location, such as a residence at night or workplace during the day. In the meantime, the surveillance effort will depart to "cool off" and debrief the operation, and then return to establish the stakeout box when target pattern analysis has indicated that the Principal can be expected to emerge from the location.

MOBILE SURVEILLANCE METHODS

VEHICULAR SURVEILLANCE

Vehicular surveillance operations are conducted to determine the Principal's activities while traveling by vehicle. Vehicular surveillance is an integral aspect of most physical surveillance operations, as the Principal rarely travels exclusively by foot. Even when operating against a Principal who travels primarily by public transportation, the surveillance team must rely on vehicles for control and mobility. Although the surveillance team will rarely observe a

Principal conducting *protected activity* while traveling by (and inside a) vehicle, it is understood that the Principal will likely travel by vehicle to reach the location where such activity may occur.

Vehicular and foot surveillance share many operational tactics. Vehicular surveillance, however, is a more exact science because routes of travel are generally restricted to, or channelized by, established roadways. This can be used to the advantage of a capable surveillance team, but in the same way, it can be used to the advantage of a resourceful Principal. There is also less maneuverability in vehicular surveillance because a surveillance vehicle has less flexibility to turn around and reposition discreetly. This disadvantage is overcome by expertise in teamwork and tactical applications.

A vehicular surveillance begins with the *stakeout* of a specified location at which the surveillance team expects to establish initial command of the Principal. The location is selected based on assumptions about when and where the Principal is likely to appear. Primary stakeout locations are the Principal's residence and workplace. The Principal is normally expected to stay the night at his residence, depart sometime during the day, and return to his residence by the end of the day. As applicable, he can also be expected to appear at his place of work with some degree of regularity. These standard patterns, established by *target pattern analysis*, provide the surveillance effort with locations that promise a high probability of establishing command of the Principal.

The tactics normally employed to stakeout an area to pick-up the Principal for a mobile surveillance follow are referred to as boxing. A stakeout box is a logical positioning of surveillance vehicles to attain initial command of a Principal as he either travels through a specified area or emerges from it. The stakeout box consists of positioning surveillance vehicles in such a manner as to control routes of travel out of a specified area. These vehicles are positioned to "pick-up" the Principal as he drives out of the stakeout box along any of the possible routes of travel. The stakeout box commonly employs a *trigger*, which is a surveillance vehicle or operator that is positioned to observe the Principal and alert the team as he departs a denied area around which the stakeout is based, or enters his vehicle to depart the stakeout location. Chapter 7 (Figures 1, 2, and 3) addresses specific tactics for the stakeout and pick-up.

The surveillance team may use an observation post to observe a specific location in support of the stakeout. Observation posts are normally positioned to observe a residence, business, or workplace. Using an observation post saves the team from having to expose a vehicle to observe the location. A surveillance team may also employ a mobile observation post, such as a van that can be parked within line of sight of the target location for observation. Again, the employment of observation posts is addressed in Appendix 5.

A surveillance vehicle normally has two operators — a driver and a navigator. The navigator reads a map and directs the driver. When in the command vehicle position, the navigator transmits the Principal's location and actions to the entire team. Otherwise, the navigator monitors the radio/communications means to track the Principal's location on the map and directs the driver to maneuver in a manner that supports the operation.

During the vehicular surveillance *follow*, the Principal's rear and side view mirrors are the key surveillance detection enablers, of which the surveillance effort is constantly cognizant. The following distance of the vehicular surveillance team is dictated primarily by the terrain and available cover from surrounding traffic. Terrain attributes impacting following distance include structural obstacles to line of sight observation (more so in built-up urban areas; less so in rural areas), and in some cases foliage. The other key terrain considerations are restrictive terrain such as traffic hazards and channelized terrain, which are addressed in detail in Chapter 4. Traffic hazards such as traffic obstacles and traffic options may deter the surveillance team from maintaining command of the Principal. Therefore, the team will normally need to maintain a closer following distance when confronted by significant traffic obstacles. Traffic hazards, such as highway and other thoroughfare interchanges, offer the Principal high-speed or multiple avenues of escape. Since it is important that the surveillance assets have command of the Principal when entering a traffic hazard, they will normally close their following distance when approaching one.

The *floating box* surveillance technique, as previously addressed, applies most directly to vehicular surveillance. Given the example of a standard city block in a vehicular surveillance, the floating box would consist of at least one asset traveling behind the Principal on the same road, while other surveillance vehicles travel along each of the two parallel roads. In addition to providing flexibility in covering multiple options of the travel the Principal may choose, the floating box and variations thereof reduce the probability of compromise by having as few vehicles as necessary following on the same route as the

Principal, which leaves fewer vehicles vulnerable to detection by maneuvers such as a sudden stop or a 180-degree turn. Again, Chapter 10 provides additional detail (with supporting figures) as it applies to the floating box and applicable surveillance detection methods.

A complete floating box formation may also include a *lead* asset, alternatively referred to as a *cheating* asset. The lead vehicle travels ahead of the Principal on the same route and can warn the surveillance effort of approaching hazards or options, and can be positioned ahead of the potential obstacles in case the following surveillance assets are held up. In some cases, the lead vehicle could be the asset responsible for command (observation) of the Principal at a given time by observing through rear and side view mirrors.

The mobile surveillance follow transitions directly to the *box phase* anytime the Principal stops, excluding normal traffic stops. This consists of the surveillance team maneuvering to box positions around the Principal's stopping point. As with the stakeout box, surveillance vehicles establish positions along each of the Principal's possible routes of departure to pick him up when he begins to move and leaves the box location. The surveillance team normally positions a vehicle (*trigger*) in a location from which its occupants can physically observe the stationary Principal vehicle and inform the team when it begins to move. When the vehicle stop location does not facilitate a secure vehicle trigger location, a foot operator may be dropped off to move into place and establish a more discreet trigger. Chapter 7 (Figures 6 and 7) describes a surveillance team establishing a box in reaction to the Principal's stop. As the Principal begins to move, the pick-up is executed and the follow phase is again initiated. The follow phase begins again after the Principal exits the box and the surveillance vehicle along his route of travel maneuvers to assume command (pick-up) for the mobile surveillance follow.

Night surveillance operations are markedly different from those conducted in daytime. The basic tactics remain the same, but darkness imposes many additional considerations. The very nature of night surveillance dictates that the surveillance team concentrate on more technically intricate concepts and tactical applications. This may include the use of night vision equipment or specialized controls to prevent the surveillance vehicle's brake lights from projecting when the brake pedal is engaged. At night, surveillance vehicles' lights are the most visible signature the team projects to the Principal, and therefore, a professional surveillance effort ensures that vehicle lights are in proper working order and do not project in an unusual manner that may bring a vehicle to the Principal's attention or make it readily distinguishable at multiple locations. In crowded urban areas, the lights of surrounding vehicles can make the surveillance team virtually invisible to the Principal. In these conditions, surveillance vehicles will likely be compelled to follow very closely behind the Principal unless the Principal vehicle has a very distinguishable rear light signature. As the hour gets later and the traffic density decreases, the surveillance vehicle's lights make it virtually impossible for it to remain discreet, but following surveillance vehicles should be able to securely increase following distance in these conditions. Appendix 6 addresses nuances of surveillance and surveillance countermeasures at night.

FOOT SURVEILLANCE

Foot surveillance operations are conducted to determine the Principal's activities while traveling by foot. Such operations normally have very specific objectives. Foot surveillance is most effective when there is specific information to indicate that the Principal will conduct significant (protected) activities that the surveillance team wants to observe and record, in an anticipated area while on the ground.

Communications equipment is an important aspect of effective foot surveillance, just as in vehicular surveillance. Concealed communications equipment enables each foot operator to transmit and receive information regarding the Principal's observed activities. Most capable surveillance operators can employ methods to communicate silently in the Principal's presence such as transmitting static codes rather than speaking. Since body communications equipment is expensive, it is not common to all foot surveillance teams. Teams that operate without it must rely on cellular phone capabilities which do not have an effective broadcast capability short of an open conference call. Alternatively, a team may use visual signals to communicate as these can be communicated to multiple operators within observation range, but this dictates that each foot surveillance operator either maintain visual observation of the Principal or another signaling operator to continue in the follow. Therefore, a team without body communications equipment must follow much more closely, which invariably results in a higher potential for exposure to the Principal for all operators.

The mobile foot surveillance employs most of the same tactical applications as vehicular surveillance and consists of the same three phases of a surveillance operation. A primary difference from vehicular surveillance is that foot operators have much more flexibility to maneuver quickly in any direction. This is a significant advantage in the *stakeout phase* because foot operators are not constrained by having to position themselves to pick-up the Principal traveling in limited and channelized directions. One other key factor that distinguishes foot from vehicular surveillance is that the Principal does not have the advantage of mirrors, and must physically turn to observe in multiple directions.

One key factor in the foot stakeout is the degree of cover and concealment available. Whereas operators manning a surveillance vehicle parked along the road have some physical concealment, a foot operator standing alongside the road runs a greater risk of exposure. For this reason, foot operators in the stakeout box attempt to maximize available cover and devise a plausible reason for being where they are (cover for action). They will also attempt to position themselves in locations that provide physical concealment from the Principal, such as inside a building looking out of the window.

During the *follow* phase, foot surveillance operators normally follow and observe the Principal from behind. They will be positioned to follow directly from behind, behind and on the opposite side of the road, or a combination of both (tandem). Following distance is largely dictated by the terrain and amount of cover. Cover in foot surveillance consists primarily of pedestrian traffic into which the surveillance operators can blend, but it may also include plausible activities that they can undertake. Chapter 11 (Figures 17 and 18) demonstrates how surveillance operators coordinate coverage to maintain a secure and effective command of the Principal.

Cover and concealment are also normally more important considerations in the foot surveillance follow because foot operators tend to be more vulnerable to unexpected maneuvers by the Principal. Foot operators must consistently assess the surrounding terrain for cover and concealment opportunities in the event of a turn, stop, or reversal of direction by the Principal. This requires a high degree of skill and discipline to react naturally to such unexpected moves by the Principal and transition to an effective cover or concealment position without drawing attention.

For the foot operator, traffic obstacles consist primarily of traffic or pedestrian density and busy roadways that are difficult to cross quickly. As with vehicular surveillance, significant traffic obstacles normally dictate that the foot surveillance team decrease its following distance.

With a more sophisticated surveillance effort, vehicles may be employed to support the foot surveillance by ferrying operators ahead of the Principal and relaying communications. As another example, an operator in a stationary vehicle can read a map and give foot operators movement instructions or other information, such as possible hazards that the Principal and operators may be approaching.

The ability for a surveillance team to operate effectively in *public locations* is key to successful surveillance operations. Public locations are readily employed by *hard targets* to enable surveillance countermeasures prior to conducting *protected activities*, and provide a Principal with a degree of *cover for action* when conducting such activities. Public locations are areas or establishments that offer open access to the public, and differ from public streets because they normally have physical or notional boundaries and a greater concentration of people. These factors impose unique restrictions on foot surveillance operators. In most cases, public locations force the operators much closer to the Principal than they would otherwise allow themselves to become.

The options for public locations to which the Principal may lead the surveillance team are unlimited, and may include restaurants, stores, malls, parks, and entertainment venues. Public locations offer varying degrees of cover, which is critical due to the confined operating area. A surveillance team is particularly vulnerable to exposure in public locations because there is a higher probability of unexpected maneuvers by the Principal. Public locations are also unique in that they may have varying levels of terrain. These are normally separated by channelized avenues of travel such as stairways, escalators, or elevators, which again may leave operators vulnerable to exposure. One other disadvantage the surveillance team encounters in public locations is multiple entrances and exits, which allow the Principal to enter and exit at any time via multiple avenues. This may require the team to commit more surveillance operators to the public location to maintain team integrity, potentially exposing multiple surveillance operators to the Principal.

Foot surveillance at night provides the surveillance team with an enhanced degree of concealment. The advantages gained by increased concealment with the darkness can be easily negated by limited visibility. Surveillance operators can maximize the advantage of darkness by employing night vision equipment. Because there are fewer pedestrians at night, surveillance operators are not as concerned with appearing suspicious to surrounding pedestrians and can therefore operate less discreetly. A team without body communications equipment at night is at a disadvantage because it is difficult to rely on visual signals in darkness; this constraint may require that surveillance operators use more overt methods to signal members such as to light a cigarette or provide illumination signals from a cell phone or other source. Again, Appendix 6 addresses surveillance and surveillance countermeasures at night.

COMBINED FOOT AND VEHICULAR SURVEILLANCE

Combined foot and vehicular surveillance operations employ all mobile surveillance disciplines comprehensively. Such operations are conducted to observe all activities of the Principal during a specified period. They require that the entire team possess a high degree of tactical and technical expertise to ensure an effective transition between vehicular and foot surveillance, and vice versa.

The most unique aspect of this method of surveillance is that as the Principal transitions from vehicle to foot or vice versa, the surveillance team must also do so while simultaneously maintaining command of the Principal and avoiding exposure. It is during these periods of transition that the team experiences the greatest difficulty maintaining command due to the sudden shift in the operation.

In the execution of the combined foot and vehicular surveillance, the surveillance team will employ target pattern analysis and other considerations to determine the balance of vehicle and foot assets. If the team anticipates that the Principal will conduct activities of interest while on foot, it will employ more operators in the foot surveillance team to concentrate its operators on the ground rather than dividing assets evenly between foot and vehicular surveillance, and accept risk in the transitions back to vehicular surveillance. When the surveillance team anticipates that the Principal's travels will be inconsequential and the surveillance will likely transition back to a vehicular follow without event, it will place a priority on establishing an effective vehicular box and maintaining command during the transition back to the vehicle follow. Determining the priority between the foot follow and the ability to transition to the vehicular follow is a key consideration in a one-person surveillance effort, or for teams with one person per vehicle, as a priority on the foot follow will significantly increase the risk of unsuccessfully transitioning back to the vehicular follow.

As the Principal stops his vehicle and transitions to ground, the surveillance vehicles attempt to drop off foot surveillance operators in positions that maximize their probability of successfully continuing the follow. The team must realize that dropping multiple operators in the same location or in the vicinity of the Principal vehicle represents an unacceptable risk of exposure. The navigators therefore analyze the area's terrain by examining the map to determine the best location for foot operators to be dropped to integrate into the follow. When the team employs the standard vehicle manning of a driver and a navigator, the navigator transitions to the foot follow as a foot operator.

As this transition is made, the tactics of foot surveillance predominate the operation. Surveillance vehicles support the foot surveillance in progress. One will be dedicated to establishing a static position (trigger) to observe the Principal vehicle. This is critical in that if the surveillance team loses command of the Principal on the ground, the surveillance vehicle observing the Principal vehicle is at least able to inform the team when he returns. The other surveillance vehicles support the foot operators on the ground. If they are equipped with body communications gear, this consists of relaying their radio transmissions as well as reading the map and providing directions. Surveillance vehicles can also transport foot operators throughout the operational area in support of the foot surveillance.

When foot operators are receiving adequate support from surveillance vehicles, any remaining vehicles establish box positions to pick-up the Principal vehicle when the transition back to vehicular surveillance occurs.

As the Principal travels back to his vehicle, all the surveillance vehicles prepare to transition to the vehicular follow by picking up foot operators and maneuvering to boxing positions around the Principal vehicle's location. As the Principal enters his vehicle and travels away, the surveillance team executes a pick-up and follow similar to that of the box phase of the mobile surveillance operation. Unless flawlessly executed, this stage risks a degradation in team integrity and strength as surveillance vehicles may be compelled to leave operators behind to effectively execute the pick-up and follow in the transition to the vehicular follow. In some cases, a specific surveillance vehicle (or vehicles) will be designated to remain behind to pick up multiple foot operators to transport and reintegrate them with their designated vehicles, or another vehicle needing a navigator, when possible.

LOST CONTACT DRILL

Over the course of a follow, the surveillance team may lose command (contact) of the Principal for any number of reasons. When this occurs, unless the team is certain of the Principal's destination based on previous travel patterns or other sources, it will execute the *lost contact drill*. When a surveillance effort initially loses contact with the Principal during the follow, it continues aggressively in the last observed direction of travel to regain contact with Principal before he reaches a traffic option that would provide multiple possible routes of travel (or escape). If the surveillance effort is unable to reestablish contact prior to the traffic option, it must initiate a *lost contact drill* in an attempt to regain contact. The lost contact drill is a standard surveillance technique that involves the systematic execution of a series of maneuvers to regain observation of the Principal. This basically involves the immediate prioritization of the Principal's likely routes of travel from the traffic option from which lost command initially occurs.

Even when the surveillance effort is confident of the Principal's route of travel, it will normally, as a standard precaution, send assets to search along alternative routes of travel to prevent losing the Principal completely and having to terminate the operation. The effectiveness of this technique is directly based on the number of assets available to search along the alternative routes. For example, if a surveillance effort is forced to initiate a lost contact drill at a standard intersection at which it is assumed that the Principal's most likely option was to continue straight, then the first asset to the intersection would continue straight in search of the Principal. The next asset to arrive at the intersection takes the second most likely alternative (left or right), and the third asset turns to check down the remaining alternative route. Chapter 13 (Figures 19 and 20) addresses the lost contact drill as it applies to advanced antisurveillance efforts.

Obviously, in the previous example, if the surveillance effort is limited to one or two assets, then one or two possible routes of travel would not be searched, potentially limiting the effectiveness of the lost contact drill. If adequate assets are available, additional assets reaching the point of lost contact would reinforce along the possible routes in the same order of priority as the initial assets reaching the point, to provide additional search capability at traffic options further along the respective routes. Committing surveillance assets to each possible route significantly degrades team integrity. Even when an asset reestablishes command of the Principal during this drill, it must continue the follow with a greater risk of exposure due to the degraded degree of team support. The fewer surveillance assets available at the outset to conduct the lost contact drill, the proportionately lower the probability of success.

4. FUNDAMENTAL SURVEILLANCE COUNTERMEASURES PLANNING CONCEPTS

The advanced concepts that are vital to the effective employment of surveillance countermeasures are based on a sound understanding of how a capable surveillance effort operates. Before entering into a detailed discussion of specific surveillance countermeasures tactics, techniques, and procedures, it is important to understand some foundational concepts which provide overarching perspective when planning to execute a surveillance countermeasures regimen.

OBSERVATION

The principles of *observation* are key to surveillance countermeasures, particularly as they apply to surveillance detection. Surveillance is the art of "hiding in plain sight." This is based on the understanding that the average individual would never suspect that the crippled homeless man, the loving couple, or the street-side vendor could possibly be surveillance assets. Surveillance professionals understand psychological factors such as perceptions and biases, and play on these factors as a form of applied science. The reality is that surveillance assets must maintain a range of vision with the Principal that is reciprocal. The art of hiding in plain sight lies in the fact that the Principal will invariably "see" surveillance assets during an operation, but unless he is acutely surveillance conscious, will not actually perceive them as such.

The effectiveness of all surveillance detection measures depends on the Principal's ability to observe his surroundings. Surveillance detection maneuvers must factor in the ability to observe the desired reaction, because obviously even the best executed surveillance detection maneuver is ineffective if the Principal cannot observe for the reaction of a possible surveillance effort. Also, the ability to observe individual and vehicle attributes and retain these observations to facilitate the future recognition of the same assets, is among the most effective means to confirm surveillance presence. Appendix 2 addresses observation methodologies in detail.

MIRRORING

The concept of mirroring warrants specific attention regarding surveillance countermeasures as they apply to a mobile surveillance operation. A surveillance team basically maintains correlation with the Principal and his movements. As surveillance assets come closer to the Principal, this degree of correlation increases, and the asset with command of the Principal must maintain the greatest degree of correlation in order to retain observation. This concept of correlation to the Principal is most basically characterized as *mirroring*. Although this is a fairly simple and intuitive concept, the requirement for the surveillance team to *mirror* the Principal's actions is the most fundamental basis of surveillance detection.

In most surveillance operations, the mobile follow phase makes up most of the operation. For this reason, it is primarily during this stage that the surveillance effort is most exposed to the Principal and is consequently most vulnerable to surveillance detection. Although there are other opportunities to detect or elude surveillance, it is generally during the follow phase that the Principal employs the most effective surveillance countermeasures techniques. Mirroring is a key aspect that the Principal attempts to detect through passive observation and active detection measures.

The degree to which a surveillance effort can conceal instances of mirroring is primarily based on the degree of training, the number of assets, and the sophistication of the effort. In fact, surveillance efforts employ tactics such as hand-offs, the floating box, and lead assets specifically to minimize the degree of mirroring. As a general rule, the fewer the assets available to the surveillance effort, the more it is required to directly mirror the Principal's movements in a manner that is susceptible to detection.

Regardless of how many surveillance assets are employed in a given operation, at any time there is always at least one asset that maintains command (observation) of the Principal, and will therefore travel in a manner that generally correlates with the Principal's movements while maintaining a secure following/stand-off distance. Mirroring is a surveillance effort vulnerability as it requires the placement of a surveillance asset in a position that best enables maintaining *command* and best positions the asset in anticipation of the Principal's next maneuver.

Normally, mirroring consists of the surveillance asset maintaining a standard speed and distance (*pacing*) with the Principal and executing like actions such as changing lanes or taking turns. At a very basic level, if the Principal is traveling on a road with two lanes in each direction and is in the left lane, the surveillance vehicle tends to position itself in the left lane as well in anticipation of a possible left turn. Alternatively, there is a tendency to follow in the right lane if this is the Principal's lane of travel. Although this form of mirroring (also referred to as *silhouetting*) has its surveillance detection vulnerabilities, it is preferable to the alternative, which is to be out of position when the Principal takes a turn and being forced to conspicuously cut across traffic in order to maintain contact. Obviously, other factors — such as the amount of traffic and following distance — impact positioning, as traveling in a different lane than the Principal does provide some advantages in regard to observation and security, if this can be accomplished in a manner that enables the surveillance asset to react appropriately. Regardless of whether the asset is following directly behind or from an offset position, the asset is mirroring to a varying degree.

RESTRICTIVE TERRAIN

The terrain and other environmental factors dictate a large part of how a surveillance effort conducts its follow of the Principal, and can therefore be leveraged by the resourceful Principal to facilitate surveillance countermeasures. Given the requirement to maintain contact with the Principal, restrictive terrain usually forces the surveillance effort to assume additional risk of detection to ensure that observation of the Principal is maintained.

Restrictive terrain is employed to isolate potential surveillance assets for surveillance detection purposes, as well as to conduct or to posture for the execution of surveillance detection and antisurveillance measures. The key enabling concept of restrictive terrain is that the Principal can lead the surveillance effort into a situation that restricts its freedom of movement, making it vulnerable to surveillance countermeasures.

Although a significant enabler for surveillance countermeasures purposes, restrictive terrain is a true double-edged sword for the Principal who may actually suspect surveillance, but does not know whether the intentions of the surveillance effort are lethal or nonlethal. This is a critical consideration when determining whether to employ these enablers, because in many cases, the restrictive terrain that the Principal can exploit for surveillance countermeasures purposes would likely be the very same restrictive terrain that a hostile element would choose to isolate and execute an attack on the Principal, if that were the intent.

Traffic Hazards

Traffic hazards are areas along a route of travel that can force a surveillance effort to slow down or come to a halt, or areas that provide the Principal multiple options of travel. As will be detailed, traffic hazards consist primarily of *traffic obstacles* and *traffic options*. Such hazards can either cause the surveillance effort to move into close proximity with the Principal or to lose contact altogether. Generally, if the Principal enters a traffic hazard ahead of the surveillance effort, or when not under observation by the surveillance effort, the risk of the surveillance effort losing the Principal is significantly increased. The surveillance countermeasures implications of traffic hazards are obvious, as they force the surveillance effort into a slow-moving or static position that may expose them as readily observable by the Principal. Particularly when moving from a relatively open area into an area with traffic hazards, the surveillance effort tends to push in closer to the Principal to avoid losing contact.

A *traffic obstacle* is any hazard that may delay or stop the movement of traffic. Common traffic obstacles are construction zones, traffic control methods (e.g. traffic lights), and dense vehicular or pedestrian traffic (particularly when further impeded by traffic controls). Even a school bus or a train crossing can be used as obstacles by the resourceful and calculating Principal. *Choke points* are traffic obstacles that generally cause traffic to slow down and concentrate in density. Various examples of choke points include construction zones, toll areas, and areas where high-traffic, multiple-lane roads merge into fewer lanes. Traffic obstacles provide several key enabling characteristics in regard to surveillance countermeasures. For surveillance detection purposes, the Principal can leverage traffic obstacles to force a surveillance effort to slow down, close distance, and concentrate, making surveillance assets more vulnerable to observation and detection. As they apply primarily to antisurveillance, traffic obstacles such as chokepoints can provide a degree of separation between the Principal and the surveillance effort. For example, when the Principal, traveling ahead of the surveillance effort, clears the obstacle/choke point, he has a window of opportunity to break away from a following surveillance effort.

A category of traffic hazards that requires additional consideration from the surveillance countermeasures standpoint is *traffic options*. Although very common, a location such as a street intersection (traffic option) that provides the Principal multiple options of travel is a traffic hazard, because if the surveillance team does not have contact with the Principal when he passes through the option, the surveillance effort is forced to degrade its integrity by fanning out assets to relocate the lost Principal, not knowing the Principal's direction of travel from the intersection (recall the *lost contact drill* from Chapter 3). Although not necessarily restrictive in the physical sense, traffic options in general do restrict a surveillance effort's freedom of movement, as assets are normally compelled to reduce following distance when approaching options in anticipation of the Principal's possible turn or change of direction.

CHANNELIZED TERRAIN

Channelized terrain consists of areas where freedom of movement is restricted to one primary route. Examples of such restrictive terrain are stretches of highway, rural roads, road construction zones where entry and exit are restricted, and roadway bridges or footbridges. The key exploitable concept of channelized terrain is that it negates a surveillance effort's ability to employ secure parallel routes or the ability to discreetly turn off of the route once committed onto it. By vehicle, one-way streets provide another dimension to a channelized route that further limits mobility for a following surveillance effort.

For surveillance countermeasures purposes, the exploitation of *channelized terrain* negates the ability for the surveillance effort to execute a secure floating box follow, and forces the surveillance effort to commit many, or perhaps all, of its assets along a single route behind the Principal. Inducing the entire surveillance effort onto a single channelized route enhances surveillance detection through observable factors such as *mirroring* and *convoying* (convoying is addressed in Chapter 7). Another potential observable is the tendency for surveillance assets to fan out at the end of a channelized corridor. As will be addressed in detail, channelized terrain is among the most effective surveillance detection enablers for the execution of surveillance detection tactics — the most effective (yet potentially overt) of which is the 180-degree turn or reversal of direction after drawing following surveillance assets into a channelized route. The exploitation of channelized terrain combined with a traffic obstacle becomes an effective antisurveillance measure.

INTRUSION POINTS

Intrusion points are locations that force surveillance assets into a close proximity with the Principal. Such locations may have a single primary point of entry and exit which further restricts maneuver for surveillance assets (but also for the Principal). Basically stated, an intrusion point is a location that forces surveillance assets to either "intrude" upon the Principal in close proximity or break contact and await the Principal's exit from the location. Common intrusion points are dead-end roads and cul-de-sacs by vehicle, and small street-side business establishments by foot.

By foot, intrusion points can be selected that enable the Principal to observe for potential surveillance operators who choose not to enter but rather linger outside awaiting the Principal's exit. Intrusion points with a secondary exit, such as a back door to a business, can be exploited to elude a surveillance effort, but such tactics may be readily perceived as overt antisurveillance measures.

As a caution, restrictive terrain such as *choke points* and *intrusion points* may also serve to isolate the Principal with the surveillance effort, making the Principal extremely vulnerable to attack if that were the intent of the surveillance effort, or if the effort feels that it must act based on being compromised (see the *fight or flight response* addressed in the next chapter).

OPEN TERRAIN

Just as the term implies, *open terrain* consists of areas where there are no, or relatively few, physical obstacles to obstruct observation for either the Principal or surveillance effort. It may sound counterintuitive to term open terrain as restrictive, but it does restrict the surveillance effort's range of options. Open terrain is restrictive terrain from the standpoint that it negates cover and concealment, and therefore restricts freedom of movement. Open terrain forces a surveillance effort to make a trade-off between line of sight observation and how closely it chooses to maintain contact with the Principal. By drawing a surveillance effort into an area where there is little vehicular or pedestrian cover and concealment, the Principal can better isolate and identify the surveillance effort. For instance, if the surveillance effort chooses close contact over distance, it makes itself immediately vulnerable to detection. Alternatively, the surveillance effort that chooses to distance itself for security purposes makes itself much more vulnerable to detection by mirroring (pacing) or a "break-away" for antisurveillance purposes. The obvious risk, however, is that if there is a danger of attack from the surveillance effort the Principal places himself in a vulnerable position by allowing the effort to isolate him in a secluded area.

BLIND SPOT

A *blind spot* is not a specific type of restrictive terrain. However, it is a key surveillance countermeasures enabling concept that primarily leverages the appropriate terrain to manipulate surveillance assets for exploitation.

A *blind spot* is any location or situation that causes a short-term loss in contact (observation) that requires movement or action by surveillance assets in order to reestablish contact. By vehicle, *blind spots* are generally facilitated by turns/bends in roads with visual obstructions such as buildings or foliage, crests or dips in roads that restrict vision, and other restrictive terrain. By foot, a common tactic to create a blind spot is the *blind turn* (blind corner), which consists of intersections or other locations at which the Principal has the option to turn, causing any following surveillance operators to lose sight of him due to structures or other visual obstructions. Such locations are particularly characteristic of urban areas, where buildings line the sidewalks on virtually every block.

As this manual progresses, the concept and applications of the *blind spot* for surveillance countermeasures purposes become very prevalent.

Transition Stages

Recall from Chapter 3 that a surveillance operation consists of three dynamic phases which have distinct transition stages between phases. Even the most capable surveillance efforts with the resources necessary to maintain synchronization and fluidity between these phases are likely most challenged during these transition stages. Transition stages (points) present challenges to the surveillance effort from the standpoint of maintaining contact with the Principal while avoiding detection. The primary transition points in a surveillance operation are when the Principal transitions from a static to mobile status and the surveillance effort transitions from a box to a follow, or when the Principal transitions from a mobile to a static position and the surveillance effort transitions from the follow to the box.

The transition stages of a surveillance operation present observable and exploitable profiles that can result in unique vulnerabilities to surveillance countermeasures. At the most basic level of observation and change detection, an observant Principal is better able to detect surveillance assets as they transition from a static to mobile status, or from mobile to static status. This, coupled with a basic understanding of how surveillance assets can be expected to position themselves to establish a box and subsequently initiate a follow, is key to detecting surveillance.

Not all transitions are associated with the transitions of a surveillance phase. Two other transition stages that may occur during the follow are the transition from vehicular surveillance to foot surveillance, and vice versa. These are also elements of the surveillance follow that present a multitude of surveillance countermeasures opportunities if properly exploited. Transition stages are addressed in detail as they apply to specific surveillance detection and antisurveillance activities.

Surveillance Countermeasures At Night

The basic surveillance and surveillance countermeasures tactics are the same for night operations as they are for operations wherein observation is less restricted. However, darkness does impose many additional considerations that must be anticipated and prepared for. Appendix 6 addresses surveillance and surveillance countermeasures at night.

5. ADVANCED SURVEILLANCE COUNTERMEASURES PLANNING CONCEPTS

Effective surveillance countermeasures planning establishes the preconditions for achieving the desired surveillance manipulation, exploitation, and detection results. Building on the fundamental concepts detailed in the previous chapter, the Principal will apply the advanced concepts detailed in this chapter to anticipate how a surveillance effort perceives the situation and acts based on these perceptions. Appropriately applied, these concepts enable the Principal to orchestrate the situation by manipulating the surveillance effort's calculus, and therefore effectively anticipating how the surveillance team will process the information and react.

TARGET PATTERN ANALYSIS

Target pattern analysis was introduced in Chapter 3 as it applies to planning and executing surveillance operations. Target pattern analysis is a process employed by a surveillance team to determine which patterns in the Principal's activities it can effectively predict and exploit. The team analyzes travel routines, specific routes used, dates and times of specific activities, and standard modes and speeds of travel. This enables surveillance assets to position themselves in the most effective manner, based on the Principal's standard, anticipated activity patterns.

At the conceptual level, since target pattern analysis is a key consideration as it applies to the planning and execution of a surveillance operation, it must also be a key driver in surveillance countermeasures planning and execution. This is the case because the "standard pattern" that the Principal projects to a potential surveillance effort is the basis for selecting the time and location of surveillance countermeasures employment.

A surveillance effort conducts target pattern analysis to maximize the efficiency and security of the surveillance. This factor becomes a key concept that can be employed for surveillance countermeasures purposes. Based on target pattern analysis, the surveillance effort tends to develop a sense of security by relying on established patterns to dictate its coverage strategy. Over time, a surveillance effort may be drawn into a sense of complacency that can be readily exploited at the time and place of the Principal's choosing. When this sense of security is suddenly disrupted by an unanticipated maneuver on the part of the Principal, the surveillance effort may be forced to react in a manner that leaves it vulnerable to detection. Chapter 13 addresses the *Chaos Theory of Surveillance* which details this and related surveillance operations dynamics.

The Principal should conduct target pattern analysis, just as the surveillance team would, to support the surveillance countermeasures process. The Principal conducts target pattern analysis on himself, which should logically lead to the same findings as a target pattern analysis conducted by a potential surveillance effort. The Principal analyzes his own activity patterns to develop a picture of what the surveillance team, if present, has observed. This analysis is based not only on the assumption that surveillance coverage is always possible, but also on the assumption that it has been present for some time, and that the surveillance team has made sufficient observations regarding the Principal's activities to conduct a thorough pattern analysis.

The effective planning and execution of surveillance countermeasures exploits the surveillance concept of target pattern analysis to develop specific strategies to detect or evade a surveillance effort based on the Principal's self-examination of established patterns of activity. This process enables the Principal to determine when and where during his routine travel patterns the surveillance effort may be vulnerable to a surveillance countermeasures maneuver, or series of maneuvers. Surveillance countermeasures maneuvers that are significantly inconsistent with the established patterns will be readily apparent as such to a surveillance effort. For this reason, the Principal's appreciation of his own target pattern analysis profile is necessary for the development of surveillance countermeasures procedures that would appear more plausible to the surveillance effort, if present. By making a comprehensive evaluation of his own activity patterns, the Principal uses his knowledge of surveillance principles and tactics to develop a concept of how a surveillance team would employ coverage.

Target pattern analysis is critical for the Principal who employs surveillance countermeasures to conduct *protected activities*. It would be a grave tactical error to diverge from an established pattern of activities to conduct surveillance countermeasures only when preparing to engage in activities that would be damaging if a surveillance team were to observe them. In conducting surveillance detection only at specific times, the Principal will probably take actions that are not consistent with the target pattern analysis the surveillance team has conducted. Any significant alteration of established activity patterns will only result in enhanced caution (and interest) on the part of the surveillance effort. Such alterations in patterns serve to confirm to the surveillance team that the Principal does indeed have something to hide — and will probably result in continued and enhanced surveillance coverage. Therefore, the Principal should integrate surveillance countermeasures activities into standard travel patterns, to make them appear close enough to the norm to discourage suspicion on the part of the surveillance effort.

The Principal should also incorporate the perceived objectives of the possible surveillance coverage into the target analysis process. A surveillance operation is conducted to observe and document activities that satisfy the objectives of the operation. Although the possible objectives of a surveillance operation are unlimited, they may involve identifying protected activity that can be used against the interests of the Principal, such as information that can be exploited as leverage against the Principal for various objectives to include business negotiations, legal prosecution, or for attack planning. A cognizance of the likely adversarial objectives of a potential surveillance effort informs the Principal regarding where and when the execution of effective surveillance countermeasures may be necessary.

The Covert-Overt Spectrum

Active surveillance countermeasures are categorized as covert or overt. Covert surveillance countermeasures are executed discreetly and are intended to detect or elude a surveillance effort without being recognized as active countermeasures. Overt surveillance countermeasures are intended to detect or elude with less or no regard whether the surveillance effort perceives them as such. Active surveillance detection and antisurveillance measures are conducted along the spectrum from covert to overt; however, there are varying degrees of each and no clear delineation regarding where the two meet along this spectrum. In fact, this delineation will be defined on a case-by-case basis, based on the objectives of the specific surveillance countermeasures effort.

As a standard principle, the more covert the surveillance countermeasure the less active it is, and the more overt the countermeasure the more active it is. In turn, the more overt (active or aggressive) the surveillance detection or antisurveillance maneuver, the more effective it will be in achieving the desired result. The potentially misleading part of this principle is that it may be read to equate "effective" with "good." Even if a maneuver is effective in detecting or evading surveillance, if the overall objective includes ensuring that the surveillance effort does not suspect surveillance countermeasures, then the maneuver may not be effective in the broader sense. An appreciation of the *covert-overt spectrum* enables the Principal to plan and execute surveillance countermeasures based on the understanding that there are varying degrees of "effectiveness" based on the specific surveillance countermeasures objectives.

Generally, the more covert or discreet the surveillance countermeasures technique, the less effective it will be in meeting immediate surveillance countermeasures goals. Conversely, the more overt or active the method the more effective it will be in meeting immediate surveillance countermeasures goals. Consequently, the more overt the method, the more identifiable it will be to a surveillance effort (if present) as surveillance countermeasures. Therefore, based on varying objectives, the covert-overt spectrum is relative to the desired results. With few exceptions, it is in the Principal's best interests, at least initially, that the surveillance effort not suspect that he is surveillance conscious or practicing surveillance countermeasures.

The covert-overt spectrum is based on the Principal's subjective professional judgment regarding the need to execute effective surveillance countermeasures, versus the acceptable risk of being observed conducting active or overt measures by the surveillance effort, if present. The determination of where along the spectrum of covert to overt the surveillance countermeasure employed will fall is normally based on an assessment of the risk versus the need to positively confirm or elude surveillance activity. If, at a certain point in time, the benefit gained by executing a successful surveillance detection or antisurveillance maneuver does not outweigh the risk of demonstrating surveillance awareness to the surveillance effort, the Principal will weigh in favor of more covert techniques. Conversely, if ensuring the execution of a successful surveillance detection or antisurveillance method warrants the risk of an aggressive display of surveillance awareness, then the measure employed will be more overt or active.

As a general rule, unless the Principal has reason to suspect that there is a surveillance effort present with immediate hostile intent, the more sophisticated approach to surveillance countermeasures is to execute them in a manner that does not disclose that the Principal is surveillance conscious. In general, the Principal has many more options and can exploit many more vulnerabilities against a surveillance effort that does not suspect that the Principal is surveillance conscious and is practicing surveillance countermeasures. This would tend to favor more covert (discreet) surveillance countermeasures.

There are various potential consequences if a Principal is observed conducting surveillance countermeasures. The perception that the Principal may have something to hide or have other concerns can likely result in a more determined approach on the part of the surveillance effort. In response, the surveillance effort may opt to use more operators or more sophisticated measures such as technical surveillance capabilities to minimize the probability of exposure. Therefore, it is generally to the Principal's long-term advantage that the surveillance team not suspect he is conducting surveillance countermeasures.

Overt methods are more applicable when the need to detect or evade a potential surveillance effort overrides any considerations regarding the need to remain discreet. There are circumstances when the need to determine for certain whether surveillance is present overrides these considerations. For example, protective services personnel providing security for a high-risk Principal may be extremely overt in attempting to detect or evade surveillance.

Although very overt and aggressive measures — illegal maneuvers that violate traffic laws — are among the most effective surveillance countermeasures techniques. Running red lights, illegal left-hand turns, and illegal U-turns are among the most basic examples of countermeasures techniques that gain their very effectiveness directly because they are illegal (overt). In many cases, not only will a surveillance effort — to maintain security — not continue to pursue the Principal after such an illegal maneuver, but, depending on the nature of the element, they may not want to risk being detected by law enforcement for mirroring this illegal maneuver. In fact, many covert or illegal elements conducting surveillance cannot risk that type of exposure. Therefore, there are various reasons why overt measures may actually degrade the effectiveness of deliberate surveillance detection effort.

Although there may be extreme cases wherein the employment of overt surveillance countermeasures may be necessary, a primary purpose of this manual is to demonstrate that countermeasures can be accomplished through sophisticated procedures that alleviate the need to carry out isolated, overt measures that may be readily identified as surveillance countermeasures. In addition, overt measures may force a fight or flight reaction which can have negative consequences on both ends of that spectrum, which is addressed next.

FIGHT OR FLIGHT REACTION

A final consideration in where along the *covert-overt spectrum* a surveillance countermeasure should be employed involves the classic *fight or flight response*. As with many factors surrounding the surveillance and countermeasures battle, there are psychological factors that apply just as they do in the most savage expanses of the wild. The fight or flight response (also called the "acute stress response") simply means that an animal has two options when faced with danger: it can either face the threat (fight) or it can avoid the threat (flight). The previous discussion regarding a surveillance effort's tendency to break contact (flight) rather than mirror an overt surveillance countermeasures maneuver (fight) reflects this concept.

Generally, a surveillance effort places a higher priority on security than on maintaining contact with the Principal, and will therefore choose flight over fight. However, it is important to understand that in some cases, depending largely on the ultimate intent of the surveillance effort, an overt surveillance countermeasure that is identified as such may force the surveillance effort into the fight mode. Any surveillance effort that continues coverage despite knowing that it has been compromised represents an immediate threat to the Principal, warranting extreme antisurveillance, anti-pursuit, and protective measures. The most extreme consequence involves a surveillance effort that perceives that it has been compromised and is compelled to react in a high-risk or violent manner, rather than run the risk of not having another opportunity with the Principal. For example, a surveillance effort that is following a Principal for the purpose of determining where he would be most susceptible to attack and kidnapping may react by moving directly into the attack phase of the operation if it observes actions by the Principal that may indicate that he is attempting to detect or elude surveillance, and they may not have another opportunity if these attempts are successful.

SURVEILLANCE-ENABLED ELICITATION AND RECRUITMENT TECHNIQUES
Recall that a surveillance operation may be conducted to develop personal, and potentially exploitable, information regarding the Principal. In some cases, a surveillance operation may be conducted solely for developing information that can be used to establish an interpersonal relationship with a surveillance asset or another adversarial agent. Such an interpersonal relationship may be established to develop additional information on the Principal, or to establish a relationship that will eventually lead to the coercion/recruitment of the Principal to act on behalf of the adversarial element. Motivation for coercion/recruitment may include money, blackmail, or fear (based on threats against self, family, or other interests). In espionage and counterspy terminology, this is referred to as "getting hooks into" the individual.

When establishing a personal relationship with the Principal, either as a supporting effort or the main objective of a surveillance effort, at some point the surveillance effort or adversarial element will place an operator/agent "up against" the Principal. This refers to the tactic of actually having a surveillance operator or adversarial agent establish contact and rapport with the Principal. This may involve a one-time-contact effort to elicit specific information, or an effort to establish a relationship that will continue to develop in the future. In either case, the Principal should be familiar with standard elicitation techniques such as "leading questions," "ego-up," and "playing dumb," to enable the employment of effective counter-elicitation methods. In many cases, adversarial elements can develop sufficient information through social media research and other public domain sources to establish an initial common interest with the Principal for the purpose of facilitating an initial degree of rapport. Adversarial agents are highly trained and experienced with building interpersonal relationships under false pretenses. In addition to the obvious establishments, such as bars and night clubs, which inherently engender social interaction, public transportation, such as planes and trains, also provide exceptional venues to establish an apparently harmless interaction.

In many cases, the adversarial element will employ innocuous appearing individuals, such as senior citizens or women disguised to be pregnant, because their appearance alone normally enables them to "disarm" and bypass the Principal's defenses. The Principal should always be suspicious of people who are immediately able to establish rapport in chance encounters based on a common professional or personal interest. Any attempts by such individuals to arrange further contact with the Principal should be regarded with extreme caution, as should any coincidental chance encounter that occurs at a later point in time.

Although the security-minded Principal should approach any "chance encounters" with caution, these circumstances also offer the opportunity to provide a possible surveillance effort with deceptive or misleading information. The Principal's primary concern in such situations is to ensure that the surveillance team cannot invalidate the information he provides through previous observations or other means, thus disclosing his deceptive measures.

A sophisticated threat element will evaluate the results of any personal encounter/interaction with the Principal to assess whether a more enduring relationship can be established under the guise of a friendship or another feasible type of relationship. Such a relationship would enable the surveillance effort to develop information to support the objectives of the surveillance operation, or the larger adversarial element objectives against the Principal. This is classic agent recruitment tradecraft, but it also provides the witting Principal an opportunity to reduce the manipulators to the manipulated. In the vein of a classical "double agent" operation, the Principal can exploit such a relationship to feed information that supports his surveillance detection, antisurveillance, or other adversarial defeat objectives.

6. PASSIVE SURVEILLANCE DETECTION OVERVIEW

Recall that the very nature of physical surveillance dictates that the surveillance team risk a degree of exposure to the Principal regardless of the Principal's actions. *Passive surveillance detection* consists of the Principal (or a security detail escorting the Principal) observing the surroundings to identify indications or instances of surveillance without taking any active measures. Passive detection is conducted in a manner that does not provide the surveillance effort, if present, any indication that the Principal is observing for a surveillance presence. Passive surveillance detection is conducted during the Principal's standard activities, when no unusual action is being taken.

A general understanding of surveillance principles and tactics facilitates the effective employment of passive physical surveillance detection. Since the Principal conducts passive physical surveillance detection during his standard activities, he will give no indication to the surveillance team that he is doing so if employed properly. Obviously, the indications of surveillance that the Principal passively observes for are equally applicable when executing more *active* surveillance detection measures as addressed in the applicable chapters.

Passive surveillance detection makes maximum use of enhanced observation practices (addressed in the Appendix 2) to detect indications of surveillance presence based on a sound understanding of the principles and tactics employed by a sophisticated surveillance effort. Anyone concerned with personal security should practice passive detection routinely as a standard, baseline security measure, even when there is no specific reason to suspect surveillance.

To facilitate passive surveillance detection, the Principal should proceed as though every surrounding vehicle and individual are surveillance assets. By employing passive detection, the Principal develops indications of surveillance if it exists. At that point, the Principal may choose to employ active surveillance detection measures or antisurveillance measures against the identified or suspected surveillance effort as addressed in Chapters 9-13. As the Principal becomes more experienced in surveillance detection, it becomes easy to initially identify suspicious individuals or vehicles and recognize them when observed again — hours, days, or weeks later.

An understanding of surveillance principles and tactics is critical to the effective application of passive surveillance detection. A Principal can exploit his knowledge of the tactics a surveillance effort employs against him for detection purposes. A surveillance team operates in a logical and systematic manner to maximize coverage and minimize exposure. A sophisticated surveillance team can operate against an unwitting Principal for extended periods without providing any indication of its presence. However, against a Principal who is surveillance conscious and capable of conducting discreet passive surveillance detection, the surveillance team tends to exercise less diligence and likely exposes itself to a much greater risk of compromise.

7. PASSIVE VEHICULAR SURVEILLANCE DETECTION

The effectiveness of passive vehicular surveillance detection is based largely on an understanding of vehicular surveillance tactics and the fact that vehicular routes of travel are generally restricted to, or channelized by, established roadways. The imperative for surveillance assets that have relatively limited maneuverability to maintain observation of the Principal makes passive surveillance detection an effective and unalarming practice. The Principal's rear and side view mirrors are the key surveillance detection enablers which provide a continuous capability to observe potential surveillance vehicles unless they are capable of employing *cover* and *concealment* at a sustained level, which is extremely challenging during the course of a comprehensive surveillance operation.

STAKEOUT AND PICK-UP PHASE DETECTION
In the stakeout, the surveillance team is positioned to pick-up the Principal as he passes through or departs the stakeout location. This requires that surveillance vehicles be positioned to observe for the Principal and pull out as he passes their location. In the vehicular stakeout, box positions are established primarily by surveillance vehicles, but foot operators may be used to observe locations that cannot be covered securely by a vehicle. The primary locations for stakeout consideration are the Principal's residence and workplace. Other possibilities include frequented establishments and the residences of relatives and associates.

Target pattern analysis is particularly effective when based against the threat of a surveillance stakeout in preparation for a mobile pick-up. By identifying which locations a surveillance team would likely select to establish stakeout box positions, the Principal can determine specific locations on which to focus surveillance detection attention. In evaluating potential stakeout positions, the Principal should also assess where fixed observation posts or mobile surveillance systems might be located to support the stakeout effort. Observation post detection is addressed in detail in Appendix 5.

A surveillance team is particularly vulnerable to detection in the stakeout phase because operators must remain in static positions for extended periods of time. Additionally, although the team will have a good general plan for where the Principal is anticipated to initially appear, the fact remains that he could appear in a location that leaves the team vulnerable to compromise.

Surveillance vehicles are positioned to observe all routes into and out of the specified stakeout area. The positioning enables a surveillance vehicle to pull out and establish command of the Principal to initiate the mobile follow along every route out of the stakeout area. Figure 1 depicts a stakeout box established to pick-up the Principal as he drives away from an enclosed parking garage in a residence (R). The surveillance vehicles are shown in simplified box positions to illustrate how they would position themselves to initiate the follow as the Principal travels out of the stakeout box. The arrows in front of each surveillance vehicle indicate the direction in which they are oriented in order to pick-up the Principal as he departs the stakeout area (See Figure 1 next page).

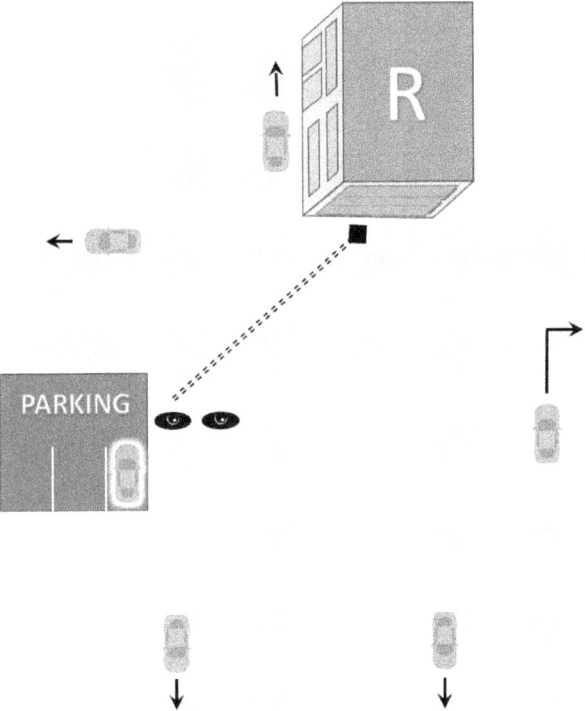

FIGURE 1

A stakeout box established to pick-up the Principal as he departs his residence by vehicle

When the Principal determines that the stakeout box may be positioned around a denied location such as a residence or workplace, he should observe for indications of a *trigger*. A *trigger* is a surveillance vehicle or operator that is positioned to initially observe the Principal and alert the team as he departs a denied area or enters his vehicle. The *trigger vehicle* in Figure 1 is depicted with the "eye" icon. Since a trigger position requires line of sight observation, the trigger is detectable by the Principal unless there is sufficient cover and concealment. In fact, in preparation for the surveillance detection process, the Principal should conduct a *line of sight analysis* based on where the trigger would likely focus observation, such as the door the Principal would be expected to exit, where the Principal vehicle is parked, or where the Principal vehicle will emerge from a garage. This level of analysis better narrows the locations most suitable for a trigger position, and therefore determines where the Principal can concentrate his limited surveillance detection opportunities as he begins to travel. An observation post may be employed to provide a discreet trigger capability. When appropriate for security or operational purposes, a foot operator may perform as a trigger to initiate the vehicular surveillance follow.

Although employing a trigger can be key to initiating a successful pick-up and follow, it is vulnerable to detection. The reason for this is that it may give the Principal a good look at the surveillance vehicle — at an angle which may allow him to see that it is manned. Vehicles with an individual or individuals inside that are parked in a position to observe the Principal should be retained as an indicator of a surveillance stakeout. The Principal can inconspicuously observe for such positions while departing the denied area, walking to his vehicle, while placing items in the vehicle, and when negotiating traffic to depart his residence drive or parking area. Although the trigger is likely to be the most vulnerable asset to detection in the stakeout box, this type box position is widely used, particularly when there is sufficient cover from other vehicles parked on the side of the road and traffic traveling on the road. Ideally, the trigger remains static during the pick-up with another vehicle establishing initial command from a more discreet location. If the Principal identifies a potential trigger that pulls out in the Principal's direction of travel after he passes, this is indicative of a single vehicle surveillance or a poorly disciplined surveillance operator/vehicle.

A surveillance effort may choose to establish a stakeout box in an area they assess the Principal will travel through, rather than around the (denied) location from which the Principal is expected to initially emerge. This may be done for security purposes or to facilitate a more effective pick-up. A stakeout box of this nature is normally established at a location where the Principal invariably passes through. For example, the Principal may reside in a residential area that only has one route in and out to the main thoroughfares, providing the surveillance team with additional stakeout box locations to choose from along the route he must travel. Even when the box is established away from the Principal's base location, a *trigger* may be established at that location to alert the team of the Principal's departure and imminent arrival at the box location.

As the Principal leaves an area that he has assessed as a possible location for a surveillance stakeout, he observes for vehicles or individuals meeting the profile of those employing stakeout tactics. He should be familiar with vehicles that are normally in the area of the possible stakeout and be able to identify those that appear alien and do not blend with others in the area. The Principal should discreetly note the license numbers of any suspicious vehicles when possible.

Among the most effective surveillance detection enablers is a strong understanding of how surveillance assets position themselves to facilitate a seamless and effective *pick-up* when transitioning from the static *box* to the dynamic *follow*. The pick-up requires that a vehicle pull out from a stationary location and follow the Principal. The tactics of surveillance dictate that there are optimum positions for a surveillance vehicle to be situated in order to establish command of the Principal securely and effectively. The most basic surveillance vehicle pick-up position is to parallel park on the right side of the road on which the Principal vehicle may pass (see Figure 2).

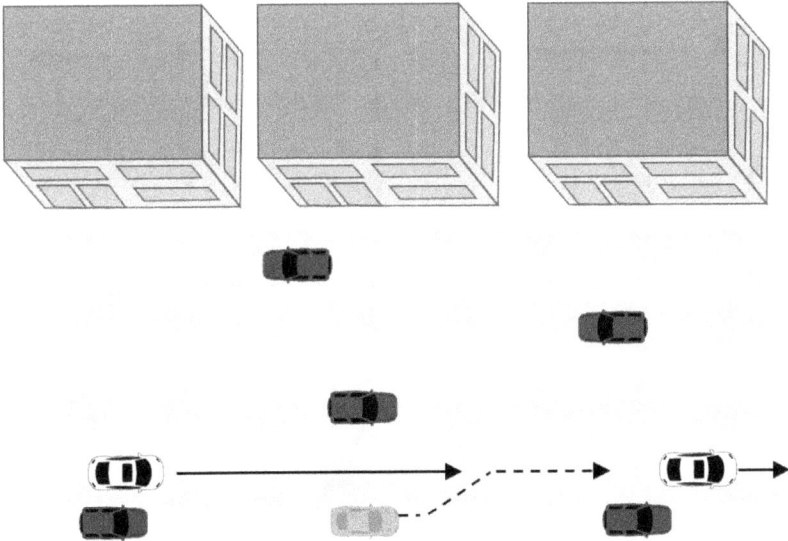

FIGURE 2

Basic parallel parking box position used by a surveillance vehicle to leverage the cover of other parked vehicles and establish command of the Principal securely and effectively

The best pick-up positions for surveillance vehicles are those which can be established off the main road of travel. Such positions allow the surveillance vehicle to complete the assignment without being in the Principal's line of sight as he passes by. Parking lots are often suitable locations for pick-up positioning. The most common and readily available locations for pick-up positions are roads that run perpendicular and join the main road of anticipated travel. By parallel parking on such roads, the surveillance vehicle can observe its designated stakeout location and pull out to establish command of the Principal (see Figure 3).

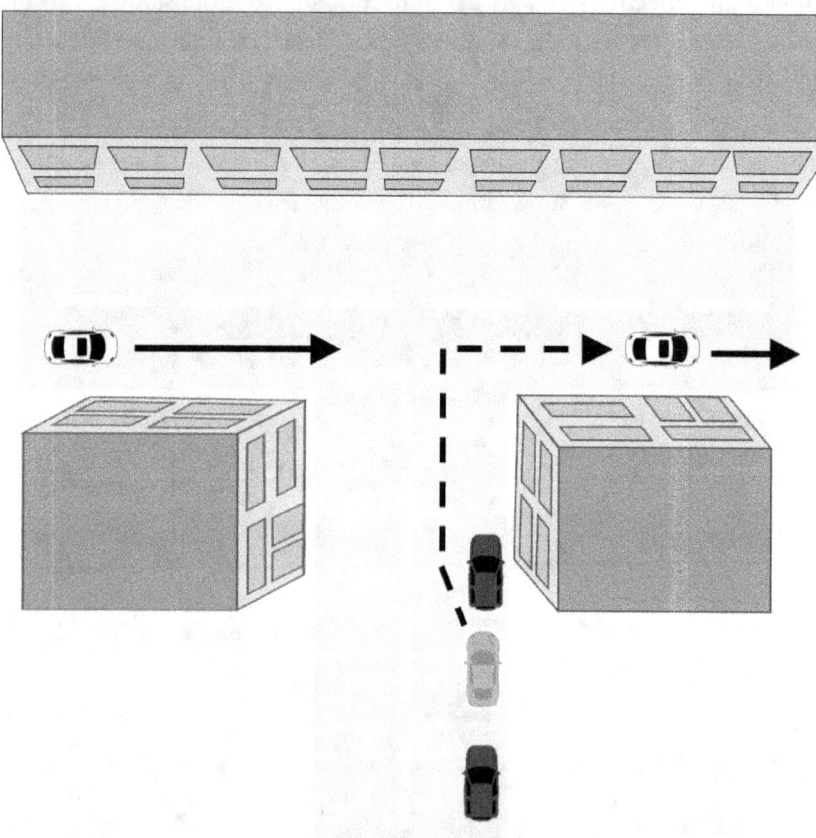

FIGURE 3

A road that is perpendicular to the Principal's main road of travel is a common location for a pick-up position that avoids the Principal driving directly by the surveillance vehicle

When selecting a pick-up position in a parking lot or on a perpendicular road, the surveillance vehicle will attempt to ensure that it can make an unimpeded entry onto the main route of travel. Surveillance vehicles will be positioned to best negotiate traffic, which is likely to be the primary obstacle to establishing the pick-up. To lower the probability that traffic impedes entry, positioning should be based on the Principal's anticipated direction of travel. On two-way roads the pick-up surveillance vehicle should always select a position that allows it to enter the main route of travel from the right side as the traffic flows to ensure that the surveillance vehicle can make a right turn onto the main route to pick-up the Principal. Making a left turn makes it more difficult to enter the main route because the surveillance vehicle is impeded by traffic traveling in both directions. This applies to a lesser degree on one-way roads because the probability encountering traffic from the road to be entered is the same from either side; however, a surveillance vehicle attempting a left turn onto a one-way road may still be impeded by oncoming traffic. These considerations are applied less rigidly in residential or rural areas where traffic is light and presents a negligible obstacle.

Based on his understanding of stakeout pick-up positions, the Principal observes for indications of the pick-up when departing or passing through the possible stakeout area. There are many indicators he should focus on when observing for surveillance vehicles parked parallel on the side of the road or on perpendicular roads where box positions may be within observation range (recall that priority should go to vehicles parked on the right side of the road that can pull out quickly to follow). As the Principal identifies vehicles that display indicators of surveillance boxing, he retains their images for subsequent recognition.

An initial specific indicator the Principal observes for is parked vehicles that are manned. The standard manning for most surveillance vehicles is a driver and a front seat passenger, but a parked vehicle with any number of occupants should be considered indicative. Surveillance operators in a vehicle on stakeout must ensure that they not only appear inconspicuous to the Principal but also to others who may approach them or notify the authorities of suspicious activity. Surveillance operators in vehicles may use the seats to block the view of passing traffic, but if they make the tactical error of forgetting to remove their seat belts/shoulder straps, passing traffic can observe them easily even though they may have employed all other principles of discretion.

At night, light from his headlights and other surrounding illumination assists the Principal in observing silhouetted persons or objects in parked vehicles. Exhaust from a running vehicle is yet another indication that it is manned and ready to maneuver. If the driver has the brake pedal engaged, even when the surveillance vehicle is not running, the brake lights project. While surveillance vehicles are in box positions during periods of inclement weather, such as rain or snow, they must keep their vehicle windows clear to observe for the Principal. They will do so primarily with windshield wipers and the vehicle defroster. Although this is necessary, it makes surveillance vehicles stand out, as they will be among the only vehicles parked along the road with clear windows that can be seen into. This is particularly true in the case of snowfall, but it also applies to icy conditions and, to a lesser degree, rainfall. The Principal should observe for these indicators when conducting surveillance detection at night and in inclement weather.

When the Principal begins to emerge from a location where a surveillance effort would establish a box, if present, he observes for indications of the stakeout box pick-up. In most cases, this involves no active measures and consists of passive surveillance detection. Observation for change detection purposes is most effective in areas where the Principal is very familiar with the normal surroundings, such as the neighborhood he lives in. The Principal initially observes for vehicles or individuals who are conspicuously placed to act as a potential trigger. Unusually placed trucks, vans, or vehicles with tinted windows are particular indicators. As the Principal begins to move, he observes for vehicles that conspicuously transition from a static to a mobile status. When the Principal departs the potential box location by vehicle, he observes for vehicles that are located in likely positions to pull out and assume the follow; focusing primarily on vehicles that pull out behind the Principal from parallel parking positions or from positions adjacent to the primary route, such as parking lots and side streets.

The detection of assets moving from static to mobile status can be very apparent to the observant Principal. After passing potential surveillance vehicles or locations from which pick-up vehicles may emerge, he observes back through the side or rear view mirror to see if the vehicle in question pulls out to follow, or if one emerges from a previously concealed location. It is much more difficult to observe for pick-up vehicles parked in parking lots or on perpendicular roads because of the additional cover this usually affords them. Additionally, it is much more obvious that a Principal is surveillance conscious when he can be observed visually checking every such location. A vehicle that the Principal observes pulling out and following from these positions offers the primary indicator of a surveillance pick-up. Again, the Principal should pay more attention to vehicles pulling out from the right side of the road, as surveillance assets would not likely assume the risk of having to cross traffic to initiate a follow.

FOLLOW PHASE DETECTION

The primary purpose of passive vehicular surveillance detection is to identify vehicles that might be indicative of surveillance coverage. The ultimate objective of passive vehicular surveillance detection is to identify the same vehicle in two separate locations that are unrelated or non-coincidental. Ideally, the Principal will detect indications of surveillance during the pick-up, but it is rarely that simple. During the follow phase, the surveillance team is constantly vulnerable to detection because at least one surveillance vehicle must maintain line of sight observation (command) of the Principal. The team must also react discreetly to maneuvers by the Principal. Due to these facts alone, passive surveillance detection can be extremely effective, even against a well-disciplined surveillance team.

Recall that with a fully-integrated surveillance team, a number of separate surveillance vehicles observe the Principal at different periods throughout the mobile follow. This dictates that the Principal concentrate not only on one or two probable vehicles, but any number of vehicles. Also recall that a comprehensive surveillance effort does not comprise only one trip or day in the life of the Principal. This dictates that the Principal remember any vehicles he observes that fit the profile of a surveillance vehicle for extended periods. For instance, if the Principal observes a suspected surveillance vehicle and then observes it two weeks later at an unrelated location, he has virtually confirmed that he is under surveillance. This example emphasizes the importance of keen observation and retention skills in surveillance detection.

As already mentioned, a well-disciplined surveillance team will only expose one surveillance vehicle at any given time during the mobile follow. For this reason, the Principal will normally observe for a single possible surveillance vehicle at any one time. An exception is when he is traveling on terrain that facilitates rear observation over a distance such as straight highways or rural roads, or when multiple surveillance assets are committed onto a channelize route of travel behind the Principal. Also, during the mobile phase of a surveillance operation, a well-disciplined surveillance team rarely provides the Principal with specific indicators of surveillance unless he takes active measures to induce a conspicuous reaction. Since passive detection involves no active measures by the Principal, detection is generally limited to multiple sightings of surveillance vehicles, suspicious activity observed when a surveillance vehicle is forced close to the Principal vehicle due to traffic hazards, or perhaps when the surveillance team mishaps and conducts an unforced, isolated tactical error.

Recall that one particular aspect of the mobile follow that the Principal may be able to detect through passive observation is mirroring. Mirroring refers to the tendency of a surveillance vehicle to duplicate the Principal's maneuvers. This results from the sometimes even subconscious tendency of a driver to continually place the surveillance vehicle in the optimum position to follow and react to the Principal's maneuvers. Although this is more significant in active surveillance detection, it may also be detectable through passive observation. As the Principal navigates through traffic he observes for following vehicles that appear to be mirroring his actions.

A passive method of eliciting such an action from a possible following surveillance vehicle is to engage the turn signal well in advance of a turn and observe for any vehicle that moves into a position to make the same turn. Engaging the turn signal on short notice — or failing to signal at all — is an active measure that rarely serves the purpose of surveillance detection against a well-disciplined surveillance team. The reason is that if the driver of a surveillance vehicle is not in a position to make a turn with the Principal securely, he should simply relinquish command (hand-off) to a vehicle that can do so from a more secure distance.

Also as it applies to mirroring, anytime the Principal makes a turn, he should observe to his rear to identify any vehicles that also make the turn. This in and of itself rarely confirms that a surveillance effort is underway, but it can facilitate surveillance detection by adding to the Principal's mental database of vehicles he may observe subsequently, again over time. The obvious exception to this is when the surveillance element consists of one or a few vehicles, dictating more frequent and less secure turns behind the Principal, leaving it much more vulnerable to detection.

During a follow, the members of a surveillance effort with multiple assets *hand-off* command of the Principal among each other to reduce prolonged asset exposure and to reduce the signature of mirroring the Principal's movements. Surveillance assets on well-disciplined surveillance efforts instinctively know when to hand-off to another asset to reduce exposure and appear unsuspicious to the Principal. The most basic example of this *hand-off* process (Figure 4) is when the Principal is traveling along a route and then takes a turn onto another road. In this case, the surveillance asset (1) traveling most closely behind the Principal continues straight at the intersection, while another surveillance asset (2) that is further out of observation range takes the turn and establishes command of the Principal.

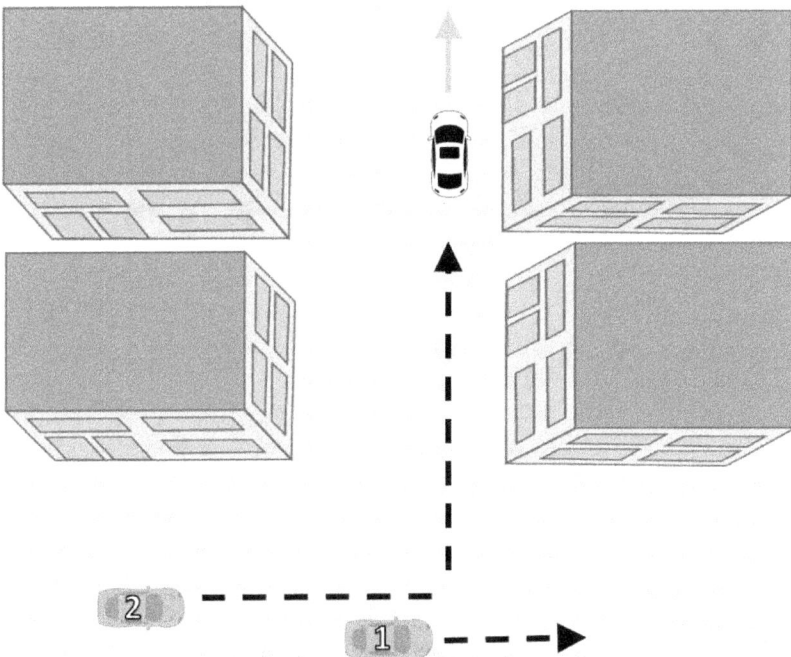

Figure 4
The basic hand-off between a command vehicle and a following surveillance vehicle in reaction to the Principal taking a turn

When the Principal is keyed in on a following vehicle as a possible surveillance vehicle, and it continues straight after the Principal takes a turn (potentially indicative of a hand-off), the Principal should observe for any vehicle which subsequently turns behind him and key on that vehicle as a potential surveillance vehicle. In this case, the Principal may observe a potential surveillance vehicle accelerate slightly after taking the turn to establish an effective follow (command) position.

An alternative hand-off tactic is employed when a command surveillance vehicle (1) assesses the need to turn off and transition control of the Principal to a follow-on surveillance vehicle (2) (Figure 5).

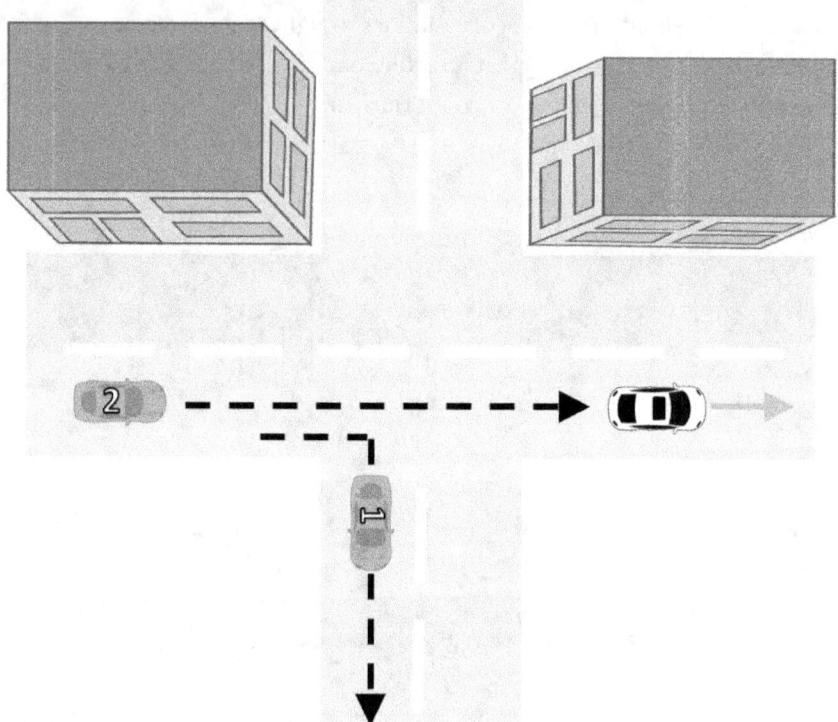

Figure 5

The command vehicle chooses to turn off of the Principal's route of travel and hand-off command to a following surveillance vehicle

In this case, the Principal may observe the vehicle taking the hand-off and assuming command (2) accelerate slightly through the intersection to establish an effective follow position.

Another indicator of surveillance that the Principal may detect through passive observation is *pacing*. This is another form of mirroring in which the surveillance vehicle tends to gauge the speed of the Principal and travel at that same general speed. In doing so, the surveillance vehicle maintains a standard following distance that may not be consistent with the surrounding traffic. An undisciplined surveillance vehicle may even provide suspicious indicators such as holding back traffic or making erratic maneuvers to maintain the established pacing distance.

Convoying is an indicator of surveillance which is detectable on roadways that afford the Principal a long look back at following traffic, such as highways and rural roads. Convoying is the tendency for surveillance vehicles to maintain an equal distance between each other. Obviously, this tendency is only detectable when the terrain allows the Principal to observe two or more potential surveillance vehicles. Over a period of time and distance, the Principal may detect surveillance vehicles because they meet the profile of maintaining the convoy effect while other vehicles pass by. Streets with a long downward or upward slope provide optimal terrain for observing for convoying vehicles and other indicators of vehicular surveillance. The characteristics of darkness which facilitate the observation of vehicle lights from a distance also enhance the detection of convoying vehicles on appropriate terrain.

Overall, in conducting passive vehicular surveillance detection the Principal should observe for any activity of surrounding traffic that appears peculiar. Even the best surveillance teams commit tactical errors — maneuvers that appear suspicious because they do not blend with the surrounding traffic. Surveillance vehicles may reduce their following distance on the Principal when approaching traffic hazards such as highway interchanges or busy intersections in order to maintain command through the hazard. This tendency is referred to as the *avoid lost contact concept* and is addressed in detail in Chapter 13. After maintaining command of the Principal through the hazard, the surveillance vehicles tend to increase following distance and reestablish a more secure following position.

At times during the follow, surveillance vehicles may lose temporary command of the Principal and be forced to travel at accelerated speeds to reestablish contact, perhaps bearing down quickly on the Principal for identification purposes and then decelerating to establish a comfortable following distance. When the Principal stops at a traffic light or stop sign, following traffic is forced in behind. In these situations, the Principal should observe for vehicles that appear to slow prematurely as though to avoid driving up behind him. Such occurrences provide strong indicators of surveillance to the observant Principal.

Traffic density, or lack thereof, may force a surveillance vehicle much closer to the Principal vehicle than desirable. It is not uncommon for a surveillance vehicle to find itself directly behind the Principal at a traffic stop. Such circumstances afford the Principal an excellent opportunity to examine potential surveillance vehicles and their occupants. One indicator might be a passenger-side occupant looking in his lap as though reading a map (again, the navigator is continuously examining the map to anticipate the Principal's actions and to identify potential traffic hazards ahead). Another might be a passenger-side occupant who is talking but does not necessarily appear to be conversing with the driver — either because his head movements are not consistent with the conversation or because the driver does not appear to be talking — indicating that the occupant is transmitting information to other surveillance vehicles. After a potential surveillance vehicle has been forced uncomfortably close, the Principal should observe its subsequent actions. If there are supporting surveillance vehicles, it will likely turn off and transfer command to a follow-on surveillance vehicle as soon as possible due to the high degree of exposure.

At dawn and at the approach of dusk, the sun can be either an asset or a liability to the surveillance detection effort. When traveling toward the sun there is poor forward visibility, forcing any surveillance vehicles to decrease their following distance. At the same time, while the Principal's visibility is obstructed to the front, it will be relatively good to the rear, which may allow him to observe following surveillance vehicles clearly. The surveillance team may attempt to overcome this disadvantage by establishing a command vehicle in front of the Principal (lead vehicle). Conversely, when traveling away from the sun the Principal's visibility is obstructed to the rear.

Adverse weather conditions such as rain, sleet, or snow generally obstruct the Principal's vision. There are some advantages in that adverse conditions normally require surveillance vehicles to decrease their following distance. In the case of heavy rainfall or snow, particularly when traveling at high speeds, visibility is generally obstructed more to the front than to the rear. This may result in surveillance vehicles following at decreased distances due to poor visibility while the Principal has relatively better visibility to the rear. Rear visibility is normally clearest through the side-view mirrors. Alternatively, a surveillance team may attempt to overcome this limitation by establishing a lead command vehicle ahead of the Principal.

BOX PHASE DETECTION

Recall from the discussion of surveillance principles and tactics (Chapter 3) that anytime the Principal vehicle stops (excluding standard traffic stops), the surveillance team establishes a box around it to ensure an effective transition back to the mobile follow. The box is based on the systematic positioning of surveillance assets around the area where the static Principal is located in order to prepare for a mobile surveillance follow when the Principal begins to move. The techniques of the surveillance box basically consist of the logical coverage of roads or routes by which the Principal can depart the fixed location.

During this transition, there is an inherent vulnerability to detection as the surveillance assets maneuver based on the Principal's actions, and may be forced to pass directly by the Principal's position. A sound understanding of surveillance boxing tactics is essential to identifying where box positions might be located. By applying such knowledge, the Principal can identify specific locations where a surveillance team would position assets to facilitate a secure and effective mobile pick-up. This assessment enhances the Principal's awareness of where he may observe assets maneuvering to establish box positions, and to focus his observation when departing any potential surveillance box area. Area knowledge is necessary to analyze possible box locations; when the Principal is not familiar with the area, he should examine a map to determine likely locations, if possible in a discreet manner.

The Principal uses any such stop as an opportunity to observe for indications of surveillance, which will likely be more evident the more unexpected the stop may be. Routine short-term stops, such as stopping at a gas station to pump fuel, offer excellent opportunities to observe for boxing surveillance vehicles. Regardless of the stop location, it should provide a plausible reason for the stop (cover for action) and the opportunity to inconspicuously observe for surveillance assets.

Figure 6 depicts the standard surveillance team reaction to a temporary stop by the Principal. Surveillance vehicles (1), (2), (3), (4), and (5) are executing a standard follow when the Principal turns into a parking lot. As command vehicle (1) informs the team that the Principal is entering a parking lot, it continues straight to establish a box position. Surveillance vehicle (2), the backing vehicle, maneuvers to establish a trigger position. The remaining surveillance vehicles maneuver to their box positions by the use of routes that allow them to avoid passing by the Principal's location.

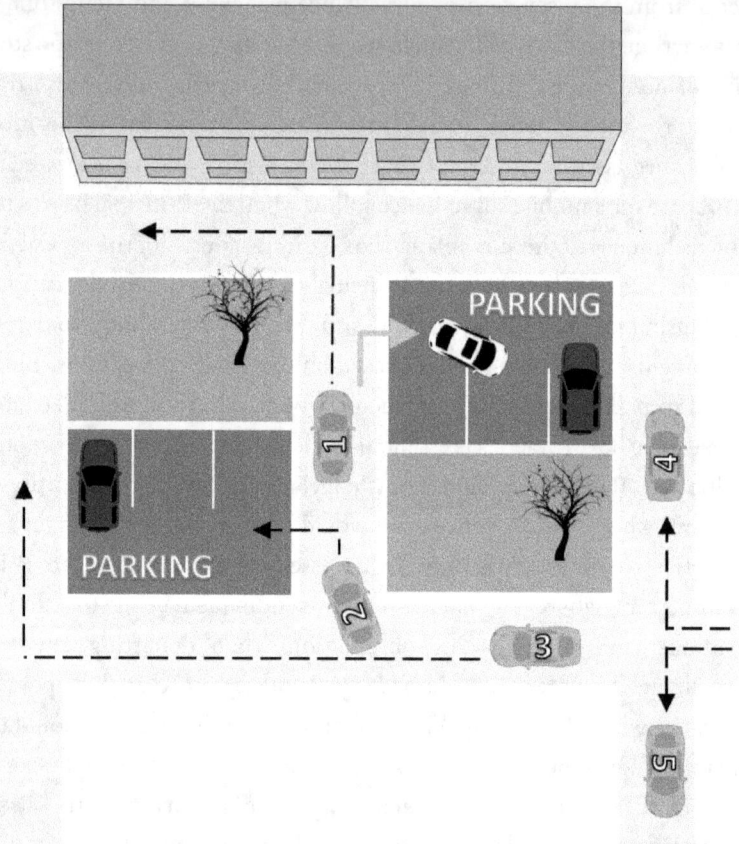

Figure 6

The surveillance team reacts to a stop by the Principal and postures to establish box positions

When stopping at any location, the Principal observes all vehicles that pass by subsequent to the stop. The command vehicle will normally continue past the Principal vehicle to defer subsequent observation duties to a surveillance vehicle that can position itself in a more discreet manner. Additionally, any other surveillance vehicles that are too close to the location of the stop to discreetly stop for an observation position must turn off prior to passing by the Principal in a potentially conspicuous manner, or continue past the Principal to avoid appearing suspicious while exposing itself to observation. This affords the Principal a free look at the command vehicle and perhaps additional surveillance vehicles. The Principal observes all passing vehicles for the purposes of subsequent recognition and to identify more specific indicators of surveillance, such as vehicle occupants who appear to scrutinize the Principal vehicle or a passenger-side occupant who is talking as if transmitting information or perhaps even bowing his head as though reading a map.

As surveillance vehicles pass the location of the Principal's stop, they will continue ahead to the first appropriate location at which to turn off and either establish a box position or circle around to establish one along another route. The Principal should observe for any vehicle that appears to turn shortly after passing his location.

The most immediate potential indicator of a surveillance box is any vehicle that stops and positions itself to observe the parked Principal vehicle. In a one vehicle surveillance this is very beneficial because a vehicle following within observation range of the Principal will be the surveillance vehicle that stops in this type position. This makes it much easier for the Principal to isolate and identify.

In a team surveillance follow, however, the surveillance vehicle that stops to observe the Principal vehicle probably will not be among those which were following within observation range of the Principal when he stopped. In such a situation, the command surveillance vehicle informs the team of the Principal's stop while continuing past the location in a natural manner. This allows another surveillance vehicle to more discreetly establish a position from which to observe the Principal vehicle. The purpose for establishing an asset within observation range of the Principal is to observe his actions while at the stop location and to inform (trigger) the team when the Principal begins to depart the box location. The observant Principal should still be able to observe the surveillance vehicle parking in his vicinity, unless surrounding cover is to the advantage of the surveillance team. Focus should be on the identification of vehicles which stop but maintain a secure distance, rather than those that park directly in the Principal's proximity when more secure (distant) parking options were available and feasible.

Figure 7 depicts the box after it is established. Surveillance vehicle (2) is established as the trigger. The arrows depict the control assignments of the remaining surveillance vehicles. Although not the case in this example, when there are not enough surveillance vehicles to cover all the Principal's possible routes of travel, the least likely routes of departure will not be covered.

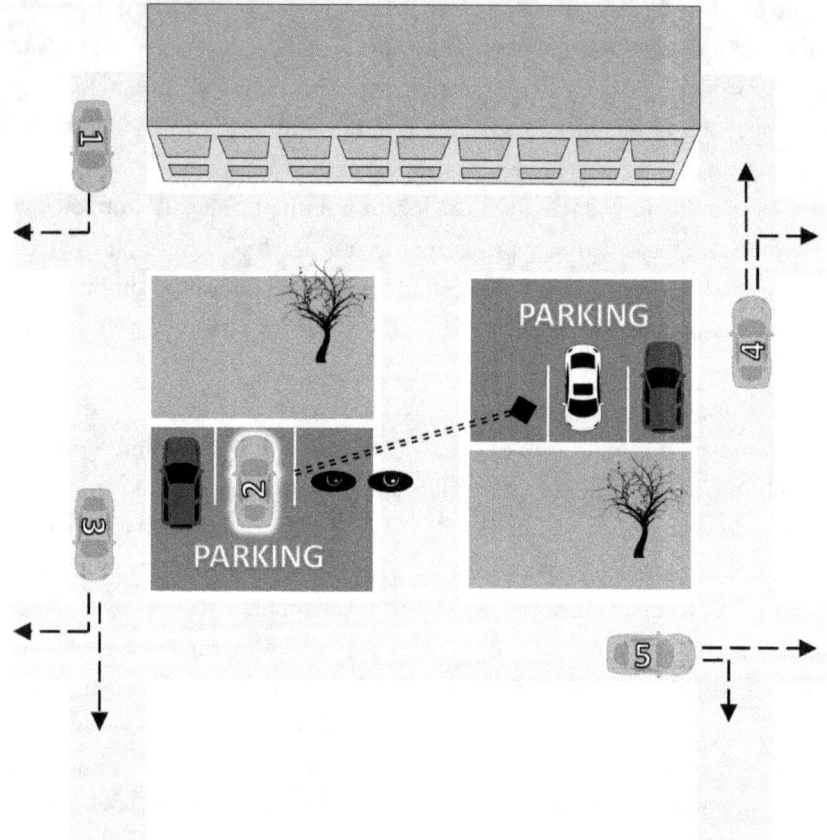

Figure 7

The surveillance team establishes a box around the Principal with a trigger vehicle established to observe the Principal vehicle

Although a trigger surveillance vehicle is ideal, it is not employed at the expense of leaving a route of departure uncovered. A box is still effective without a trigger if all routes of travel are covered. When the surveillance team is unable to establish a secure trigger, and depending on the duration of the stop, a surveillance vehicle may periodically pass by the location of the stop to confirm that the Principal is still stopped at that location. The Principal will observe for vehicles meeting this profile.

If surveillance vehicles are limited or there are simply too many routes to be covered, further adjustments must be made. The least desirable is to leave routes uncovered. When this is necessary, the selection of the route(s) to remain uncovered is based on a prioritization of the least likely routes of departure. Another option is to collapse the box in closer to the Principal in an effort to decrease the possible routes of departure. This option decreases the degree of security by bringing additional surveillance vehicles closer to the Principal's location. The Principal employs the understanding of these concepts to facilitate observation as the team establishes the box, and to plan his efforts to detect surveillance vehicles positioned in and emerging from box positions as he travels out of the likely box area.

When the Principal vehicle begins to depart, the team executes a pick-up and follow as the box is broken, similar to that of the stakeout pick-up and follow. As the Principal departs the stop location, he observes for indicators of surveillance vehicles in box positions or pulling out to follow. The methods for detecting surveillance assets in box positions addressed in the previous stakeout box section apply to the detection of box positions during this phase.

8. PASSIVE FOOT SURVEILLANCE AND COMBINED SURVEILLANCE DETECTION

Passive foot surveillance detection is conducted to identify specific indications of foot surveillance. The ultimate objective is to identify the same individual in two separate locations that are non-coincidental. This method of surveillance detection is more difficult than vehicular surveillance detection for a number of reasons. Foremost, the Principal on foot does not have the range of vision that is afforded by mirrors in the vehicle surveillance detection process. The only reliable method of observation is by line of sight, which is difficult if not impossible to disguise from possible surveillance operators. Virtually the only way to observe for following surveillance operators is to turn and look to the rear. This makes it much easier for the surveillance element to identify a Principal who is unusually observant of his surroundings.

Another disadvantage is that foot travel is less channelized. Vehicular surveillance is restricted to established roadways, whereas foot surveillance generally affords surveillance operators more flexibility in travel. This flexibility is further enhanced beyond that of vehicular surveillance because foot operators can more readily maneuver in any direction with equal speed and security while vehicles are relatively restricted in their maneuverability. However, concepts of restrictive terrain do apply and are detailed in the discussion of active foot surveillance detection (Chapter 11).

Passive detection of combined surveillance activities employs detection techniques associated with foot and vehicular surveillance, but largely exploits the difficulties associated with a surveillance effort's transition from a vehicular surveillance to a foot follow, and vice versa.

STAKEOUT AND PICK-UP PHASE DETECTION

Perhaps the best opportunity for foot surveillance detection through passive observation is during the stakeout or box phases. During a foot stakeout the surveillance operators' greatest concern is adequate *cover* or *concealment* to man a box position securely while effectively observing a specified location. A vehicle parked on the side of the road with operators inside is even more plausible than a person standing out in the open for no apparent reason. For this reason, foot surveillance operators attempt to maximize existing cover while on stakeout. The longer the duration of the Principal's stop, the longer they must remain static or loiter in the area. Anyone who is standing around for no discernible reason should be readily apparent to the observant Principal. In most circumstances, people on foot are moving with a purpose or destination; those who are not are easily isolated from the surrounding populace. Such individuals should be observed for retention purposes and to identify other indications of foot surveillance.

Unlike the vehicular surveillance box wherein individual asset box locations are primarily dictated by the road network from which the Principal is expected to emerge, and it is relatively easy for the Principal to determine where they will be located based on an understanding of boxing tactics, foot box positions are established more so by where the surrounding area provides cover and concealment to foot operators. Whereas surveillance vehicles can normally blend with other parked vehicles for cover, foot surveillance operators must be more enterprising and adaptive when establishing box positions. Even when the Principal's travel is restricted by established road or walkways, and the appropriate box locations are largely dictated by the terrain, foot surveillance operators may not have the cover necessary to establish a secure box location and may be forced to accept additional risk of compromise or establish a suboptimal box position.

For reasons primarily related to the Principal's range of maneuver options by foot, establishing an effective *trigger* is usually essential to the stakeout box, to ensure that *command* is established before the Principal is able to move in a direction that the team may otherwise not be prepared for. In addition, and contrary to vehicular surveillance, the trigger operator is often in the best position to execute the pick-up and initiate the follow in a secure manner, cover and concealment permitting. Again, this factor is due to the Principal not having the range of observation on foot to detect a following operator that is enabled by vehicle mirrors.

When departing a possible stakeout location, the Principal should focus on locations that would provide surveillance operators with their needed cover. Such locations include benches, bus stops, and outside shops or newsstands. Street-side shops and eateries provide excellent locations for surveillance operators to establish concealed positions from which to man a box position and observe for the Principal. A parked surveillance vehicle may provide the best concealment for foot operators to box and observe for the Principal, but the appearance of an individual (or individuals) in a sitting vehicle may be conspicuous to an observant Principal and may expose both the vehicle and operators(s) to scrutiny.

The circumstances of the Principal's activities will determine how much time is available to observe surroundings. Individuals should be observed to determine whether their actions and mannerisms are consistent with the surroundings, or if they appear more focused on observing other activities rather than conducting plausible activities themselves. This applies to the observation of virtually any activity. People who are casually window shopping should receive particular scrutiny because this is a very shallow cover that is easily detected. Individuals waiting at a bus stop should be observed if the circumstances of the Principal's activities allow continuous observation or the opportunity to recheck the location periodically. In this case the Principal observes for any individuals who remain at the stop after one or more buses have stopped to pick up passengers.

Foot surveillance teams operating without concealed broadcast communications capability use visual signals to communicate among each other. Visual signals normally reflect mannerisms or actions that would appear natural to the casual observer, such as scratching the head, checking the watch, or placing a hand in a pocket. The Principal will observe for individuals who display idiosyncrasies that are indicative of visual communications signals.

Foot operators wearing body communications equipment may display awkward actions and mannerisms that can be indicative of surveillance to the observant Principal. To conceal their equipment, foot operators may wear baggy or loose-fitting clothing that is not consistent with their overall build. Body communications equipment may be operated by the use of a key button for transmitting. The most common place for this button is inside the operator's pocket, so the Principal should observe for individuals with their hands in their pockets or who periodically insert and remove a hand. Since communications equipment is normally worn on the upper body, surveillance operators may periodically adjust it for comfort and concealment. The equipment includes an earpiece, which the operator may need to readjust by raising a finger to the ear.

Communications equipment may also include a microphone, which may be concealed under the clothing and positioned near the center of the chest. Even though the microphone is sensitive enough to pick up an operator's speech regardless of the position of his head, he may still have a tendency to lower the chin toward the chest when communicating. Yet another tendency is for the operator to stop moving and stare aimlessly when listening to communications transmissions. Experienced operators are capable of disguising the fact that they are speaking over the communications system, but the Principal should still observe for individuals who appear to be talking without reason.

When departing or passing through a possible stakeout location, the Principal should observe for individuals who transition from a static to mobile status. This involves a consciously developed perceptive process of observing surroundings and isolating individuals who move from static positions. Through concentration and the filtering out of all unnecessary distracters, the "mind's eye" perceives movements that would normally be beyond the Principal's peripheral vision limitations. This enhanced perceptive acuity, coupled with concentrated hearing, can assist in detecting individuals who exit an establishment after the Principal passes by, as might be indicative of a surveillance operator manning a box (or trigger) position inside an establishment and maneuvering for the pick-up. Again, surveillance vehicles may be employed to provide concealment for foot operators in the box, so individuals exiting vehicles in a manner potentially coincidental with the Principal's movements are indicative of surveillance.

FOLLOW PHASE DETECTION

During the course of passive surveillance detection, the Principal will rarely be close enough to a surveillance operator to distinguish specific facial features for retention and subsequent recognition. For this reason, the observation of clothing and mannerisms, which can be observed at a greater distance, is particularly important. The Principal should remain constantly aware that surveillance operators alter or disguise their appearance and alter mannerisms to deceive the surveillance detection effort. Observation techniques for disguise and mannerisms are addressed in Appendix 2.

Since passive foot surveillance detection involves only those observations made during the course of standard travel, the Principal will have few natural opportunities to observe to the rear for surveillance operators when traveling. Therefore, it is most difficult to discreetly observe for surveillance operators following directly behind and at a secure distance from the Principal.

Perhaps the best opportunity for passive observation of following individuals is when the Principal stops for traffic at an intersection or another travel option to make a turn. The surveillance operator in this situation is detectable by passive observation when the Principal stops at an intersection to negotiate traffic to make a turn and cross the road. As the Principal turns to negotiate traffic, it may be possible for him to observe following individuals through peripheral vision or by a slight glance to the side.

A surveillance operator following directly behind the Principal is highly vulnerable to a *180-degree turn* by the Principal, which is an active surveillance detection technique that is addressed in Chapters 10 and 11. The 180-degree turn is an effective measure because it compels a following operator to either move out of the Principal's path of travel in a potentially conspicuous manner, or pass directly by the Principal with exposure to face-to-face observation. To mitigate this risk, a surveillance operator may conduct the follow from an offset location, such as the other side of the street.

In addition to the vulnerability to the 180-degree turn, a surveillance operator following directly behind the Principal is highly vulnerable to an active surveillance detection method of the Principal turning a *blind corner*, a technique that is commonly enabled on most city streets by structures that obstruct observation. As is detailed in subsequent chapters, the Principal may turn a blind corner and stop to observe potential operators and perhaps identify potential operators who act conspicuously when turning the corner and finding themselves suddenly in close proximity to the Principal (which is an *active* detection technique). To mitigate this risk, two operators may follow the Principal in tandem to enable the operator on the opposite side of the street with a better stand-off position and a better range of observation to ensure that the Principal did not stop after a blind turn before the operator following directly behind the Principal commits to the blind turn. Chapter 11 provides a detailed discussion of how surveillance operators following in tandem will likely react to a potential blind corner turn by the Principal.

Although an operator following at a distance on the opposite side of the road can be effective in mitigating the risk of active surveillance detection techniques (180-degree turn, blind turn), he is still vulnerable to detection; an operator in this position is vulnerable to detection by passive observation when the Principal increases his field of view by stopping to observe traffic.

Figure 8 depicts the standard tandem surveillance positioning for two surveillance operators. To reduce the amount of time the Principal is unsighted if he takes a blind right turn and to reduce the amount of exposure of surveillance operator (1) if the Principal does so, the offset operator (2) may accelerate and reduce his following distance to increase range of observation prior to the Principal reaching the corner. As such, the offset operator becomes increasingly vulnerable to observation when the Principal stops at the corner and observes or turns left, as he is caught more directly in the Principal's field of vision if he has no plausible cover under which to stop in reaction to the Principal's actions.

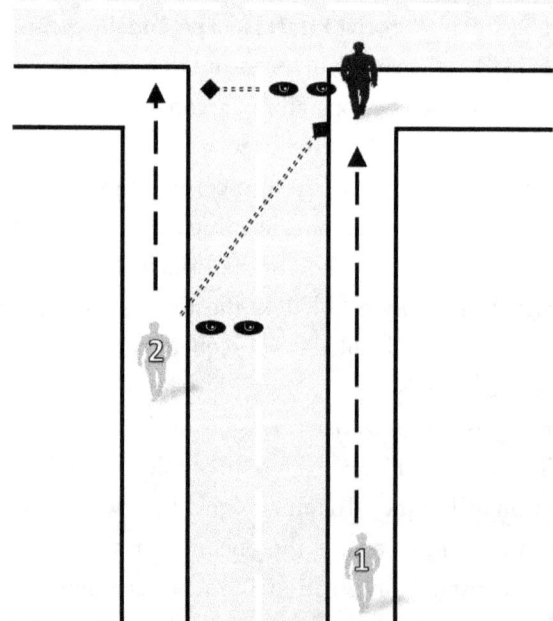

FIGURE 8

The standard tandem surveillance positioning for two surveillance operators

As the Principal turns to negotiate traffic, he can observe pedestrians who are approaching the intersection on the opposite side. At this point, the Principal should observe for individuals who either slow their pace to avoid crossing his path or quicken their pace to complete the intersection prior to his crossing. In such instances, a surveillance operator may stop suddenly using a shallow cover for action such as window shopping, move abruptly to enter an establishment, or move behind a physical structure for concealment, which are reactions that may be indicative of surveillance.

An important aspect of passive (and active) surveillance detection is that the surveillance effort will likely endeavor to record the Principal's activities when traveling by foot, particularly when conducting activities potentially constituting *protected activities*. Operators will usually prefer to leverage the concealment of a vehicle or other physical structure from which to video tape or photograph the Principal in a discreet manner, but this is not always practicable. Therefore, the Principal will observe for instances or indicators of such surreptitious activities among his surroundings, to include groups or partners who orchestrate videos or photographs which could coincidentally capture the Principal in the background.

Box Phase Detection

When the Principal stops during the course of standard foot travels, he observes for surrounding individuals who appear to transition from a mobile to static status. As the Principal approaches the location of the stop he should observe all individuals already in the area and eliminate them from primary consideration as surveillance operators. He can then focus on those who subsequently appear in static positions and who were not in the area when he made the stop. The Principal also observes for individuals who meet the profile of a surveillance operator as addressed in the section on foot stakeouts detailed previously.

As the Principal stops, surveillance operators will transition into cover positions as an operational necessity and therefore may not appear completely natural with the activity that is used as cover. At a point, identifying an individual who appears out of place becomes an almost intuitive perception.

Passive surveillance detection in public locations is extremely effective in identifying indications of surveillance as well as specific surveillance operators. In fact, public locations are among the points in a foot surveillance operation where operators are most vulnerable to detection. Since many of the passive observation principles applicable to public locations are similar to those involved in active detection, they will not be addressed at this point. One point of note regarding public locations is that anytime the Principal enters a public location, the surveillance team establishes a surveillance box outside the location to reestablish the mobile follow when he departs. For this reason, when departing a public location, the Principal employs the same passive observation tactics as addressed previously for the foot stakeout box.

PASSIVE DETECTION OF COMBINED VEHICULAR AND FOOT SURVEILLANCE
When the Principal stops and parks his vehicle, he observes for the indicators of surveillance as addressed in the previous section on vehicular surveillance detection. When the Principal stops to park and gets out of his vehicle to travel by foot, he employs passive detection measures that are unique to the transition from a vehicular surveillance to a foot surveillance. The primary consideration the Principal should concentrate on is the fact that the surveillance team will attempt to maintain a continuity of observation during this transition.

The surveillance team will attempt to place foot operators on the ground as quickly as possible. This is a difficult task to accomplish without coming to the attention of the Principal. At this point the Principal should observe for possible foot operators exiting vehicles. In an effort to find secure locations to drop foot operators, surveillance vehicles may reconnoiter the Principal's location, making them vulnerable to detection. The Principal will continue to observe for these indicators after he has departed the location of his vehicle because the surveillance team may continue to drop foot operators anywhere along the Principal's identified route of travel.

In almost any environment, surveillance vehicles are more readily detectable as they maneuver to transition foot operators to the ground. Additionally, the detection of boxing surveillance vehicles by both sight and sound is enhanced as the Principal exits his vehicle and enjoys a 360-degree range of observation. This transition is extremely difficult for a surveillance team to execute discreetly in less densely trafficked or desolate areas. At night, the factors of less traffic on the roads, better observation of vehicle lights, and an enhanced sense of hearing facilitate the detection of the transition from vehicular to foot surveillance.

Specific indicators of the transition from a vehicular to foot surveillance include the sound of doors shutting and perhaps the observation of interior vehicle lights as surveillance operators exit vehicles. In open terrain or in close proximity to a surveillance vehicle, communications transmissions may be audible as surveillance operators get out of the vehicles. At night or in inclement weather, a poorly disciplined surveillance vehicle may turn off its lights for enhanced concealment while maneuvering but disregard the fact that the reverse and brake lights will still activate.

As the Principal travels by foot, he employs passive detection measures addressed previously with regard to passive foot surveillance detection. As the Principal begins to return to his vehicle, he observes for indications that the surveillance team is preparing to reestablish vehicular surveillance. For a sophisticated surveillance effort with multiple assets to operate by foot or vehicle, the foot to vehicle transition is standard and will cause no significant problems. However, this normally requires that foot assets move at a faster pace as they anticipate the Principal's return to his vehicle. This sense of urgency to return to the surveillance vehicles and be in position to assume the vehicular follow presents a profile that is susceptible to surveillance detection.

During this transition phase, surveillance vehicles may attempt to pick up foot operators. The Principal observes for individuals who enter vehicles in an unnatural manner or location. Again, the Principal observes for vehicles that appear to be surveying the area, either in an effort to find foot operators or to establish a box position. Multiple individuals observed entering a single vehicle may be indicative of a well-coordinated surveillance effort and transition. As the Principal approaches his vehicle, enters the vehicle, and pulls out to drive away, he observes for indicators of a stakeout box as discussed in the sections on the stakeout and box phases of vehicular surveillance detection.

When the use of public transportation is among the Principal's standard modes of travel as established by previous travel patterns, the applicable transportation mode can be incorporated into the combined vehicular and foot surveillance detection process. Appendix 7 (Surveillance Tactics and Surveillance Countermeasures on Public Transportation) includes passive surveillance detection methods applicable to public transportation.

9. ACTIVE SURVEILLANCE DETECTION OVERVIEW

Active surveillance detection consists of specific, normally preplanned maneuvers executed by the Principal to enable the observation of potential surveillance assets, and ideally, to elicit an isolating reaction from a surveillance asset. By orchestrating an unanticipated situation to which the surveillance asset must react, the Principal potentially isolates that asset for identification. As with passive detection, active surveillance detection is based on a knowledge of how a surveillance team operates. Such an understanding allows the Principal to employ active measures that invoke compromising actions by surveillance assets.

Active surveillance detection is normally employed when the Principal has identified specific indicators of surveillance. The Principal executes surveillance detection maneuvers to confirm any suspicions. He may also use active surveillance detection as a standard security practice prior to conducting *protected activity*. This allows the Principal to confirm the absence of surveillance before conducting any activity that would be damaging to him if observed by surveillance. The most common practitioners of active surveillance detection are espionage agents and other covert operators, who engage in extensive detection drills prior to any operational meetings or activities. These time-proven methods employed by the most highly trained and capable practitioners are equally effective when employed by the range of risk-averse and security conscious individuals (Principals).

Active surveillance detection is dependent on the principles of observation for success. No surveillance detection maneuver is effective in exposing surveillance unless the Principal is in position to observe the reaction. Active surveillance detection will rarely expose surveillance with each maneuver. In most cases, the Principal will at best develop specific indicators to focus on for observation and retention. For instance, although a surveillance detection maneuver may elicit a suspicious reaction from a nearby vehicle, it is normally not until that vehicle is observed subsequently at a non-coincidental location that surveillance can be confirmed.

There are two general categories of active surveillance detection methods: overt and covert (discreet). These are broad categories which reside along the covert-overt spectrum as addressed in Chapter 5. The Principal employs overt methods when he is not concerned that surveillance detection tactics will be identified as such. Overt surveillance detection tactics are generally associated with overt Principals (as defined in Chapter 2). Although it is usually in the Principal's interest to disguise the fact that surveillance detection tactics are being employed, at times the need to determine for certain whether surveillance is present may override these considerations. For example, protective security personnel employing surveillance detection for executive protection purposes are extremely overt in attempting to detect surveillance.

Overt detection tactics generally involve more aggressive maneuvers designed to provoke a more conspicuous reaction. In relative terms, the more overt the surveillance detection maneuver, the more effective it is in exposing surveillance. The negative impact that overt tactics can have on the overall effectiveness of the detection effort should influence the selection of the method of surveillance detection. Although overt maneuvers may be effective in forcing a suspicious reaction from a surveillance asset, they may have negative impacts based on the Principal's objectives, or could be altogether counterproductive. When a surveillance asset assesses that it has received a high degree of exposure to the Principal due to an overt surveillance detection maneuver, the particular vehicle or operator at issue may be removed from the operation due to security/compromise concerns. This deprives the Principal of an opportunity to confirm surveillance by observing that asset at a subsequent time and location.

Discreet (covert) surveillance detection tactics are employed in a manner that disguises the use of detection measures. As previously addressed, it is (almost) always to the Principal's advantage if a surveillance team does not identify the active employment of surveillance detection measures.

ACTIVE SURVEILLANCE DETECTION PLANNING

Active surveillance detection is based on the Principal conducting a maneuver to elicit a reaction that exposes/isolates a potential surveillance asset to observation. To this end, the planning of surveillance detection maneuvers must always take into consideration the anticipated or desired reaction of the surveillance asset if present. This allows the maneuvers to be assessed in advance as to their effectiveness in satisfying the objective and whether their effectiveness offsets the risk involved in conducting them. The risk involved consists of the probability that surveillance assets, if present, will identify the fact that the Principal is conducting active surveillance detection against them.

In determining the effectiveness of a surveillance detection maneuver, the Principal must factor in his ability to observe the desired surveillance reaction. Obviously, the best-executed surveillance detection maneuver is ineffective if the Principal is unable to observe the surveillance asset's reaction to it. The aforementioned considerations emphasize the importance of preparation and planning in surveillance detection practices.

It is important to deliberately plan surveillance detection activities in advance. Planning may be conducted to support immediate surveillance detection needs or for contingency situations when the Principal suspects surveillance and needs to spontaneously implement pre-planned surveillance detection measures. Area knowledge is necessary for the effective execution of active surveillance detection measures, as it informs the planning of active surveillance detection activities. The Principal must be intimately aware of traffic patterns throughout the area and how these patterns may affect the surveillance detection effort. The plan will include the incorporation of restrictive terrain, transition points, and specific surveillance detection techniques as detailed in the following two chapters.

TARGET PATTERN ANALYSIS

As with passive detection, active physical surveillance detection uses the concept of *target pattern analysis*. The Principal evaluates his own activities and travel patterns to determine how a surveillance team would employ coverage. Based on this concept of the surveillance strategy, he identifies those specific locations where active detection methods can be employed with the highest probability of success. The pattern analysis process progresses beyond that conducted in support of passive detection by actually identifying routes of travel and specific terrain characteristics along those routes that facilitate active detection maneuvers. As specific detection tactics are addressed in subsequent chapters, the importance of advantageous terrain becomes increasingly apparent.

To conduct discreet active surveillance detection effectively, the Principal must develop specific surveillance detection maneuvers based on established patterns of activity. Recall that the target pattern analysis process is based on the assumption that the surveillance team has made sufficient observations of the Principal's travels and activities to develop a comprehensive picture of his standard patterns. Surveillance detection practices involving activities that are notably inconsistent with these established patterns will be readily apparent to a surveillance team, if present. Therefore, it is necessary to develop specific surveillance maneuvers that are consistent with established patterns. The Principal's target pattern analysis ensures that surveillance detection practices meet this criterion.

This is a particularly important concept because it enables the Principal to use the target pattern analysis the surveillance team has previously conducted in support of its operation against it. A surveillance team generally becomes more efficient and effective against a Principal after it has observed him for a period of time and has become familiar with the activities and travels incorporated into the pattern analysis process. This allows the team to better anticipate the Principal's intentions. For example, if the Principal establishes a pattern of leaving the workplace at a standard time and traveling directly home by a specific route, the surveillance team will anticipate this activity and coordinate its surveillance coverage accordingly. Even though the surveillance team is prepared to react to unanticipated travels, it instinctively assumes that the Principal will conform to the previously established pattern. This enables the surveillance effort to operate in a more effective and less exposed manner. However, this can work against the surveillance team from the active surveillance detection standpoint, because the team will tend to develop a sense of security by relying on established patterns to dictate its coverage strategy. When this sense of security is suddenly disrupted by an unanticipated maneuver on the part of the Principal, the team may be forced to react in a manner that leaves it vulnerable to detection (this concept is applicable to the *Chaos Theory of Surveillance* which is addressed in Chapter 13).

A Principal with a wide and varied pattern of activities and travels has much more latitude with which to incorporate natural active surveillance detection measures than one with a relatively restricted pattern. Most people conform to the latter because they are restricted by a standard day-to-day routine. The more active someone is in his travels and activities, the more the pattern is expanded. If the Principal determines through target pattern analysis that his patterns are too narrow in scope to accommodate the necessary surveillance detection activities, he should make a conscious effort to gradually expand them. This is accomplished by making activities more frequent and varied, such as going to a different location for lunch every day or varying the route of travel home from work. In doing so, however, the Principal must ensure that a plausible reason for the variation is apparent in case surveillance is present. For example, if varying the route home from work, a plausible reason might be a stop at a particular store along the alternative route when appropriate.

SURVEILLANCE DETECTION ROUTE

A surveillance detection route (SDR) is a (usually) preplanned route around which a formalized detection plan is based. There are two general types of SDRs. The first type of SDR is one that that follows a *logical route* but incorporates aspects such as restrictive terrain or areas facilitating a broad range of observation to detect potential surveillance assets when conducting surveillance detection measures. The other general type incorporates an *illogical route* to facilitate the isolation and identification of surveillance assets that are detected traveling the same illogical route.

LOGICAL ROUTE SDR

The previously addressed concept of target pattern analysis is the basis for the logical route SDR. The primary reason for developing this type of SDR is to ensure that surveillance detection activities are well conceived and follow a logical pattern of travel. Whether developed graphically on a map or mentally, the SDR applies the understanding of surveillance detection concepts and principles to specifically planned maneuvers along a given route.

This type of SDR consists of a logical route of travel that maximizes existing terrain and traffic characteristics to incorporate surveillance detection measures. Ideally, the logical SDR follows a standard route that would have been established through target pattern analysis, or at least one that is consistent with standard travel activity and would not cause the surveillance effort to perceive it as an abnormal travel activity. In most cases, an SDR incorporates active surveillance detection maneuvers throughout that are executed in locations that appear plausible and maximize the observation of surrounding traffic at their points of execution.

The active surveillance detection measures detailed in the following chapters are available for consideration for incorporation into the *logical* SDR. The ultimate objective of a logical SDR is to execute sequential detection maneuvers that initially identify potential surveillance assets and subsequently isolate those assets to confirm a surveillance presence.

ILLOGICAL ROUTE SDR

This type of SDR is an advanced method of surveillance detection that is performed to induce a surveillance effort into mirroring the Principal's broad movements in a manner that facilitates the isolation and multiple sightings of surveillance assets. The underlying concept behind this technique is that the Principal travels from one point to another by *not* taking the most direct and logical route. In some cases, the execution of this type of SDR may be the only active measure taken in regard to surveillance detection. To this end, the SDR may simply involve a route that enhances the effectiveness of passive observation and detection activities.

One of the more basic examples of this type of SDR is the *three sides of a box* technique. This involves the Principal traveling a route that follows three sides of boxed terrain, such as a city block, and observing for any potential surveillance asset following this otherwise illogical route. For illustration purposes, Figure 9 depicts how the Principal, suspecting surveillance, is approaching Point A from the lower left of the figure. If Point E is the Principal's intended destination, he would continue through Point A and turn left at Point B or turn left at Point A and travel along the other most direct (logical) route by turning right at Point F. However, as a form of surveillance detection, the Principal takes an illogical route along the *three sides of the box* from point A through points B, C, and D to reach (and turn right at) point E. Any person or vehicle observed following the Principal through this indirect and illogical route is immediately identified as a possible surveillance asset.

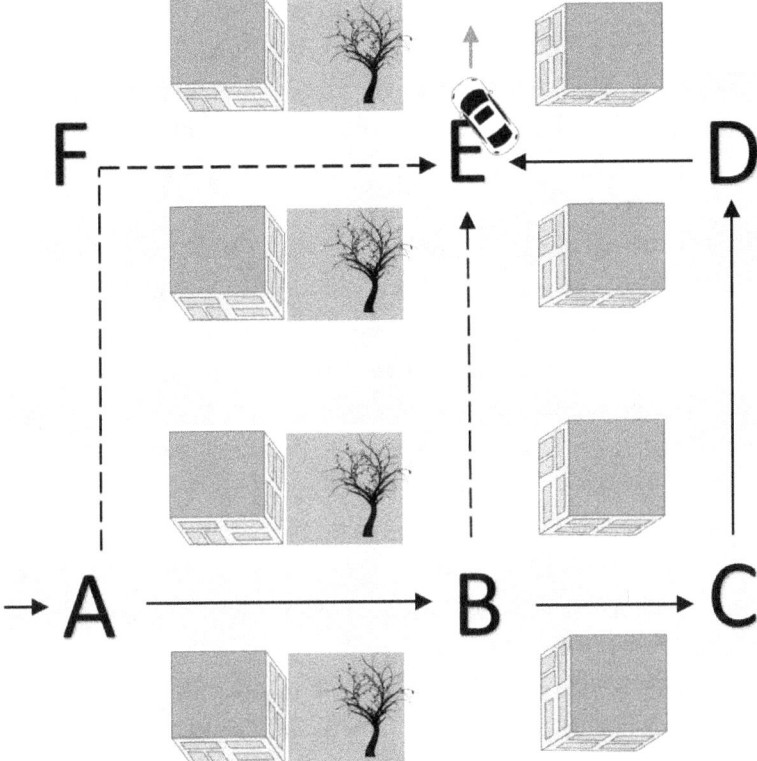

FIGURE 9

The Principal, suspecting surveillance, executes the three sides of a box SDR by taking the less direct/logical route from point A to point E

As a less overt approach, taking the route through Point F is less logical than turning left at Point B, so taking the route through Point F would serve surveillance detection purposes, but would not provide as strong a confirmation as an asset following three sides of a box.

The example in Figure 9 is the simplest possible application and should generally only be employed when needed as an expedient, as it may be perceived by a surveillance effort as an overt detection maneuver. Although this simple example of an SDR may be easily identified as such, there are many routes that can incorporate three sides of a box that are not as easily recognizable. As such, it does not need to be executed in a linear fashion as the name implies, as there are many less linear and less discernible variations applicable to both foot and vehicle SDRs.

If in keeping with target pattern analysis, an excellent time for the Principal to execute this type of SDR is when he has lured a possible vehicular surveillance team to unfamiliar terrain and then departs the vehicle by foot. At this point the foot surveillance operators may follow the Principal more readily through three sides of a box because they have little knowledge of the area.

The most effective (yet complex) form of illogical SDR is one that incorporates a *theme* to make an otherwise illogical route of travel appear logical. Common themes include traveling to numerous stores as though shopping for (or pricing) a particular item. Another effective theme is to plan an SDR around properties advertised for sale and use the guise of property hunting as a logical reason for an otherwise illogical route of travel. Visiting car dealerships is another good example. The stop locations represent the surveillance detection points (SDPs) where the Principal observes for potential surveillance assets. While providing a feasible reason for the unique travel pattern, this method effectively isolates potential surveillance assets following the same, otherwise illogical, route of travel.

Countersurveillance operations as detailed in Appendix 3 (third-person surveillance detection support), are normally planned and executed around an SDR with SDPs.

10. ACTIVE VEHICULAR SURVEILLANCE DETECTION MEASURES

The surveillance principles and surveillance detection methods addressed in the previous passive surveillance detection chapters apply to active surveillance detection measures as well. In fact, active surveillance detection efforts build on these concepts and significantly enhance the effectiveness of surveillance detection by incorporating specific techniques and procedures. However, this incorporation of active measures invokes concepts addressed in regard to the *covert-overt spectrum* and *fight or flight response* for consideration (Chapter 5).

ACTIVE STAKEOUT AND PICK-UP PHASE DETECTION

The stakeout is the phase of a surveillance operation in which the surveillance team is potentially most vulnerable to detection. Here the team must establish basically static positions for extended periods of time with a degree of uncertainty regarding exactly when and where the Principal will initially emerge. The Principal takes advantage of this factor in the employment of surveillance detection measures.

A surveillance team may employ an observation post either for a *fixed surveillance* of a specified location or as a *trigger* in support of the mobile surveillance stakeout. Appendix 5 details active observation post detection measures.

The target pattern analysis process used to determine how a surveillance team would establish a stakeout to cover a Principal is much more extensive for active physical surveillance detection. Recall that a stakeout box is devised to establish initial command of the Principal as he either passes through or emerges from within the stakeout box. Surveillance vehicles are positioned to observe all routes into and out of the specified stakeout area. The positioning enables a surveillance vehicle to pull out and establish command of the Principal to initiate the mobile follow along every route out of the stakeout area.

A surveillance stakeout may be established around a location the Principal is expected to pass through, but they are most commonly established around a denied area, such as a residence or workplace where the Principal is known or assessed to be housed. A stakeout established around a location the Principal is anticipated to pass through shares the same characteristics as a surveillance box established when the Principal stops during a mobile surveillance follow.

The Principal employs his knowledge of surveillance stakeout tactics to anticipate how a surveillance team will position itself. He will determine likely stakeout coverage tactics for every area he identifies as a possible stakeout location, thereby identifying where surveillance vehicles would be positioned if a surveillance stakeout is present. At this point the Principal is prepared to employ active measures of physical surveillance detection. The Principal employs a basic understanding of surveillance box position and pick-up tactics as addressed in Chapter 7; but in the case of active surveillance detection, the Principal takes measures to seek out or draw out surveillance assets for detection.

There are some proactive measures the Principal can employ before even giving the surveillance effort the opportunity to trigger the vehicular operation and execute the pick-up. An effective active surveillance detection measure to identify a trigger vehicle or any surveillance vehicle in a box position is for the Principal to take a walk when he anticipates that there may be a stakeout. This should be done at a time when, based on pattern analysis, the surveillance team would not anticipate such an action. The Principal will design the route to cover suspected locations where surveillance vehicles may be positioned. If he does so in a logical manner, the purpose for the walk will appear natural to the surveillance team. Even a simple walk around the neighborhood for exercise should follow a logical route to avoid meandering in a conspicuous manner. Such a surveillance detection technique is more credible if it incorporates a plausible destination into the walk, such as an associate's house, a nearby store, or a park.

When the stakeout is based around a home in a residential area, it is many times difficult, if not impossible, for the team to observe the rear of the residence, or all exits other than the one commonly used by the Principal. If the Principal establishes a pattern that leads the team to assume that he only departs from the front or another regular point of departure, which is normally the case, the team will not attempt to position a trigger to observe the rear of the house or other unlikely departure routes. An aggressive active measure is for the Principal to depart the denied location from the rear by foot so that he cannot be observed by surveillance vehicles/operators positioned for forward observation. By traveling back to another street without being detected by the surveillance team, the Principal can walk throughout the area to identify possible surveillance vehicles in stakeout box positions. This tactic leaves the surveillance team particularly vulnerable to detection because it will adopt a more relaxed security posture in assuming that the Principal is still inside the denied location. The Principal must exercise discretion, because if the surveillance team observes him maneuvering throughout the area after having departed the denied location covertly, it will certainly assume that he is practicing surveillance detection. If this tactic is employed under the cover of darkness it affords the Principal an additional degree of concealment.

The concept of walking to identify vehicular stakeout box positions around a residence is equally applicable to most possible stakeout locations.

As the Principal prepares to depart the location where a stakeout may be established by vehicle, he observes for a vehicle or individual meeting the profile of a trigger position. However, the team may use an observation post to serve as the trigger, negating the need for a vehicle or operator to support this aspect of the operation. When the stakeout location is situated in an apartment complex, the surveillance team may have more flexibility and concealment with which to establish a trigger position. When the Principal resides at a hotel, the surveillance team may position a trigger operator inside the lobby to provide it with early warning regarding the Principal's activity and to inform the team of the exit by which he is departing. When residing at a hotel, the Principal should observe for individuals in stationary positions in the lobby or other common areas.

Recall that the Principal should have conducted a *line of sight analysis* to identify potential trigger positions around any location assessed to be a likely stakeout location. An appropriately placed trigger is positioned to observe the exit to the denied location or the Principal vehicle without being visible from inside the denied area. If the trigger meets these criteria then the Principal will not have an opportunity to observe it until he has exited the denied location, and will therefore have only a limited time to observe for a trigger in an inconspicuous manner. If a trigger must park on the road in front of the denied area location, it will make every effort to be positioned in the direction that the Principal is least likely to travel.

When possible and applicable, the Principal should subscribe to a local morning newspaper and request that it be left in the yard near the street or in a mailbox at the street. By establishing a pattern of going out to get the paper and then returning to the residence about five minutes before leaving the residence for the day, the Principal creates a plausible reason for being in position to observe for a trigger. In fact, a surveillance team may welcome this activity — not realizing the actual surveillance detection purposes it serves — because it provides an indication that the Principal is preparing to leave for the day.

If the Principal vehicle is parked in a driveway or on the road outside the denied location, it provides a degree of early warning and predictability for the trigger and team. However, the Principal can exploit this situation for surveillance detection purposes by establishing a pattern of conducting activities which provide an opportunity to observe for a potential trigger vehicle. Establishing a pattern of regularly opening the trunk to emplace a briefcase or hanging a jacket in the back seat are examples of activities that provide additional observation opportunities and facilitate surveillance (trigger) detection.

If the Principal parks his vehicle in the garage or driveway of his residence, he should establish a pattern of always backing into the parking position. This gives him a better field of view to observe for a trigger when driving out to the street and departing. This is particularly important when the vehicle is parked in a garage that adjoins the residence, because the opportunity to observe for a trigger is generally limited to the time between the vehicle exiting the garage and its entering the street.

An appropriately established trigger should be positioned in a location away from the direction in which the Principal is expected to travel upon departing the stakeout location. Ideally, from the surveillance team's standpoint, the trigger will be positioned off the road in an area such as a parking lot, but this is not always possible given the surrounding terrain. When a trigger must be parked on the street that runs in front of the denied location, it will be positioned opposite to the Principal's anticipated direction of travel to minimize the possibility of his driving past the trigger and getting a "free look." On a one-way street, this is an easy judgment, but normally the trigger must determine positioning based on other factors. Target pattern analysis is used to determine the direction in which the Principal usually departs the stakeout location, or that in which he normally departs at a given time. If the Principal parks his vehicle on the street in front of the denied location, the trigger may position itself opposite the direction in which the vehicle is facing, assuming that the Principal will depart in that direction rather than turn around.

Based on this reasoning, the Principal should avoid establishing a pattern of parking his vehicle facing the same direction every time it is parked on the street. This forces the trigger to position itself with a degree of uncertainty. If the trigger bases its position on the assumption that the Principal vehicle will depart in the direction which it is facing when parked, then the trigger is vulnerable to detection if the Principal then turns around and departs in the opposite direction. The Principal should employ this tactic when he believes there is a good probability of success in detecting a potential trigger asset. If this detection method is employed, it should be done frequently enough to not appear to be an unusual travel pattern, but not so frequently that the surveillance effort would commonly anticipate it, rendering the maneuver ineffective.

A slightly overt application of this concept is initiated as the Principal approaches the possible stakeout location where the surveillance effort would be expected to establish a stakeout box after the Principal parks. Assuming that surveillance is present, the Principal executes a U-turn to orient the vehicle in the opposite direction from which it approached and then parked. Based on this action, the observing surveillance team may assume that the Principal has consciously predetermined his next direction of travel. The Principal then enters the stakeout location for a short period of time, but long enough for the surveillance team to maneuver its vehicles into stakeout box positions. When he departs the stakeout location, the Principal executes a 180-degree turn (U-turn) and travels in the opposite direction to detect a trigger vehicle that was positioned based on the Principal's earlier deceptive indication of his intended direction of travel.

As a general practice, the 180-degree turn is among the most effective surveillance detection maneuvers against the stakeout. This maneuver should be based on an analysis of where surveillance vehicles are likely to be positioned and its expected results. One application of the 180-degree turn is for the Principal to depart the denied location by vehicle and drive until he believes he has broken the stakeout box. At this point, under the guise of having to return to the location, he turns the vehicle around. In this case he should do so by making an actual 180-degree turn (U-turn) rather than circling a block, in order to retrace the route he traveled out of the box. The objective of this doubling back is to encounter a surveillance vehicle that has left its box position to pursue him.

The Principal should observe any vehicles he encounters along the route in returning to the location. This maneuver may also elicit a suspicious reaction from the surveillance vehicle that may be surprised and left vulnerable by the maneuver. Possible reactions include speeding up to pass by the Principal more quickly, turning quickly onto a side street to avoid crossing paths with the Principal, or behaving unnaturally, perhaps by making too much of an effort to maintain forward focus and avoid looking in the Principal's direction. This maneuver should be concluded with an action that provides a plausible reason for the Principal's return to the location, such as locking the door or retrieving an article he forgot.

Another aggressive detection maneuver is to depart the possible stakeout location, circle the block, and return to the location with a plausible reason to return. When the surveillance team is determining box locations, it bases the positioning of vehicles on roads which it does not expect the Principal to use. Normally it will select one of the streets on the side of the block the stakeout is covering as a secure position, for the very reason that the Principal would not logically circle his own block. This applies to either the block which the Principal's location is actually on or the one on the opposite side of the street, whichever is determined to be the Principal's least likely route of departure. If effectively planned, the Principal should at least pass directly by the vehicle positioned to establish the initial pick-up facing in the opposite direction. This maneuver also provides a good opportunity for the Principal to observe a trigger vehicle still in the box position or beginning to maneuver as the Principal passes back by. Again, the plausible reason for the maneuver should be one that rationalizes the otherwise unusual travel pattern. The more overt (yet effective) variation of this technique is to circle the block, but rather than stopping at the point of origin, pass by and continue with the planned travel. This is a very overt detection measure because there is little logical reason for such a maneuver, but the fact that it confounds logic is precisely why it is effective. This concept of detecting surveillance vehicles in adjacent side street box positions is similar to the scenario depicted in Figure 15.

ACTIVE FOLLOW PHASE DETECTION

Active vehicular surveillance detection during the follow offers the Principal the greatest variety of detection maneuvers. During the follow phase of a surveillance operation, the team is in a reactive mode, dictated by the actions of the Principal. For a sophisticated surveillance team this is not a disadvantage because the operators are disciplined to react to virtually any maneuver in a systematic manner. It is only when the Principal maneuvers in a nonstandard manner that the surveillance team's reactions are thrown out of synchronization. This complication forces the surveillance team to rely on resourcefulness rather than its standard tactical applications. Active surveillance detection is employed to enable observation of potential surveillance assets, and when most effective, force a surveillance asset to react in an unnatural and detectable manner, when encountering an unanticipated maneuver by the Principal.

Active vehicular surveillance detection should be planned and conform to the Principal's established travel patterns (target pattern analysis). One travel pattern that enhances the ability to conduct surveillance detection is fast and aggressive driving. However, this should only be used if it conforms to the Principal's normal pattern. A Principal who drives in a conservative manner on most occasions and then drives aggressively only when intending to conduct active surveillance detection sends an undesirable, and potentially counterproductive, signal to a surveillance team. One reason fast and aggressive driving is an advantage is that it forces the surveillance team to drive in a similar manner. When the Principal is maneuvering through traffic aggressively, it is easy to observe to the rear for vehicles that are following (mirroring/pacing) in a similar manner.

In relation to aggressive driving, a Principal who establishes a pattern of using expedient shortcuts such as maneuvering through back streets or cutting through parking lots to avoid traffic signals has more flexibility in conducting surveillance detection maneuvers. Additionally, the Principal who establishes a pattern of violating traffic laws such as taking illegal left-hand turns, illegal U-turns, or running red lights when no traffic is coming opens additional surveillance detection options. Such driving habits also serve the purposes of antisurveillance, as addressed in Chapter 12.

At the other extreme is slow and conservative driving. The Principal who drives in this manner inherits some surveillance detection advantages as well. Here too, if the Principal drives in a slow and conservative manner, the surveillance team is forced to conform to this pattern as well. If the Principal drives 5 miles per hour below the speed limit, he may upset a number of other vehicles, but he can easily isolate following vehicles that are maneuvering in a similar manner (mirroring/pacing).

Driving patterns are used for detection purposes because a surveillance team attempts to maintain mobile observation of the Principal from the rear. This requires that at least one surveillance vehicle maintain a following distance that is within observation range of the Principal but still provides a degree of security from detection. In most cases, this is dictated by the traffic density and prevalence (or lack of) restrictive terrain. In open terrain such as on highways or rural state roads, a surveillance vehicle can increase the following distance because there is a greater observation range for both the surveillance vehicle and the Principal who may be observing to the rear. In denser city traffic, a surveillance vehicle will normally follow more closely for observation and to ensure that traffic hazards do not obstruct it from remaining with the Principal. Whatever the circumstances may be, the following surveillance vehicle normally travels at a pace that is similar to the Principal's in order to maintain a standard secure following distance.

The Principal employs various methods to exploit the operational imperative (and vulnerability) of mirroring/pacing for detection purposes. For example, by gradually fluctuating from faster to slower speeds and vice versa, the Principal can observe for vehicles that mirror this driving pattern. If done gradually, this detection tactic should go unnoticed by the surveillance vehicles.

The brake lights of the Principal vehicle can be modified to facilitate this and other surveillance detection maneuvers. By installing a button that, when depressed, disengages the brake lights, the Principal can decrease vehicle speed without displaying the overt indicator of brake lights. The system should be installed so that the Principal must manually depress the disengage button the entire time it is in use to prevent the Principal from accidentally leaving the system engaged, thus creating a suspicious appearance and a safety hazard. In employing this system, the Principal must ensure that his slowing activity is not so extreme that the malfunction is detectable by a surveillance team. Such a system is particularly effective at night, when it is more difficult to judge distance, possibly causing a surveillance vehicle to inadvertently close distance and then decrease speed in an unnatural manner. Manual transmission vehicles can similarly decrease speed by downshifting rather than braking and projecting the brake lights.

More overt variations in speed can be employed on favorable terrain. In areas where there are bends in the road that would force a following surveillance vehicle to temporarily lose sight of the Principal, the Principal can travel at a faster speed going into the bend and then decrease his speed when completing it. If successful, this results in a surveillance vehicle pursuing quickly around the bend and then bearing down on the slower-moving Principal when completing it. This forces the surveillance vehicle to either decrease its speed in an unnatural manner or pass the Principal. A poorly disciplined surveillance vehicle may even decrease its speed to reestablish a secure following distance, which is very indicative of surveillance to the observant Principal. This tactic can also be used as the Principal passes over the crest of a hill and temporarily out of sight of a following surveillance vehicle. This technique of exploiting a *blind spot* is further detailed in Chapter 13 as it applies to advanced surveillance detection procedures.

Probably the most effective vehicular surveillance detection maneuver is the logical 180-degree turn (U-turn). Note the term logical, implying that the circumstances of the turn should appear plausible to an observing surveillance team, if present. One example is to execute a 180-degree turn as though to back-track and travel to a location that was missed. Intersections at which it is difficult to execute a left turn due to heavy oncoming traffic or other obstacles provide 180-degree turn opportunities as a logical maneuver to overcome this obstacle. In this circumstance the Principal continues straight through the unsafe or difficult left turn until there is an opportunity to make a safe U-turn and return to turn right into the location where the left turn was bypassed. A perfect location for an alternative application of this technique is one where there is a median that obstructs a left turn, making a 180-degree turn to back-track to a location that was not accessible by a left turn completely plausible. In any case, the 180-degree turn should be planned so that there is a plausible purpose and conclusion to justify the maneuver.

The objectives of a logical 180-degree turn are to provide the Principal with an opportunity to observe following vehicles head-on and to elicit suspicious reactions from surveillance vehicles. When a surveillance team encounters a U-turn by the Principal, it should react in a standard manner. After observing the U-turn, or being informed of the maneuver by the command surveillance vehicle, any surveillance vehicles that can do so will attempt to pull off the road prior to the Principal's doubling back and passing them head-on. Surveillance vehicles that are able to pull off onto adjacent roads or into parking lots will immediately establish box positions to pick-up the Principal and continue the follow as he passes back by.

Since the most effective pick-up positions are established from the right side of the road in the Principal's direction of travel, surveillance vehicles will attempt to turn off the road to the left in reaction to the U-turn. The next standard reaction is for vehicles that are unable to turn off prior to being forced past the Principal to turn off the road at the first possible opportunity in order to circle back and rejoin the follow. Only a poorly disciplined surveillance vehicle would execute a U-turn to rejoin the follow. Figure 10 depicts the standard reaction of surveillance vehicles to a U-turn by the Principal.

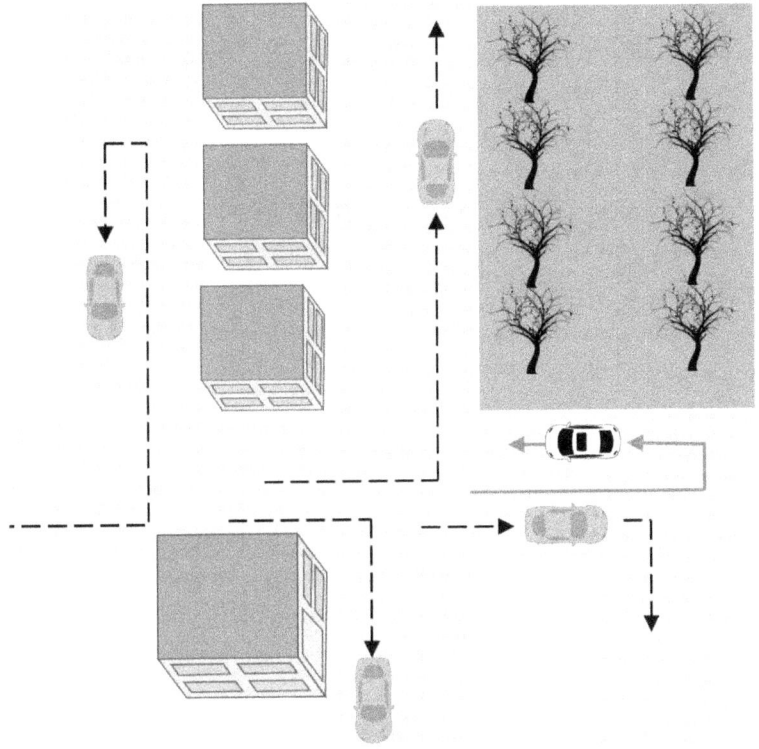

FIGURE 10

The standard reaction of surveillance vehicles to a 180-degree turn (U-turn) by the Principal

After executing the U-turn as depicted in Figure 10, the Principal observes oncoming vehicles for retention or recognition. While doing so, he also observes for any vehicles that appear to turn off the road in a hasty manner. If any vehicles are observed reacting in this manner, the Principal will observe for those vehicles when passing back by where they turned off the road, to determine whether the vehicles continued through the turn in a natural manner, or whether any of the vehicles can be observed subsequently maneuvering to position themselves to rejoin the follow, which would be highly indicative of a surveillance vehicle. During the course of this maneuver, the Principal also observes to the rear to identify any vehicles that turn off the road after passing by, or in the case of an undisciplined team (or single vehicle surveillance), execute a U-turn at the same or a proximate location.

As a follow-on to the scenario in Figure 10, if the Principal detects a vehicle turning off to the left in a manner indicative of one evading direct observation, the Principal can turn right at that location as a plausible reason for having conducted the U-turn, and observe for additional suspicious actions. In this scenario, observation of the surveillance vehicle (far left) turning around to establish a box/pick-up position would essentially confirm surveillance activity.

The Principal should plan a U-turn based on the desired results. For example, if he is primarily concerned with observing following vehicles, he will execute the maneuver in a channelized location that provides no roads or parking lots for following traffic to turn into — forcing all following traffic to cross his path. This method is effective in providing a good look at all following vehicles, but it does little more in the way of surveillance detection unless a surveillance vehicle displays poor tactical discipline. When the Principal wants to observe how specific vehicles react to the 180-degree turn, he must do it in a location that provides options for surveillance vehicles to react, such as side streets or parking lots to turn onto (as in Figure 10).

A more overt but effective variation of the 180-degree turn is to combine it with a *blind spot*. Again, blind spots are facilitated by turns/bends in roads with visual obstructions such as buildings or foliage, crests in roads that restrict vision, and other restrictive terrain. This maneuver may require that the Principal accelerate into the blind spot location to ensure that any possible surveillance vehicles temporarily lose sight of him. When he executes a 180-degree turn within sight of the command surveillance vehicle, that vehicle has ample opportunity to inform the team and provide vehicles with more time to react. By exploiting the *blind spot* when temporarily breaking contact (observation) with the team, the command vehicle is caught completely off guard when it regains observation and is unexpectedly confronted by the Principal, who has executed a 180-degree turn while in the blind spot.

The many variations of the 180-degree turn technique effectively enhance the possibility of an unnatural reaction on the part of the command vehicle and may also deter it from informing the team of the maneuver until it has passed the Principal, to avoid appearing suspicious within observation range of the Principal. This, in turn, increases the possibility of other surveillance vehicles being unprepared and reacting unnaturally. It may also enable the Principal to observe indications that the surveillance vehicle navigator is transmitting immediate information to the team.

There are a number of active surveillance detection maneuvers that can be employed on the highway. Highways are normally favorable for surveillance detection because they are generally open and provide good fields of observation. Also, due to the fast rates of speed on highways, surveillance vehicles have little time to react to surveillance detection maneuvers. Although the following techniques are scoped for highway travel, the applications apply to the range of vehicle roadways.

One terrain feature that facilitates surveillance detection on highways is a rest area or a similar location such as a state welcome area or highway-side service station. As the Principal exits the highway and enters a rest area, he observes to the rear for any vehicles that enter behind him. He can then take a position in the rest area to observe any vehicles that enter shortly after him. He also observes the reactions of vehicles as he departs the area.

A more overt variation of this tactic is for the Principal to continue slowly through the rest area and reenter the highway, observing for any vehicle that entered behind him and does the same thing. This maneuver can be employed in another way as well; if a suspected surveillance vehicle has other vehicles in support, it will continue past the rest area when the Principal enters to allow a vehicle that is in a more discreet position to enter behind the Principal. As the Principal slowly travels through the rest area, he will continue moving through the area while observing the suspected surveillance vehicle as it passes by on the highway, and then reenter the highway behind the suspected surveillance vehicle, at a non-intimidating distance, for observation purposes. If the vehicle is in fact a surveillance asset, it will likely exit the highway at the earliest possible opportunity to avoid additional exposure and to position itself to rejoin the follow. If/when this occurs, the Principal has further validated that the vehicle is a likely surveillance asset that should be retained for future recognition.

Another surveillance detection maneuver involving highway travel is for the Principal to simply exit the highway and observe for vehicles that exit behind him. This is particularly effective if employed immediately after passing a vehicle and then shifting right across both lanes of traffic to exit the highway. The act of passing another vehicle just prior to the exit provides a plausible reason for the abrupt maneuver. The primary objective of this maneuver is to isolate any vehicle that also shifts from the passing lane to exit the highway behind the Principal. Although any abrupt exit from the highway can be effective in isolating vehicles that mirror this activity by also exiting suddenly, it may be identified as an overt surveillance detection maneuver if there is no plausible reason to justify the action.

An overt variation of this maneuver can be executed on long highway exit lanes that allow vehicles to enter up to the point of the exit ramp. If the Principal decreases his speed and enters the exit lane at the earliest possible point, surveillance vehicles will have the opportunity to enter the exit lane before the Principal actually reaches the exit ramp. Just before reaching the exit ramp, the Principal will shift back onto the highway and observe for any vehicles that mirror this action as depicted in Figure 11. Again, this technique is not unique to highways, and is applicable on many multi-lane roadways.

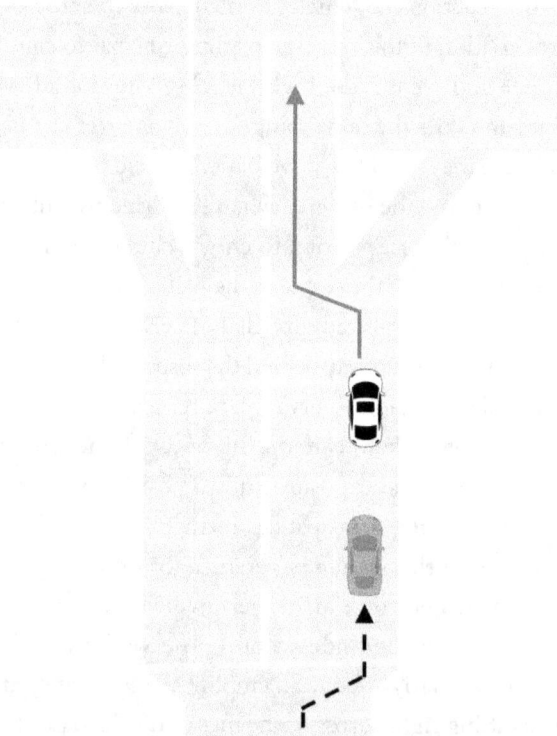

FIGURE 11

A long exit lane allows the Principal to enter early, wait for surveillance vehicles to enter, and then shift back onto the highway and observe for any vehicles that mirror this movement

Anytime the Principal wants to observe the vehicles that are traveling behind him on the highway, he can simply pull over into the breakdown lane and stop. This is a particularly overt maneuver, but it is effective in allowing the Principal to observe following vehicles as they pass. When he conducts this maneuver within observation range of a highway exit, the Principal should focus on vehicles that leave the highway at that exit, which would be the standard reaction of a surveillance vehicle. A variation of this tactic is to pull over into the breakdown lane after entering a highway exit ramp. This extremely overt maneuver is effective in isolating, for observation purposes, vehicles that exit the highway behind the Principal. It is particularly effective when the characteristics of the exit ramp obstruct the view of following vehicles so that they do not realize the Principal has stopped (in the blind spot) until they are already committed to exiting the highway.

Another option when using a highway exit ramp for surveillance detection is to continue straight through the exit and back onto the highway traveling in the same direction, in locations where possible. A poorly disciplined surveillance vehicle may continue straight through as well. This maneuver is also effective in that a surveillance vehicle with adequate back-up will continue past the exit, allowing the Principal to reenter the highway from behind for observation purposes.

A variation of this technique can be very effective at complicated highway interchanges, the most common of which is the cloverleaf. Many major interchanges are characterized by nonstandard road networking due to the number of avenues involved. By studying such interchanges in advance, the Principal can enter the interchange and then circle around and reenter the highway in the same direction as he was previously traveling. A surveillance vehicle that relies more on following the Principal than reading the map may mirror this action without realizing, until it is too late, that the route is illogical. Even traveling and exiting after three of the four loops on a standard clover leaf exit exchange is an illogical route that reflects the *three sides of a box* SDR concept.

One final example when using a highway exit ramp for detection is for the Principal to exit, pass over the highway (usually by turning left), and then reenter traveling in the opposite direction. This is an interesting challenge to a surveillance team, because in order to cover the Principal in a tactically sound manner, the team must expose at least two and possibly three surveillance vehicles. If the team does not counter the maneuver in a tactically sound manner, or does not have the surveillance vehicles necessary to rotate positions securely, the Principal can easily identify any vehicle that duplicates the maneuver in part or completely. When the Principal incorporates a plausible rationale for making such a maneuver — such as backtracking to reach a specific (logical) location — then this maneuver serves as a plausible three sides of a box SDR.

Highway interchanges provide many conceivable alternatives to the resourceful Principal for surveillance countermeasures, and this manual emphasizes these type applications because experience has proven that espionage agents and other intelligence operatives employ these type options as the most exploitable for surveillance detection (and antisurveillance) purposes. Although many of these tactics are addressed as they apply to highway travel, the principles involved can be applied to virtually any type of vehicular road travel. Variations can be conducted on any type of street in both city and rural areas. For example, the tactic of rolling through a rest area and reentering the highway can be executed in any number of city roadside parking lots and shopping areas. The Principal can also make unexpected maneuvers along any road, or in any number of locations to observe the reactions of surrounding vehicles or to observe passing vehicles that are channelized or otherwise restricted by the terrain.

Turn-only lanes are very common on city streets. These can be used in the same manner as long exit lanes on the highway. The Principal enters the turn lane, giving any following surveillance vehicles an opportunity to follow behind. Prior to making the mandatory turn, the Principal reenters the main thoroughfare and observes for any vehicles that also shift out, similar to the example in Figure 11. This may be even more effective if the Principal engages his turn signal early into the maneuver, inducing a following surveillance vehicle to engage its signal, thus making any subsequent mirroring of the Principal particularly suspicious. There are also any number of opportunities on city streets to shift quickly across traffic and make a turn while observing for any vehicles that mirror this action.

Through area knowledge the Principal should be aware of back-street shortcuts that can be used to avoid traffic obstacles, of which lengthy traffic lights are among the most common. Although others may also be aware of such shortcuts, most people are patient and conservative enough to travel by the main streets through the traffic obstacle. As the Principal maneuvers through back streets or parking lots to avoid a traffic obstacle, he should observe for other vehicles that take the same route. When the Principal has established these type travel trends as standard travel activities through target pattern analysis, they appear more plausible when executed for surveillance detection purposes.

Restrictive terrain such as channelized terrain and choke points facilitate surveillance detection. Channelized terrain refers to limited routes of travel available to a following surveillance team, and can be leveraged to force the surveillance effort into a sub-optimal security posture. Channelized terrain can force the surveillance team to increase vulnerability or risk losing command of the Principal. The Principal can force the surveillance team to channelize its vehicles by traveling on routes such as rural roads and bridges over waterways with no paralleling avenues. Channelized terrain offers no adjacent roads for surveillance vehicles to escape onto to avoid passing the Principal and being exposed by surveillance detection maneuvers. Many of the previously addressed tactics demonstrated the channelizing of following vehicles on the highway for surveillance detection purposes. Off the highway, such channelizing renders the surveillance team vulnerable to detection through passive observation or active measures such as the sudden stop or 180-degree turn. Refer back to Figure 10, which depicts the standard reaction of a surveillance team to a 180-degree turn by the Principal. Note that if this maneuver were conducted along a channelized route with no side streets on which to turn, all of the surveillance vehicles following along this same route would be forced to continue straight and pass by the Principal face-to-face.

Choke points are terrain features that cause traffic to concentrate in density. In such locations, surveillance vehicles may be forced in behind the Principal closer than would otherwise be appropriate while also slowing or stagnating their movement, thus making them more vulnerable to observation from the Principal. Common examples of choke points are construction zones, school zones, and busy merge lanes. An overt detection tactic associated with the use of a choke point involves the Principal turning onto an unmarked dead-end road or cul-de-sac (intrusion points) to observe for any vehicles that follow and then react in an unnatural manner. As a caution, such an aggressive maneuver may induce an equally aggressive *fight or flight response*.

Toll booth plazas are choke points that are generally associated with highways. These provide unique opportunities for surveillance detection. As the Principal approaches a toll booth barrier, he should enter the longest line if traffic is backed up. He then observes for any other vehicles that enter the longer line rather than a shorter one. Any vehicle meeting this profile will be isolated and observed as a possible surveillance vehicle. When entering the line, the Principal also observes the vehicles that pass by to enter a shorter line — which would be the tactically sound reaction of a surveillance vehicle concerned with security. If the Principal encounters no lines when reaching the toll booths, he should fabricate a reason to delay passing through, such as fumbling for money or his pass, to allow any surveillance vehicles to pass through other available booths ahead of him. In this case, the Principal should observe the other vehicles to facilitate subsequent recognition. After passing through the toll booth, the Principal observes for vehicles that pull out behind him from subsequent interchanges, rest areas, and other likely box/pick-up positions, to determine whether they were among those that passed by at the toll booths. The delays associated with traditional toll areas will continue to be less common due to virtual pay technology, but these concepts apply to other locations where travel may be delayed through multi-lane checkpoints, such as border control points, entry into a large event (e.g. sports event parking), or other enclosed facilities with controlled entry points.

Although streets generally restrict vehicular travel along established routes, most street networks, particularly in urban areas, provide a high degree of maneuverability when conducting a surveillance operation. An understanding of how a surveillance effort leverages a higher degree of freedom of maneuver can enhance the Principal's surveillance detection efforts. For example, to avoid mirroring and avoid continued exposure, a command surveillance vehicle may opt to relinquish command of the Principal when the Principal takes a turn by continuing straight at the turn while a follow-on surveillance vehicle takes the turn from a more secure distance and continues the follow. This *hand-off* tactic prevents the vulnerability to detection that exists anytime a surveillance vehicle within observation range of the Principal takes a turn behind him. When the Principal detects a potential surveillance vehicle that continues straight when he turns, he can exploit an understanding of that vehicle's most likely subsequent maneuvers for surveillance detection.

Recall from the discussion of surveillance tactics that the *floating box* is a surveillance method that is characteristic of a more sophisticated surveillance effort. This method involves surveillance assets supporting the command asset by moving at a pace with the Principal while traveling along parallel routes for a more secure and effective reaction to a turn in either direction. The floating box also enables the paralleling assets to more effectively continue the follow if the command vehicle and any other following surveillance vehicles are stopped by an obstacle on the Principal's route of travel.

Figure 12 depicts how the surveillance effort takes advantage of a right turn by the Principal to prepare to establish the floating box. After the Principal turns right at intersection A, the command vehicle (1) continues straight at the turn option to hand-off command to surveillance vehicle (2).

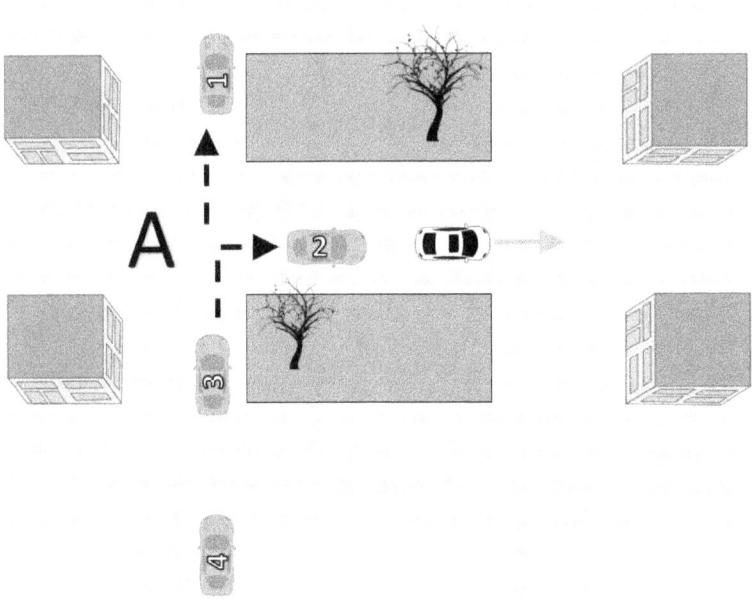

FIGURE 12

The command vehicle performs a hand-off of command with a following surveillance vehicle and the team prepares to establish a floating box

The most common and logical subsequent maneuver by the surveillance vehicle (1) that continued straight is to continue to the next possible intersection and turn in a direction to parallel the Principal to continue in support of the surveillance operation (floating box concept). When practicable, the surveillance effort establishes the *floating box* to increase flexibility and reduce exposure. Figure 13 depicts how surveillance vehicle (1) and surveillance vehicle (4) maneuver to parallel routes to establish the floating box, with surveillance vehicle (2) in command and surveillance vehicle (3) backing the command vehicle.

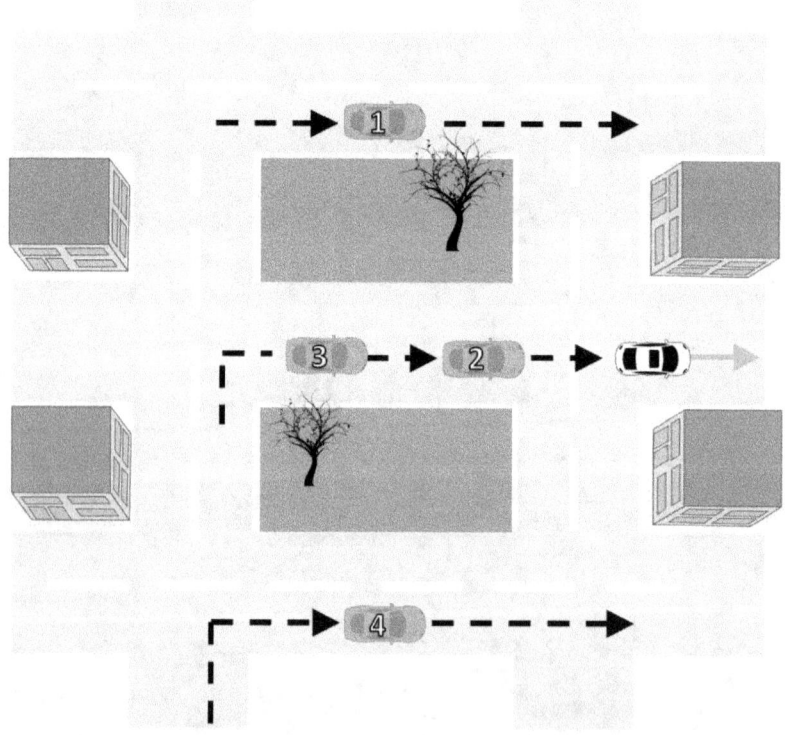

FIGURE 13

The surveillance team establishes the floating box to facilitate secure, flexible, and redundant coverage

When the Principal observes that a suspected surveillance vehicle has continued straight after he has turned, at the first possible opportunity, he will turn in the direction of the road a surveillance vehicle would use as a parallel route. This tactic is designed to detect the suspected vehicle traveling on the paralleling route, which would be highly indicative of surveillance. Figure 14 depicts an example of this active surveillance detection maneuver.

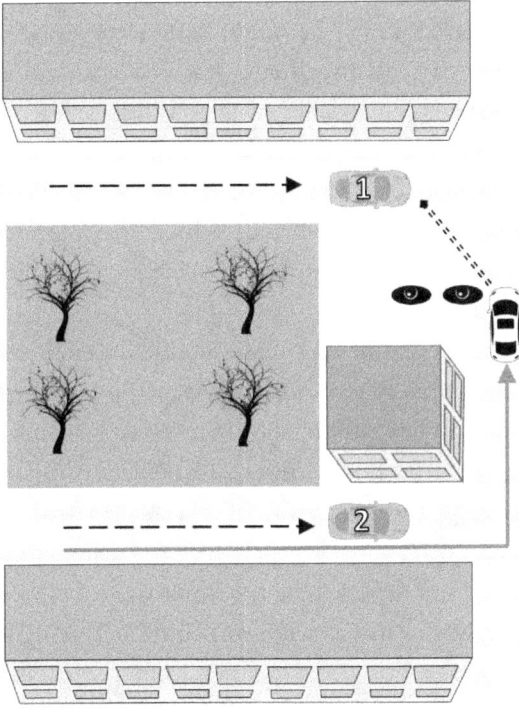

FIGURE 14

The Principal leverages the understanding of the floating box surveillance technique to observe a suspected surveillance vehicle traveling along a parallel route

A general rule that applies to passive surveillance detection — but is one that can also be actively exploited — is that surveillance team vehicles will likely have license plates that blend with the local area in which they anticipate to operate. Any opportunity for the Principal to lead surveillance vehicles into an area (e.g. interstate travel) where surveillance vehicle license plates or other location-specific attributes may stand out, provides an opportunity to isolate potential surveillance vehicles. As a caution, however, sophisticated surveillance efforts may have a variety of surrounding area license plates with "quick-change" capabilities in anticipation of such circumstances.

ACTIVE BOX PHASE DETECTION

When the Principal stops during the course of his travels, the surveillance team maneuvers to establish a box, similar to the stakeout box, to position vehicles along each route on which he might resume travel. These positions are prioritized based on the direction(s) the Principal will likely travel when resuming movement. Surveillance vehicles will attempt to position themselves at the first possible location away from the Principal's stop point, in order to minimize the avenues onto which he can travel undetected before he reaches the location of a boxing surveillance vehicle. Chapter 7 (Figures 6 and 7) describes the surveillance team maneuvering and establishing a box around the Principal's stop location.

When the Principal stops, he should determine which routes the surveillance team would cover (box) for the pick-up. If there are locations that meet the profile of a box position, he can travel to them in an effort to identify a boxing surveillance vehicle. Figure 15 depicts two surveillance vehicles located in pick-up box positions. Each vehicle is parked to observe the Principal along either/both of his likely routes of departure. Since it is assumed that the Principal will depart along the major route and travel toward Point A or Point B, the surveillance vehicles are positioned along the first secondary roads adjacent to the main route to observe him pass by and then pull out for the pick-up. Recognizing these as likely box position locations, the Principal selects and turns onto one of the secondary roads, thus exposing a surveillance vehicle. This tactic is significantly enhanced when the Principal actually observes a suspected surveillance vehicle turning into a road, parking lot, or other location that might serve as a box position as he stops. By then executing the maneuver depicted in Figure 15, he effectively confirms surveillance if he detects the vehicle in a box position.

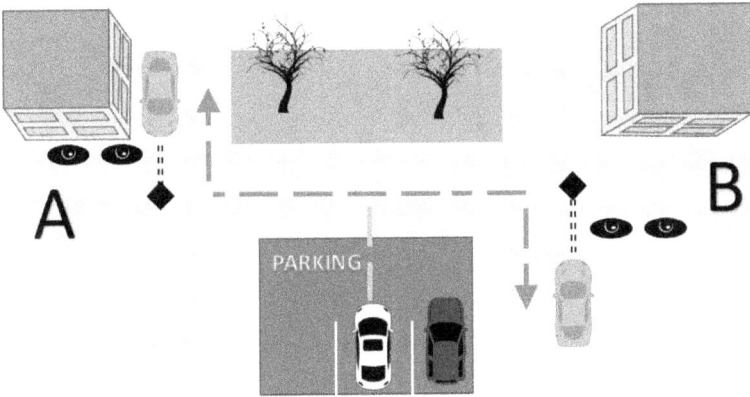

FIGURE 15

The Principal departs a stop location and drives to what he determines is a likely location of a surveillance vehicle box position

An overt variation of this tactic that the Principal can execute on a highway (or other applicable location) is to pull over in the breakdown lane prior to a rest area or similar location. After he stops, he observes the following vehicles as they pass by. After a short delay, he will resume travel on the highway and pull into the rest area ahead. He observes the vehicles inside the rest area to determine if any of them are among those which passed by on the highway. This is an effective maneuver because a rest area or similar location would be a logical location for a surveillance vehicle to establish a box position in reaction to the Principal's stop.

Another variation is to stop in the breakdown lane within observation range of the rest area. From this vantage point, the Principal can observe for any following vehicles that pass by and enter the rest area. He can then travel into the rest area to get a good look at the suspected surveillance vehicle for retention purposes. In this situation, he can create a plausible reason for the maneuver by checking under the hood as though experiencing mechanical problems.

11. ACTIVE FOOT AND COMBINED SURVEILLANCE DETECTION

Active foot surveillance detection shares many of the principles of vehicular surveillance detection. As with passive foot surveillance detection, a primary disadvantage is the limited ability to discreetly observe to the rear. This disadvantage is offset, however, by terrain that is better suited to surveillance detection and the increased degree of flexibility with which the Principal can maneuver by foot. By vehicle the Principal is generally restricted to traveling on established roadways; by foot he has many more travel/maneuver options to facilitate surveillance detection.

ACTIVE STAKEOUT AND PICK-UP PHASE DETECTION

The active detection of foot stakeouts builds on the principles of passive surveillance detection addressed in Chapter 8. When it is possible for the Principal to travel by either foot or vehicle from a stakeout location, a surveillance team places priority on positioning surveillance vehicles for a vehicular follow. This is because if the Principal departs the location by vehicle the surveillance team has less time to react and therefore must be prepared initially for a vehicular follow. If, however, the Principal departs the location by foot, surveillance operators will simply exit the surveillance vehicles and transition into a foot surveillance. The tactics addressed in the section on stakeout detection in Chapter 10, in which the Principal departs the possible stakeout location by foot and walks through the area to identify surveillance assets, applies to foot surveillance stakeouts as well.

When the Principal stays at a hotel, a surveillance team may attempt to get a room next to or on the same floor as the Principal's. Although this is normally done to support technical surveillance operations, the team also uses this placement as a *trigger* for the physical surveillance stakeout. An aggressive detection method that can be employed in this situation is for the Principal to stand in the hallway for a period of time after he exits and locks his room, observing for other guests who depart their room shortly after he does and identifying their room number. The Principal will focus on this room as a potential base of surveillance activity and may have a subsequent opportunity to identify the individual registered to the room. Any opportunity for the Principal to identify a surveillance operator by name enables him to detect surveillance at its source through some investigative effort.

ACTIVE FOLLOW PHASE DETECTION

The Principal has few natural opportunities to observe for surveillance operators when traveling by foot on public streets and thoroughfares. Therefore, active surveillance detection techniques are largely based on increasing the field of observation through methods such as by stopping, turning perpendicularly, or turning 180 degrees to change directions.

One important note for this and all other foot surveillance detection maneuvers is that when observing possible surveillance operators at close range, the Principal should avoid making eye contact. Surveillance operators are generally paranoid about compromise, and eye contact with the Principal is viewed as an extreme degree of exposure. In many cases a surveillance operator will pull himself out of the operation if eye contact with the Principal occurs. This has a negative impact on the effectiveness of surveillance detection, because if the surveillance operator withdraws from the operation after the Principal gets a good look at him, the Principal loses the opportunity to observe him later and confirm surveillance. Therefore, observation for surveillance detection purposes should always be conducted in a discreet manner that does not cause surveillance operators to feel compromised. In fact, it takes great composure for the Principal to know and observe that a surveillance operator has been compromised, but to act in an unalarming and unassuming manner that convinces the operator that he was not.

Probably the oldest yet most effective method of foot surveillance detection is for the Principal to turn a *blind corner* and stop. *Blind turns* consist of intersections or other locations at which the Principal has the option to turn, causing any following surveillance operators to lose sight of him due to structures or other visual obstructions. Such locations are particularly characteristic of urban areas, where buildings line the sidewalk on virtually every block. The objective of this maneuver is to observe for possible surveillance operators after taking the blind turn and stopping. The Principal focuses on anyone who reacts in an unnatural manner when turning the corner and finding himself within exposure range of the Principal. Even a surveillance operator who maintains composure when confronted with such a situation is exposed, thus facilitating future recognition by the Principal. Any stop made after a turn should be planned in advance with a plausible reason for the stop incorporated into the maneuver.

Whether it is a single (lone) surveillance operator or two or more operators conducting the follow, the tactically correct approach to the blind corner turn is to "clear the corner" prior to an operator taking the turn behind the Principal. Figure 16 depicts how a surveillance operator without immediate backup reacts most securely to a blind turn. In situations where there is adequate cover, the operator will continue straight in a natural manner while observing (clearing the corner) to determine whether the Principal has continued through the turn in a normal manner, or has stopped in a manner consistent with the blind corner surveillance detection maneuver. In either case, the operator continues straight through the intersection in a natural manner, crossing the street and turning in the same direction as the Principal on the opposite side of the road to continue the follow (See Figure 16 next page).

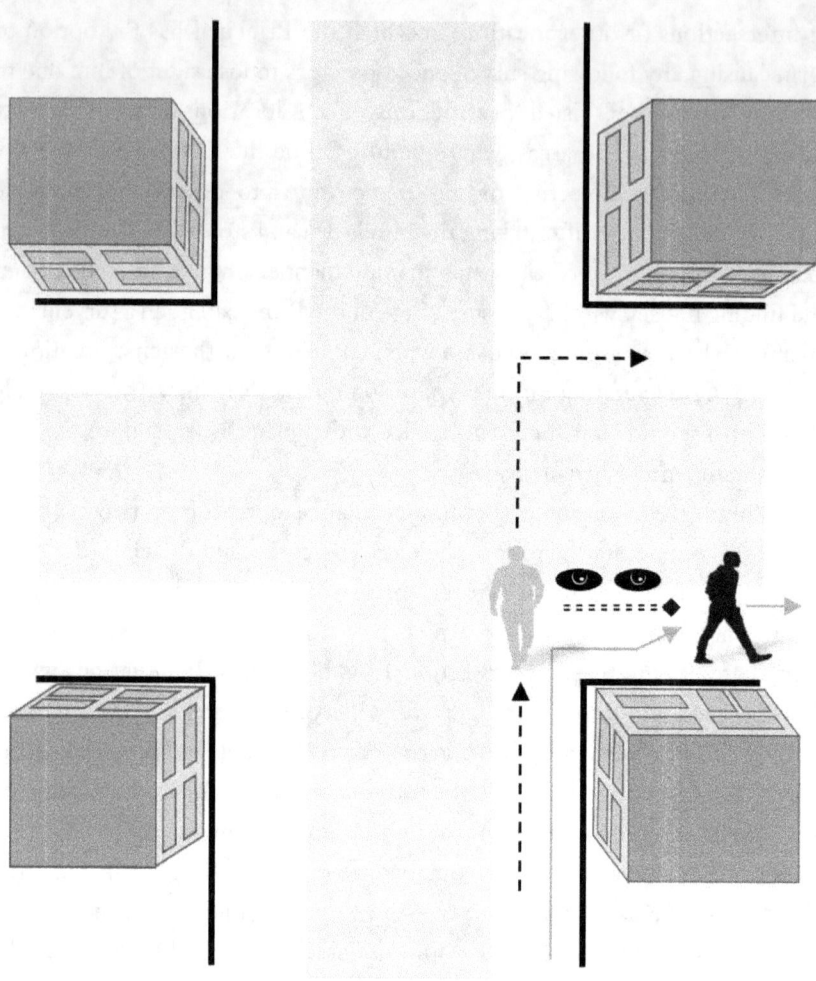

FIGURE 16

The surveillance operator without immediate backup reacts to a blind turn in a secure and tactically correct manner

A well-resourced and coordinated surveillance team will approach any blind turn taken by the Principal with caution — being aware of the surveillance detection implications. For this reason, the Principal must employ a higher level of surveillance operations understanding to prevent any false assumptions that a simple blind turn immediately exposes surveillance to detection. Alternatively, the Principal should never underestimate the threat, and must observe for surveillance at the second-

and third-higher levels of execution. In reaction to a potential blind turn, a tactically capable surveillance team with multiple operators will commit the first following surveillance operator to continue straight at the location of the turn. This prevents his turning blindly into the Principal while still allowing him the opportunity to observe and determine whether the Principal has continued naturally through the turn (clear the corner). This operator either informs the team that the corner is clear, or that the Principal has stopped and that no operator should turn the corner. In either case, the surveillance operator must inform the team of the Principal's status. Based on this application, when stopping after a blind turn the Principal should observe for individuals who glance in his direction when passing through the location of the turn. The Principal should further observe for indications of the use of concealed body communications equipment, phone communications, or visual communications signals.

Figure 17 depicts how a foot surveillance team establishes tandem follow positions to posture for the potential blind turn. Surveillance operator (1) continues straight at the location of the Principal's turn while observing to determine the Principal's status. Surveillance operator (1) signals/communicates the status to surveillance operator (2), who has the option to turn directly behind the Principal if he has continued through the turn in a normal manner, or to cross the road and continue the follow from the opposite side of the road if the Principal did execute a blind turn stop. Surveillance operator (1) has the option to continue straight and temporarily out of the surveillance follow to appear completely inconspicuous if the Principal had stopped after the turn, or to cross the road and turn right to support the follow from the opposite side of the road in support of surveillance operator (2), who assumes command and continues the follow directly behind the Principal (See Figure 17 next page).

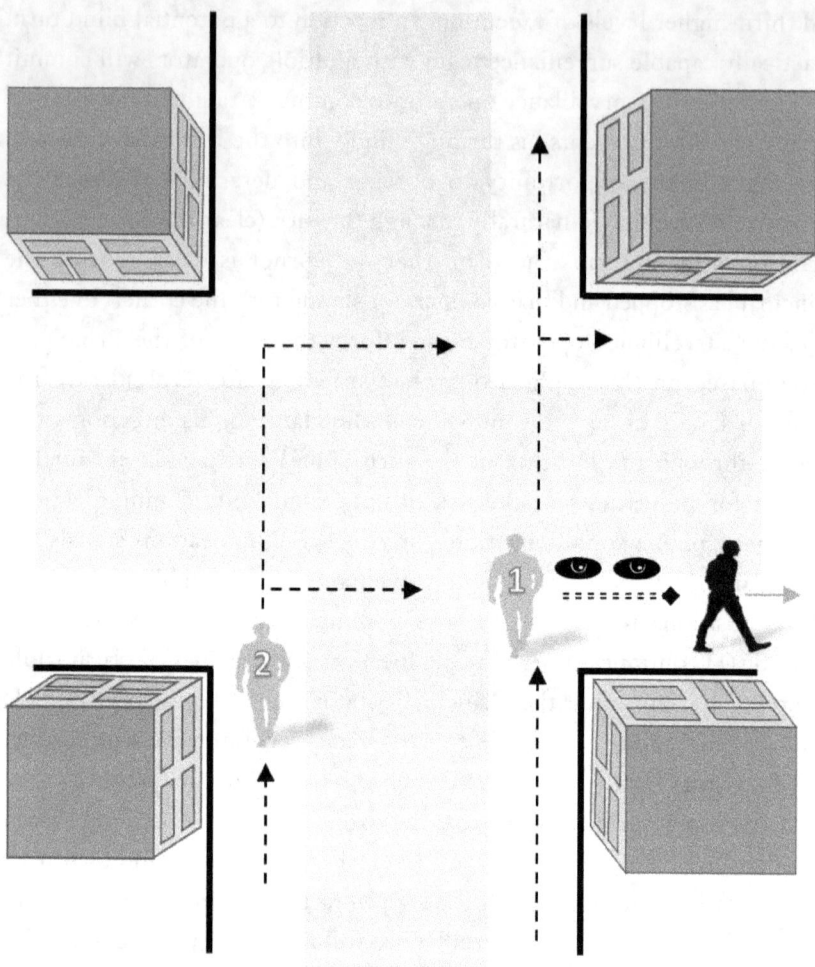

Figure 17

Foot operators conduct a tandem follow and posture for/react to a blind burn by the Principal

An alternative tactical application of clearing the blind turn is depicted in Figure 18. Again, with two operators following in tandem, surveillance operator (2) reacts to the potential blind turn by observing the Principal's actions from a stand-off location. If the Principal has continued through the turn in a normal manner, surveillance operator (2) signals/communicates to surveillance operator (1) that it is secure for him to turn directly behind the Principal and continue the follow. If the Principal stops after turning the blind corner, surveillance operator (2) signals/communicates this to surveillance operator (1) who then continues straight to avoid turning directly into the Principal. Surveillance operator (2) positions himself to turn and assume the follow when the Principal resumes movement.

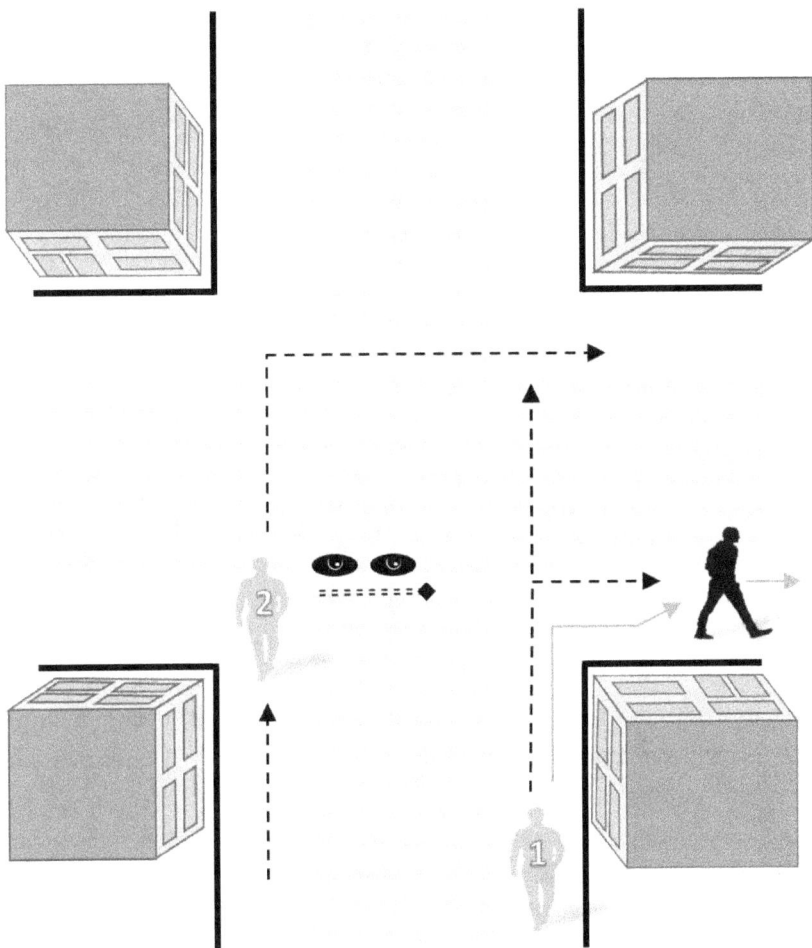

Figure 18
Two surveillance operators operating in tandem react to the potential blind turn by observing the Principal's actions from a stand-off location

When executing the *blind turn* surveillance detection technique, the Principal takes the turn in a manner that prevents observation from any following individuals. The Principal then stops and undertakes a plausible activity while observing for pedestrians taking the turn behind him or continuing straight through the turn location but demonstrating indications of the activities addressed in Figures 17 and 18.

Through prior planning the Principal may incorporate entry of a public location into the blind corner surveillance detection maneuver. After taking a blind turn he immediately enters a public location, such as a store, which affords outside observation through a window. As he establishes a position from which to observe outside while conducting a natural activity, such as shopping, he observes people who turn the corner. The Principal will focus on anyone who reacts suspiciously, meeting the profile of a perplexed surveillance operator who has lost his Principal. Such an individual may also begin scanning the area for locations where the Principal may have entered. Again, the Principal should observe for indications that an individual is communicating with others on the streets. In such a circumstance, the surveillance effort will quickly deduce that the Principal did likely enter a street-side location and may choose to commit operators to search likely such locations. In this case, the Principal employs public location surveillance detection methods as addressed later in this chapter.

The *logical 180-degree turn* is executed on foot to achieve the same objectives as by vehicle. Here again, the Principal should incorporate a plausible reason for his action. The 180-degree turn is an essential foot surveillance detection technique because it provides the most effective method for the Principal to observe what is behind him when executed with a feasible (logical) purpose. When the Principal is traveling by foot, there are many options, to include advantageous terrain, that facilitate this maneuver, particularly with prior planning. When executing the 180-degree turn, the Principal observes, for retention and recognition purposes, all individuals who had been following, as well as those who appear to maneuver out of his path to avoid detection.

A variation of the 180-degree turn is to cross the street at an intersection and then backtrack in the previous direction of travel on the opposite side of the street. Again, the Principal should incorporate a logical reason for backtracking, such as to enter a store. However, unless target pattern analysis demonstrates that the Principal is commonly predisposed to cross streets more safely at controlled intersections, rather than "jaywalk" as an expedient, such a maneuver may be perceived as anomalous and therefore be counterproductive in the overall scheme of the surveillance detection effort. Such a maneuver can also serve as a hasty three sides of a box SDR if a surveillance operator continues to follow along this route.

RESTRICTIVE TERRAIN — FOOT SURVEILLANCE DETECTION APPLICATIONS

Surveillance countermeasures principles and techniques generally apply equally to vehicle and foot surveillance. However, by foot the Principal does not have the range of vision that is afforded by a vehicle's mirrors for surveillance detection, making efforts to observe the surroundings for the presence of surveillance more difficult to conceal, if the Principal is in fact being observed. This makes it easier for a surveillance effort to identify surveillance detection when a Principal appears unusually observant of his surroundings. Another disadvantage to foot travel is that it is generally less channelized. While vehicular surveillance is restricted to established roadways and thoroughfares, foot surveillance affords more flexibility in travel, and foot operators are better able to maneuver in many directions with equal speed and security. Therefore, the Principal's surveillance detection efforts will largely incorporate restrictive terrain which enables observation and detection.

On foot, the Principal can use *channelized terrain*, *choke points*, and *intrusion points* for the same objectives as addressed with regard to active vehicular surveillance detection. Channelized terrain may consist of any restricted walkways, street overpasses, bridges, and even elevators or escalators if employed with caution. The channelized terrain may facilitate rear observation, but it is also normally exploited through the incorporation of a surveillance detection tactic such as a 180-degree turn or stop.

Some channelized terrain may offer the Principal a natural opportunity to observe to the rear. An example of this is a bridge over a river. Since such a terrain feature may provide surveillance operators with the only nearby location to cross the water obstacle with the Principal, they may have no other option but to commit surveillance operators onto the bridge behind him. As the Principal reaches the crest or middle of the bridge, he stops as though to enjoy the view. At this point he will have the opportunity to observe to the rear for possible surveillance operators. He should focus on anyone who also stops as though to enjoy the view rather than continuing toward him. At this point he may also choose to execute a 180-degree turn to further observe the reactions of suspicious individuals. It is plausible that the Principal simply entered the bridge to enjoy the view and return. This tactic is applicable to many types of channelized terrain.

Open terrain such as a park or large city square provides surveillance detection opportunities. Since following the Principal over open spaces exposes surveillance operators, they may choose to walk along the perimeter of the open terrain where more adequate cover and concealment may be available. By doing so, however, they may make themselves more noticeable by walking at a faster rate in order to maintain pace and to be positioned to close distance with the Principal when moving out of the open terrain area.

Foot Surveillance Detection in Public Locations

Public locations such stores, malls, business complexes, entertainment venues, and parks as are characterized by nonstandard terrain because the possibilities of maneuver are so varied. Public locations generally offer variations of restrictive terrain that provide among the best opportunities for surveillance detection. Public locations are choke points (and even intrusion points) to varying degrees, and provide relatively more opportunities to channelize movement. Public locations can be leveraged to force surveillance operators to concentrate and stagnate, rendering them vulnerable to detection. The presence of restrictive boundaries and nonstandard terrain imposes unique constraints and vulnerabilities on surveillance operators. One further consideration is that a public location with multiple exits normally compels a surveillance team to send in more operators because of the difficulty involved with the stakeout of multiple exits. In many cases, public locations force surveillance operators closer to the Principal than they would otherwise allow themselves to become.

The nonstandard terrain associated with public locations generally works to the benefit of the Principal for surveillance detection purposes because it forces the surveillance team to use special tactics. Public locations force a surveillance effort to rely more on adaptability and resourcefulness than on a standard systematic formula of tactics, rendering surveillance assets more vulnerable. For example, a surveillance team can operate very effectively against a Principal on foot or by vehicle out on the streets, because it can employ its tactics systematically on relatively predictable terrain. In public locations, however, it must adapt its tactics to the specific circumstances encountered.

Variations of the previously discussed tactic of entering a public location after a blind turn to observe outside for surveillance operators can be employed in many public locations. As the Principal enters the public location he can observe outside for surveillance operators as they maneuver to box positions to make the pick-up when he exits. The Principal should select a secure position — such as a seat near the window in a restaurant, cafe, or bar — that offers good outside observation while appearing natural to surveillance operators who may enter behind him. The Principal will observe for individuals who pass the location in an unnatural manner or even pass by it more than once.

Public locations require surveillance operators to react immediately to a situation in a natural manner. In most circumstances, people on foot are moving with a purpose or destination. Those who are not, are easily isolated from the surrounding populace. This is another key aspect of public locations that can be exploited for surveillance detection purposes. When individuals go into a public location, such as a store, they do so with a purpose. When surveillance operators follow the Principal into a public location, they must immediately contrive a plausible and natural reason for being in the location (cover for action), leaving them immediately vulnerable to detection if they are not able to rapidly adapt. This forces them to be resourceful in maintaining an unsuspicious appearance. Remaining inconspicuous while observing a Principal in unfamiliar terrain is a difficult task for the surveillance operator. For this reason, the Principal should observe for people who appear out of place. In many cases this is an instinctive assessment rather than a specific observation.

Following on the concept that surveillance operators must seamlessly adapt to the surroundings of a public location to appear natural, a technique that may force surveillance operators into a position that leaves them vulnerable to isolation is to enter a location that is more difficult to adapt and "fit in" with. By entering a location characterized by the unique dress of its clientele, the Principal can then observe for and isolate those whose clothing style does not conform. College bars, biker bars, and exclusive clubs/restaurants are only a few such locations that a surveillance team may have difficulty reacting to in a quick and natural manner. If the surveillance team feels that the activity to be conducted inside the location is worthy of observation, it may commit operators inside who are not adequately dressed to blend with surrounding individuals. If his intent is to remain discreet, the Principal must select locations that will appear plausible to the surveillance team based on established patterns.

Another way to force surveillance operators into a situation they may be unprepared for is to enter a public location where a specific type of action is required to blend with the surroundings. This enables the Principal to isolate and observe individuals who are not comfortable with the required activity; in the case of a potential surveillance operator, not being able to establish an effective *cover for action*. One example of such a location is a pool hall. A surveillance operator may not be able to enter a pool hall behind the Principal and appear natural without actually playing pool. Perhaps the surveillance operator is comfortable with a pool cue, but it is just as likely that he will be among the least proficient players in the hall. By identifying individuals who appear to be novices at the activity required, the Principal can isolate possible operators. Locations that involve some type of unique (usually physical) activity are ideal, but there is a range of options for locations which would challenge a surveillance operator's ability to "fit in" if not prepared. Again, any location selected should appear plausible to the surveillance team.

When entering a public location such as a restaurant for the purposes of surveillance detection, the Principal should position himself in a manner that provides a wide field of view of the other people inside. If possible, he should sit in an area that allows him to see the entrance and observe for anyone who enters after him, isolating those who enter after him as possible surveillance operators. He will focus on those who sit in a position that facilitates their observation of him and who enter and sit alone. In establishments with hosted seating, surveillance operators must identify where the Principal is seated and ensure that they are also seated appropriately to observe — which may require that they conspicuously request a specific table or ask to move after being seated. An operator may "scout" for the Principal's location by going the restroom or employing some other feasible cover for action prior to being seated. An individual entering to join someone else who is sitting alone may also be an indicator of surveillance if the surveillance team has committed another operator into the restaurant to sit with the fellow operator in order to provide a more natural appearance. This also enables the operators to transmit information to team members outside while appearing to converse with each other.

An overt detection tactic employed in a restaurant scenario is for the Principal to remain seated long enough for any surveillance operators to enter and get positioned, and then leave without ordering, as though he were not pleased with the menu selection. He then establishes a position outside of the restaurant to observe for individuals who also depart in this manner. A variation of this is for the Principal to order a meal that can be served and consumed quickly. Any surveillance operators in the restaurant will order a meal to appear natural. By leaving quickly, the Principal may catch them off guard and in the middle of a meal. The guise of receiving an emergency phone call provides a plausible reason for this action, or even for paying the bill and departing before the meal is finished. The Principal will observe for other restaurant patrons who end their meals quickly and depart behind him.

The Principal can use very small and confined public locations as choke points/intrusion points to force surveillance operators close in for observation. A surveillance team, however, will rarely commit surveillance operators into an extremely confined public location unless the expected benefit outweighs the consequences of exposing the operators to the Principal. Moderately sized public locations, such as shops and convenience stores, provide excellent surveillance detection opportunities. The location selected should be one that has sufficient space to give surveillance operators enough of a sense of security that they will enter behind the Principal, but small enough to allow the Principal to observe everyone inside with relative ease. It is always important to note that surveillance operators try to avoid making eye contact with the Principal because when this occurs, the asset is considered "burned" and of no further use to the surveillance effort. This phenomenon results in an almost instinctive or compulsive reflex to avoid eye contact in close quarters that is readily detectable and highly indicative of surveillance.

As the Principal enters the location with size permitting, he should travel to the rear while observing those who were there before him. He eliminates these people as possible surveillance operators. After he is satisfied that he has identified all the individuals who were there prior to his entry, he gradually moves toward the front in a natural manner. This allows him to isolate all those who entered after him. He observes these individuals for retention or recognition and to identify whether they display any other indicators of surveillance, such as appearing unnatural in the surroundings. Single-entry/exit establishments (intrusion points) are best for use with this tactic because they limit the avenues by which individuals can enter without observation by the Principal.

Single entry/exit establishments are also conducive to surveillance detection because a single entrance serves to channelize surveillance operators through an effective detection point. Given appropriate cover, the Principal can enter such a location and establish a position that enables him to observe anyone else who enters. He observes everyone for retention purposes and for indications of surveillance, such as an individual immediately scanning the location when entering as though searching for someone.

Many public locations have features such as elevators, escalators, and stairways that are characteristic of channelized terrain. Elevators are channelized terrain with intrusion points which force the surveillance effort to expose at least one surveillance operator to the Principal or risk losing contact. The Principal should be suspicious of anyone who enters an elevator with him and immediately selects the top level or perhaps even asks the Principal which level he would like, offering to push the button for him. When there are multiple occupants on or entering an elevator with the Principal, he should not select a level until all occupants have chosen their destinations, and select a previously unselected level, if possible. He should observe which levels specific individuals select so he can subsequently identify anyone (potential surveillance operator) who does not disembark at the level selected. Another technique for multi-level elevators with multiple occupants wherein potential surveillance operators may be entering the elevator with the Principal, is for the Principal to enter the elevator but not select a level, as though his level had already been selected by another occupant. At a level of his choosing, the Principal will depart the elevator as the doors are closing, which may prompt undisciplined or aggressive surveillance operator to exit in this manner as well.

Public locations are also excellent for surveillance detection because they offer various opportunities for logical 180-degree turns. Consider the degree of unpredictability that the Principal can incorporate into his maneuvers in a mall or department store. While such locations provide excellent opportunities to observe surveillance operators if present, they can rarely serve to confirm surveillance unless an operator acts in a particularly suspicious manner. The reason for this is that it is not uncommon to observe the same individual any number of times when moving through such locations.

Stairwells and escalators are effective in channelizing potential surveillance operators for detection purposes. The design of most escalators provides the Principal with the opportunity to channelize and observe possible surveillance operators while executing two or more sequential 180-degree turns. By approaching an escalator in the direction opposite of that in which it moves, he naturally executes a 180-degree turn in order to get on, which allows him to observe following individuals in an inconspicuous manner. Upon getting off, he turns 180 degrees again, creating another natural opportunity to observe those who stepped on the escalator behind him. Sequential escalators (or stairways) in multi-level structures provide multiple, sequential 180-degree observation opportunities.

ACTIVE BOX PHASE DETECTION

The detection of a surveillance box that is established after the Principal stops during the course of a foot surveillance again builds on the passive measures addressed in Chapter 8. When there is sufficient concealment and cover for action provided by the surrounding pedestrian and business activity, overt detection methods may be the only effective measures, as opposed to the primary passive measures such as change detection as potential foot surveillance operators transition from a static to mobile status. However, active measures to identify/isolate potential surveillance assets and corresponding efforts to elicit a conspicuous response require relatively overt tactics, which may not be in the best interests of the Principal's overall surveillance detection objectives. As with vehicular surveillance detection, the most active approach to detecting foot operators in box positions is to identify the most likely such positions, conceive and employ a plausible reason for walking by these locations, and observe them for indications of surveillance operator presence.

ACTIVE DETECTION OF COMBINED VEHICULAR AND FOOT SURVEILLANCE

When the Principal vehicle parks and the Principal transitions to foot travel, the surveillance effort conducts a similar transition. To avoid conspicuously stopping and dropping surveillance operators off, or when the driver must exit the vehicle to transition to foot surveillance, surveillance vehicles will park in locations prior to or shortly after the Principal's stop location. To exploit this tactic, the Principal observes in the likely stop directions to identify any vehicles fitting the profile of a surveillance vehicle expeditiously parking. The Principal will walk in the direction of any potential surveillance vehicles and observe for vehicles that park but whose passenger(s) remain in the vehicle as though to avoid exiting when determining that the Principal is in the direct vicinity. In the case of potential parking surveillance vehicles with passengers exiting the vehicles, the Principal will walk in the direction of the potential surveillance operator(s) and observe for any suspicious actions on their part when discovering that they have exited the vehicle directly in the Principal's line of travel.

Shopping areas where the Principal can park in a parking lot and enter a small establishment are excellent for surveillance detection. Surveillance operators choosing to enter the establishment are vulnerable to detection as addressed in foot surveillance in public locations/intrusion points. By entering an establishment that is small and innocuous, the surveillance effort will likely choose not to enter and will prepare for the Principal's next move. This affords the Principal the opportunity to observe the parking area for activity that is indicative of surveillance. Vehicles that travel through the area without parking will be observed for subsequent recognition if detected moving from likely box positions as the Principal returns to his vehicle and drives out of the area.

The Principal can plan his travel (and stop) to integrate a feasible reason to stop and exit the vehicle and then return shortly to the vehicle, such as traveling to a store to find that it is not open. In such circumstances, the Principal observes for foot operators who exit vehicles, linger in the area, and then return to vehicles as the Principal does.

The more elaborate surveillance detection effort is to plan a stop at a location at which the Principal can exit the vehicle and walk a route that logically passes by locations where surveillance vehicles would likely establish box positions to establish the pick-up and follow when the Principal vehicle departs the stop location. The Principal will identify potential surveillance vehicles and subsequently observe for further indications when the Principal vehicle departs the box location.

Travel by public transportation (e.g. bus, taxi, train, plane) requires that a surveillance effort execute modified tactics of combined foot and vehicular surveillance. Appendix 7 (Surveillance Tactics and Surveillance Countermeasures on Public Transportation) includes active surveillance detection methods applicable to public transportation.

12. ANTISURVEILLANCE

Antisurveillance consists of actions taken to elude or evade possible, suspected, or identified surveillance. Since surveillance is always possible, antisurveillance can be employed even when there is no specific indication that surveillance is present. The Principal normally employs antisurveillance methods to enhance security when he has reason to believe he is under surveillance and his activities must be protected.

Espionage agents invariably follow this practice because of their extreme need to ensure that their activities go undetected. Although they may not have identified any indications of surveillance, the fact that it is always possible dictates that they conduct antisurveillance before conducting any type of operational activity. This ensures that they elude ("clean off") any possible surveillance effort before conducting activity that would provide evidence of operational, illegal, or other protected activities. Terrorists and sophisticated criminal elements employ these same tactics to elude discovery by counterintelligence or law enforcement elements; but antisurveillance is by no means restricted to the criminal element. Even "good" agents operating in "bad" countries employ such techniques as a matter of security and survival. Secret Service agents, bodyguards, and other protective services personnel conduct antisurveillance as a standard part of their executive security duties. In addition to executing complex methods as part of a routine security regimen, they must also be prepared to employ evasive measures to the extreme of eluding violent surveillance efforts such as those associated with a terrorist attack. The antisurveillance tactics, techniques, and procedures detailed in this manual are based on the methods employed by the world's most sophisticated practitioners — good and bad.

ANTISURVEILLANCE OVERVIEW

As with all surveillance countermeasures, antisurveillance is based on an understanding of surveillance principles and tactics. The driving principle of most antisurveillance efforts is that a surveillance team will normally break contact with the Principal rather than accept a high risk of exposure. Most surveillance teams make operational security their highest priority, because if the Principal becomes aware of coverage, the surveillance effort is hindered severely if not rendered completely ineffective. Antisurveillance strives to capitalize on this by placing the surveillance team in a position that forces it to either terminate the surveillance or risk compromise (recall the fight or flight response from Chapter 5).

Many of the tactics used for surveillance detection can be applied effectively to antisurveillance. This is a key principle to understand as many surveillance detection maneuvers are equally effective antisurveillance techniques against a surveillance effort that places the avoidance of detection/compromise above maintaining contact with the Principal. This directly relates to the tactical imperative that at some point the surveillance team must determine whether the probability of compromise exceeds the benefit of continuing the surveillance operation. Surveillance detection tactics are executed for the purpose of placing a surveillance asset in a compromising position. A well-disciplined surveillance asset will normally make the split-second decision to break contact rather than risk exposure. This point illustrates that there is a vague distinction between many surveillance detection and antisurveillance maneuvers. The surveillance asset's reaction to a given maneuver — or decision not to react — may determine which surveillance countermeasures purpose the maneuver actually serves.

Antisurveillance is the most difficult of the surveillance countermeasures to conduct discreetly. As with active surveillance detection, antisurveillance tactics range from discreet to overt. Generally, the more aggressive/overt a surveillance detection measure rates along the covert-overt spectrum, the more effective the measure will be in meeting antisurveillance objectives. At the same time, the more overt the tactic, the more aggressive and identifiable it will be to a surveillance team if present.

An *overt* surveillance effort that is not concerned with compromise requires much more aggressive antisurveillance measures to evade. This discussion is limited to antisurveillance principles and tactics as they apply to protecting personal privacy. Extreme antisurveillance measures, such as defensive driving to avoid a violent pursuit, are beyond the scope of this manual.

As is the case with surveillance detection, the number of possible antisurveillance maneuvers is unlimited. This chapter focuses on the principles that facilitate effective antisurveillance as a basis for understanding while addressing general tactical applications.

TARGET PATTERN ANALYSIS

The *target pattern analysis* process significantly enhances the effectiveness of antisurveillance. As a surveillance operation progresses, the team identifies activities and patterns that are indicative of the Principal's intentions. When the Principal's activity or travel pattern is consistent with past observations, the team tends to take a more relaxed posture. This is due to the assumption that since the surveillance team is confident that it can anticipate the Principal's activity or travel destination it can loosen its coverage to decrease the probability of exposure. The team accepts this increased risk of losing command of the Principal because it is confident both of his destination, and that if he is lost, operators can simply relocate him at locations identified through target pattern analysis. For example, if the Principal has established a pattern of taking the same route to work each day, the surveillance team will avoid the risk of undertaking aggressive maneuvers to maintain command because it assumes he will go to his workplace. If operators are forced to relinquish command due to traffic or other circumstances which might otherwise risk bringing them to the Principal's attention, they will simply travel to the assumed destination and reestablish the surveillance.

When the Principal undertakes a unique activity or travel pattern, the surveillance team intensifies its coverage because it must be prepared to react to unanticipated actions. Any such indication that the Principal may be "switched on" will raise the team's acuity and enable it to be better prepared for antisurveillance maneuvers. Therefore, the Principal's actions should appear normal (standard) up to (and ideally including) the actual antisurveillance maneuver.

The Principal bases antisurveillance planning on target pattern analysis to identify the times and activities that may bring about a relaxation of the surveillance team's vigilance. The Principal evaluates routes or circumstances that fit this profile to determine how antisurveillance applications can be incorporated most effectively. When he intends to conduct protected activity, he should begin his travels with a previously established pattern. At the appropriate time, he will conduct an (ideally plausible) antisurveillance maneuver that will catch the surveillance team off guard — enhancing the probability of success.

DISGUISE AND DECEPTION

Disguise and deception can enhance antisurveillance because a surveillance team must recognize the Principal in order to follow him. The Principal can manipulate the concepts of recognition that a surveillance team relies on to maintain observation to elude surveillance. Disguise and Deception are discussed in Appendix 8.

VEHICULAR ANTISURVEILLANCE

Antisurveillance maneuvers are normally based on target pattern analysis. The Principal identifies activity patterns and favorable terrain that facilitate antisurveillance at locations identified during pattern analysis. Vehicular antisurveillance is restricted somewhat by the established avenues of travel and the maneuverability of vehicles. Antisurveillance tactics are based largely on an understanding of these limitations and how they also apply to surveillance vehicles.

STAKEOUT AND PICK-UP PHASE VEHICULAR ANTISURVEILLANCE

A primary consideration for the Principal in employing antisurveillance tactics against a stakeout is that if he eludes a stakeout, he defeats surveillance. A stakeout is based on the assumption that the Principal will either depart or travel through a designated location. Based on this calculated assumption, the surveillance team will remain in the stakeout location until it observes the Principal. However, if the Principal can elude the surveillance effort at the point of stakeout, he will be able to travel without the threat of surveillance. This applies whether the Principal departs the stakeout location observed, or unobserved, by the surveillance effort.

Appendix 5 addresses the practice of alerting authorities to a suspected fixed or mobile observation post. Regardless of the result of the response to the call, if it is in fact an observation post, the surveillance team will consider the location or vehicle compromised and discontinue its use. This neutralization of the surveillance asset is an effective antisurveillance measure.

A Principal can elude a vehicle stakeout by foot in many locations. Recall that a surveillance team employs target pattern analysis to determine its stakeout locations. When the Principal establishes a pattern of consistently departing a stakeout location in the same manner, the surveillance team will position assets accordingly. In some areas, such as residential neighborhoods, it is difficult if not impossible to maintain 360-degree observation coverage. For most residences, a surveillance team prioritizes its efforts on the primary points of departure that have been established through target pattern analysis. Based on this concept, the Principal first analyzes established patterns to predict how a surveillance team will position assets and then identifies routes of departure that are unlikely or impossible for the surveillance team to observe. This allows him to depart the stakeout location undetected and travel (normally by foot) to conduct any activity without the risk of observation. With proper planning, he can do so and return without the surveillance team realizing he was ever gone.

It is virtually impossible to depart a stakeout location by vehicle without detection. A vehicle can depart only by established roadways, and a surveillance team will certainly maintain observation of at least the primary, and to the degree practicable, any other possible routes of departure. Annex 8 (Disguise and Deception) addresses the employment of a decoy vehicle as a stakeout antisurveillance method.

When beginning movement within the potential surveillance box, the Principal generally begins movement first, so there is a degree of initial separation and momentum that can be exploited for antisurveillance purposes by acceleration out of the suspected box location. However, this may appear overt and would only be successful against a single asset or relatively small surveillance effort.

Recall that when establishing a vehicular stakeout box, coverage of the potential routes of travel are prioritized based on the Principal's most likely utilization. This prioritization process is a key concept because if there are not enough surveillance assets to cover all possible routes, then a corresponding number of routes will not be covered based on the assessment that the Principal is least likely to take these routes. This prioritization is largely based on target pattern analysis. When less likely routes must go unboxed, holes are created through which the Principal can escape. Given this understanding, the Principal can use reverse logic to confound the surveillance effort by traveling from the stakeout location along a route that would likely have been given a low priority for coverage. This maneuver is particularly effective when followed by a quick turn, or succession of turns, off the established route of travel. The *break and disappear* antisurveillance procedure discussed in Chapter 13 provides a detailed explanation of this "reverse logic" methodology.

Follow Phase Vehicular Antisurveillance

The Principal vehicle's appearance has a significant impact on vehicular surveillance. The vehicle should be as indistinguishable as possible to better blend with standard vehicle traffic. Any unique feature that makes the vehicle easier to identify assists the surveillance effort. Conversely, a vehicle that blends with others on the road and has no distinguishing features such as dents, bumper stickers, distinctive license plates, or unique paint patterns, is more difficult for the surveillance team to distinguish from similar models, which detracts from the effectiveness of surveillance (and serves antisurveillance). The vehicle's light signature is also a significant distinguishing factor, and should therefore be one that readily blends with surrounding vehicles. Malfunctioning tail lights make the Principal vehicle much more distinguishable; and in fact, a surveillance team may covertly disable a light on the Principal vehicle for this very purpose.

The ability to accelerate quickly when necessary is a characteristic of vehicular travel that has a positive impact on antisurveillance. Fast and aggressive driving supports antisurveillance by making it difficult for a surveillance team to maintain integrity and command of the Principal. However, if employed for antisurveillance, fast and erratic maneuvers should conform to a standard driving pattern that would have been observed during target pattern analysis. A Principal who establishes a pattern of fast and aggressive driving has the flexibility to conduct more aggressive antisurveillance maneuvers without drawing as much suspicion.

Traffic obstacles also support antisurveillance. It is difficult for a surveillance team to maintain command of the Principal when traveling through dense traffic. The Principal can apply this concept effectively by traveling through dense traffic, into a relatively open area, and then back into dense traffic. Breaking out of the dense traffic allows him to place distance between himself and the surveillance effort. By entering another area of dense traffic ahead of the surveillance effort, he can effectively lose surveillance. A more overt application of this tactic is to accelerate prior to entering the dense traffic. When breaking out of a dense traffic area, the Principal should use a route of departure that the surveillance team would not anticipate. This is based on the likelihood that the surveillance team will lose command of the Principal in the dense traffic and attempt to reestablish it after breaking free of the obstacle. To do so, the team must anticipate the Principal's likely route or possible routes of travel as addressed in the *lost contact drill*. The surveillance effort may choose, or be compelled to, disregard less likely routes due to resource limitations. This concept is addressed in detail in Chapter 13.

Traffic lights are another obstacle the Principal can use for antisurveillance. Particularly in dense urban traffic, they can facilitate antisurveillance by allowing the Principal to place distance between himself and the surveillance team before breaking out of the dense traffic area. By studying traffic light patterns, the Principal can travel in a manner that allows him to clear stop lights just before they turn red. A more overt tactic is to run a red light. Although this maneuver will certainly alert the suspicions of the surveillance effort, a surveillance vehicle will rarely risk detection by repeating this maneuver behind the Principal. Another option is to wait at the green light until it is about to turn red and then proceed. Again, this is an overt tactic, but the Principal can incorporate a somewhat plausible reason for such an occurrence, such as being distracted by some other activity. It is interesting to note that in such a situation, a surveillance vehicle would likely restrain from alerting (honking at) the Principal to move because it would certainly draw the Principal's attention back to the surveillance vehicle. Ironically, by not acting in this situation as most vehicles would, this restraint actually serves to make the surveillance vehicle conspicuous to the cognizant Principal. A similar but less overt method is employed when stopped at a stop sign or at a traffic light that allows right turn on red, wherein the Principal waits until traffic approaching from the left is close enough to allow the Principal to turn right before the traffic reaches the intersection, but then obstructs any potential following surveillance vehicles from making the turn behind the Principal.

Trains can serve as obstacles to a surveillance effort as well. By crossing the tracks just before the train passes, the Principal can escape while following vehicles are obstructed from moving or observing beyond the train. International boundaries can serve the same purpose, because many surveillance teams will not cross international lines. Surveillance vehicles normally have unique equipment that would not pass the scrutiny of customs inspections. Even if the surveillance vehicle can be sanitized, the delay involved should give the Principal a sufficient lead on the surveillance team. Government law enforcement or investigative agencies must coordinate operations into another country; therefore, they would not continue the operation unless they knew the Principal's travel intentions in advance and conducted the necessary coordination.

Cross-country (off road) travel presents another obstacle to surveillance. Surveillance vehicles are selected based on their ability to blend with others on the road and will therefore be models designed for standard terrain. Although not generally associated with restrictive terrain, land areas without roadways are obstacles to common vehicles. Whether or not the Principal vehicle is built for off-road travel, the Principal can drive across unimproved terrain to elude surveillance. This technique is more feasible if the Principal vehicle is a four-wheel drive vehicle commonly used for off-road travel. As a related concept, a virtually insurmountable antisurveillance technique is to unexpectedly travel to a private boat or airplane and depart across terrain that a surveillance team would be completely unprepared for, with no readily available options.

Choke points and channelized terrain also facilitate antisurveillance. Choke points such as construction zones or toll areas are generally characterized by traffic obstacles that may allow the Principal to break away from the surveillance team, when the movement of assets is obstructed. During antisurveillance planning, the Principal identifies how he can exploit the characteristics of specific choke points. The concept of using dense traffic — which is characteristic of many choke points — to obstruct the surveillance team while quickly breaking out of traffic was addressed previously. A traffic jam presents another opportunity to apply this concept. Although it is illegal and potentially dangerous, moving to the shoulder to bypass the traffic jam enables the Principal to distance himself from the surveillance team. He should do this in a location that allows him to reach a major interchange (e.g. highway exit) before the surveillance team has time to react. In very slow-moving, congested city traffic, the Principal can turn off the road at virtually any option, and unless a surveillance asset is directly behind him, the effort will be delayed in following him until traffic allows an asset to reach the option.

Channelized terrain normally forces the surveillance team to commit multiple/all assets to a single route behind the Principal, or accept risk in maintaining contact. Recall from Chapter 10 that a surveillance team will attempt to place surveillance vehicles on parallel routes in order to overcome any traffic obstacles encountered (floating box concept). Channelized terrain deprives the team of this flexibility in coverage. It also leaves the team susceptible to having all of its vehicles delayed by a traffic obstacle while the Principal drives away. By drawing the surveillance team into channelized terrain, the Principal can use a traffic obstacle such as a stop light to obstruct the entire team while he escapes. Again, after the breakaway he should travel by a route that the surveillance team conducting a *lost contact drill* would not anticipate.

Anytime the Principal makes a turn, he forces the surveillance team to rotate command vehicle positions (hand-off) or risk detection by taking the turn directly behind him. The fewer surveillance vehicles involved in the follow, the less flexibility the team has to use such tactics. The Principal should identify logical routes of travel that incorporate successions of quick turns to exploit this vulnerability.

When the Principal makes a 180-degree turn, he forces surveillance assets to either pass by him face-on or react immediately to avoid close observation. Since most surveillance teams give discretion priority over maintaining command of the Principal, they focus first on avoiding detection by not reacting in a conspicuous manner. In many cases, it is difficult for a surveillance team to react to such a maneuver in an inconspicuous manner while maintaining command of the Principal. This security consciousness dynamic makes the 180-degree turn an effective antisurveillance tactic.

There are many variations of the 180-degree turn that are best described as they apply to highway driving, but are equally applicable to a wide range of vehicle roadways. Among the possible tactics is a 180-degree turn consisting of exiting a highway and taking the overpass to reenter in the other direction. An overt variation of this is to take a highway exit where traveling to the overpass is an option. The Principal stops at the option, allowing any following surveillance vehicles to close in. Then, rather than turning in the direction of the overpass, which is normally left, the Principal turns and travels away from it. After traveling a short distance (but out of sight of the overpass), he executes a 180-degree turn and returns to the highway. This maneuver enables him to reach and reenter the highway traveling in any direction, unobserved by the surveillance team, which is reacting to the 180-degree turn. This forces the team to split in two directions to reestablish contact with the Principal, who by that time should have established a substantial lead. The Principal should take the next possible exit and travel again along an unlikely route. The less time the surveillance team has to catch him before he exits, the better. Again, fast driving enhances the effectiveness of the maneuver. This tactic is applicable to many city street options as well.

Service roads that allow authorized vehicles to turn around on a highway (or other applicable roadways) by crossing the median can serve as very effective, yet overt, antisurveillance routes. The Principal should identify the locations of service roads to determine which are appropriate for antisurveillance. The most effective locations enable the Principal to execute a 180-degree turn on the highway and travel only a short distance before he has an opportunity to turn off the highway and escape along an unlikely route. This technique should be executed in a location that allows the Principal to observe to the rear for any vehicle that also turns at the option, which should deter any security conscious surveillance vehicle from mirroring the maneuver, or would alternatively identify an overt surveillance effort.

An even more overt variation of this tactic is for the Principal to execute a 180-degree turn on a service road and then pull over in the breakdown lane of the highway facing in the other direction. By stopping within observation range of the service road, he forces any following surveillance vehicles to continue past it rather than repeat this overt maneuver within his observation range. This ensures that a surveillance vehicle cannot use the service road to execute a 180-degree turn after the Principal is out of observation range, as is possible with the first method. The Principal executes this maneuver in a location that requires bypassing surveillance vehicles to travel a long distance before reaching an option to turn back around. This should provide the Principal ample time to reach a traffic option in the other direction to take and complete the antisurveillance process. Yet another variation of this is for the Principal to stop in the breakdown lane of the highway just prior to the service road. After waiting a short time to allow any following surveillance vehicles to pass by, he reenters the highway and executes the 180-degree turn on the service road.

Another overt highway antisurveillance method is for the Principal to exit the highway on a ramp and immediately stop in the breakdown lane of that ramp. After waiting a short time to allow any following surveillance vehicles to exit the highway and pass by, he will carefully back up in the breakdown lane to reenter the highway. A variation of this is to stop in the breakdown lane immediately after passing an exit ramp, and after allowing any following surveillance vehicles to pass by, back up, and take the highway exit. These maneuvers are most effective at interstate highway (or similar) interchanges at which exiting or bypassing vehicles are committed onto another roadway for a considerable distance before reaching an option to turn around. For example, the first exit option at a major interstate interchange normally requires that the exiting vehicle enter directly onto the other highway.

Many of the previously addressed tactics involving stops on the highway are applicable to city antisurveillance as well. Stopping on channelized terrain and then executing a U-turn after following vehicles have passed is one example. The Principal can also stop immediately after passing an intersection and back up or turn around to take one of the other routes off the intersection after vehicles have passed.

One final vehicular antisurveillance tactic exploits a surveillance team's anticipation that the Principal will stop. Again, based on insight gained in target pattern analysis, the surveillance team attempts to minimize exposure by relaxing coverage when the Principal's travel activities appear standard based on previously observed patterns. Understanding this, the Principal can exploit it for antisurveillance purposes. Since a surveillance team is particularly vulnerable when the Principal stops and departs his vehicle with an enhanced field of vision, it will identify when this is likely to occur and alter coverage accordingly to enhance security. As mentioned earlier, the residence and workplace are the most common such locations, but the Principal's travel patterns dictate the number of possibilities. As it identifies appropriate locations, the surveillance team normally establishes a point prior to the assumed destination at which to terminate coverage. This enables operators to begin establishing a surveillance box without committing a surveillance vehicle past the destination and thus unnecessarily exposing a surveillance asset. By assessing locations at which the team is likely to terminate coverage, the Principal can facilitate antisurveillance by traveling to the location, but rather than stopping as the surveillance effort would anticipate, he continues past the location and then executes a series of evasive maneuvers. Even when the surveillance team has an asset in place to observe that the Principal did not stop and continued through the location, this technique is still an effective antisurveillance measure in that it exploits the *Chaos Theory of Surveillance*, which is detailed in Chapter 13. This technique is an effective method of breaking contact to initiate the *break and disappear* antisurveillance procedure, as detailed in Chapter 13.

Again, many of the tactics associated with *surveillance detection* of the vehicular surveillance follow are also effective antisurveillance maneuvers because the surveillance team may opt to break contact with the Principal rather than react in a detectable manner. Whenever a maneuver forces the surveillance team to break contact for security reasons, it is validated as an effective antisurveillance maneuver. Having achieved an understanding of antisurveillance principles and tactics, review the tactics addressed in Chapter 10 (Active Vehicular Surveillance Detection), from the perspective of how those maneuvers become effective antisurveillance measures if the surveillance team chooses to break contact rather than risk detection. The 180-degree turn on a channelized route is a perfect example, as most surveillance efforts will opt to break contact rather than mirror such a maneuver in a detectable manner.

Box Phase Vehicular Antisurveillance

The Principal should leverage his knowledge of how a surveillance team reacts to a stop during the mobile follow to conduct effective antisurveillance measures. A surveillance team reacts to a stop by the Principal in a secure and systematic manner. At this point, the team must maneuver to box positions by routes that are undetectable by the Principal.

When the Principal stops, surveillance vehicles maneuver to establish box positions along his possible routes of departure. The Principal should select a stop location that has multiple possible (as many as possible) routes of departure to reduce the probability that the surveillance effort can cover all possible routes, and proportionately increase the number of routes that may go uncovered by a surveillance asset. As with the stakeout box, coverage of the potential routes of travel from the location of the Principal's stop are prioritized based on the Principal's most likely utilization. When the number of possible routes exceeds the number of available surveillance assets, this prioritization drives which routes are covered by assets and which routes will not be covered. This prioritization may be based on target pattern analysis, but is more likely based purely on a situational assessment of the Principal's most logical routes of travel from the stop location.

Establishing an effective box after the Principal stops is rarely an instantaneous process. This creates a *window of vulnerability* for the surveillance effort while it maneuvers to establish a hasty box when the Principal stops. This also represents an antisurveillance *window of opportunity* for the Principal. This window of opportunity enables the Principal to go on the offensive by stopping and then reinitiating movement before a surveillance effort would have had the opportunity to establish secure box positions. By stopping just long enough to force the surveillance team to initiate the boxing process and disperse, the Principal may be able to maneuver away by a route that is not yet covered. This dynamic can facilitate a break in contact with a desynchronized surveillance effort. However, this can be a relatively overt technique, so in most cases it is more discreet to posture for antisurveillance while temporarily stopping in a more natural and unalarming manner.

Recall that when the Principal stops the surveillance team will attempt to position a vehicle in a static position to observe the Principal when stopped (trigger). In selecting the appropriate stopping location for antisurveillance purposes, the Principal should identify one that offers no inconspicuous locations for the surveillance team to position a *trigger* vehicle for observation. If the surveillance team has no discreet options for a trigger position, it will normally forego positioning a vehicle that would be vulnerable to detection. At this point the team will focus on positioning vehicles along possible routes of departure. This puts the surveillance team at a significant disadvantage because assets are unable to observe the Principal until they pick him up along a given route of travel — if there is a surveillance vehicle covering that route. Again, the surveillance team may be forced to leave less likely routes of departure unboxed due to limited resources. In this situation, by taking an unlikely or unanticipated route, the Principal can depart the stop location without the surveillance team's knowledge. This approach reflects a key antisurveillance concept, which is to leverage an understanding of surveillance tactics and to use the surveillance effort's system and standard methodology (logic) against it. To this end, the Principal uses *reverse logic* to confound the surveillance effort by traveling from the box location along a route that would likely have been given a low priority for coverage. In many cases, this may involve making an immediate 180-degree turn to travel away in the direction from which he approached. This maneuver is particularly effective when followed by a quick turn, or succession of turns, off the established route of travel — again, traveling in the least logical direction to evade a surveillance team that will think and react in a logic-based manner.

Even a well-established box presents vulnerabilities to the surveillance effort when the Principal begins to transition from a static to a mobile status. When the Principal departs the box, surveillance assets must pull out into traffic to establish the follow. Obviously, the faster the Principal is moving, the more difficult it is to establish positive contact in the follow in a timely manner. A pure "brute force" approach to evade surveillance during the box phase is for the Principal to rapidly break the box and reach an option by which he can evade/confound the surveillance team's efforts to regain contact. Although this method does largely employ the element of acceleration, the fact that it is coupled with a transition stage makes it more discreet and effective. In addition, by breaking the box in this manner the Principal essentially creates a *blind spot* that can be exploited by various methods to include the *break and disappear antisurveillance* procedure as detailed in Chapter 13.

FOOT ANTISURVEILLANCE

Antisurveillance by foot is generally more difficult than by vehicle, mainly because of the limitations of speed, and the fact that the movement of surveillance operators is relatively less restricted. By foot, the slower speed of travel makes it easier for surveillance operators to react to the Principal's movements in a natural manner. Additionally, the effectiveness of virtually all vehicular antisurveillance maneuvers can be attributed to the restricted maneuverability. Since foot surveillance operators encounter fewer of the obstacles and restrictions that vehicles do, they are better able to overcome similar antisurveillance maneuvers by the Principal on foot. This increased maneuverability can, however, facilitate the Principal's antisurveillance efforts when exploited effectively. Foot antisurveillance is most effective when the Principal selects and dictates an environment that best restricts/manipulates the movement of the surveillance effort.

Previous sections emphasized the principle that most surveillance detection maneuvers may also be effective antisurveillance maneuvers, depending on the reaction of the surveillance team. Although still a valid principle, it is much less applicable to foot antisurveillance because the limitations to observation that restrict foot surveillance detection maneuvers also restrict their effectiveness when applied toward antisurveillance. Recall that the three primary aspects to be exploited in foot surveillance detection are turns, stops, and public locations, while also incorporating the concepts of restrictive terrain. The tactics involved here are integral to antisurveillance as well, but their applications differ considerably.

The previously addressed concepts of using restrictive terrain such as traffic hazards and channelized terrain also apply to foot antisurveillance. Although these features are not limited to public establishments, such locations do provide a proportionately higher number of natural choke points and channelizing options. These characteristics are key considerations in examining public locations for antisurveillance applications during the planning phase.

The exploitation of pedestrian traffic is the most discreet method of foot antisurveillance. A foot surveillance operator's observation is restricted by line of sight. Pedestrian traffic creates a natural obstacle to both the vision and movement of surveillance operators. By moving from a relatively open area that forces surveillance operators to distance themselves to a congested pedestrian location, the Principal can readily elude observation. In many public areas there is a high concentration of people, which enables the Principal to blend into the crowd and disappear.

By foot the Principal can exploit blind turns (as addressed in Chapter 11), which are characteristic of virtually any downtown city block, to facilitate antisurveillance. Such locations to be leveraged for antisurveillance purposes should be identified and planned for in advance. By taking a blind turn and then taking another immediate turn while obstructed from the view of any possible surveillance operators, the Principal can elude surveillance. Public locations, such as stores, are common turning locations that are readily available after blind turns.

Many public locations are also conducive to antisurveillance because they have multiple exits by which the Principal can escape after entering. When the

Principal enters a public location, there will normally be a short delay before a surveillance operator enters, due to the coordination involved. This period of lost command allows the Principal time to maneuver to elude surveillance. Building on this idea, when the Principal enters a public location, it will take some time for the surveillance team to identify and cover all exits to the location from the outside. Also, the number of exits it can cover is limited by the number of operators. The Principal should exploit these vulnerabilities by departing the location quickly by an unlikely or difficult to find exit.

Elevators, available in many public locations, are a type of channelized terrain — and potentially an intrusion point within the channelized terrain — that places unique restrictions on a surveillance team. The more levels associated with an elevator the more effective its use for antisurveillance. To follow the Principal on an elevator, a surveillance operator must get dangerously close. With a suspected surveillance operator on the elevator, the Principal can employ more overt tactics to elude surveillance. When initially entering an elevator, the Principal will not select a level until all occupants have chosen their destinations. He will observe which levels specific individuals select so he can subsequently identify anyone who does not disembark at the level selected — making this an effective surveillance detection tactic as well. After all other occupants have selected their levels, the Principal will select a previously unselected level if possible. If this option does not exist, he should select the top level (or bottom depending on direction of travel), to maximize the exposure of any potential surveillance operator, and perhaps compel any potential operator to expeditiously exit to avoid prolonged exposure and possible detection. If able to orchestrate a scenario wherein he can exit the elevator at a level that no one else selected, the Principal eludes any potential surveillance operator — unless that operator compromises security and disembarks with the Principal — thus serving surveillance detection purposes. Another technique for multi-level elevators with multiple occupants wherein potential surveillance operators may be entering the elevator with the Principal, is for the Principal to enter the elevator but not select a level, as though his level had already been selected by another occupant. At a level of his choosing, he will depart the elevator as the doors are closing, which should elude all but the most undisciplined or aggressive surveillance operators. When the Principal is forced to select the top level because no other option exists, an overt method of antisurveillance is to remain on the elevator after it has reached the top. Any surveillance operator who remains with the Principal at this point has no regard for security and should be considered a threat. At the first indication that the other individual intends to remain on the elevator as well, the Principal should exit immediately and aggressively elude him because of the threat of attack. If the surveillance team does not place a surveillance operator on the elevator, it will lose command of the Principal and have a degree of uncertainty regarding his intentions. Even when operators are able to observe the level indicator light, they cannot be certain whether the Principal disembarks when the elevator stops or if the stop is for other individuals to enter or exit. At this point the Principal can take the elevator to an appropriate level and then elude surveillance by exiting via a different route. The surveillance team will establish a trigger on the ground floor elevator, anticipating the Principal's eventual return. Therefore, the Principal should use an alternative elevator or stairs to evade the surveillance effort.

Any location that incorporates specific types of security measures is effective for antisurveillance. This is based primarily on the fact that a surveillance team is not only concerned with detection by the Principal but also by third parties. Security personnel or systems provide the third party for antisurveillance purposes. Even a surveillance team that is operating under official authorization must be sensitive to compromise by well-intentioned security personnel. Security personnel are trained and employed to identify suspicious activity, rendering any surveillance team vulnerable to detection. Additionally, security systems such as metal detectors and body scanners will obstruct or delay the entry of surveillance operators with communications equipment or firearms. Through prior planning, the Principal can exploit such locations for antisurveillance purposes.

When traveling by foot, the Principal can transition to public transportation, which can be among the most effective modes to enable antisurveillance. Appendix 7 addresses surveillance countermeasures employing public transportation.

COMBINED FOOT AND VEHICULAR ANTISURVEILLANCE
Combined foot and vehicular surveillance requires that the surveillance team transition from a vehicular surveillance to a foot surveillance, or vice versa.

During these periods of transition, a surveillance team must move foot operators out of or into a vehicle, normally after the Principal has already begun or completed this transition. The process is further complicated by the fact that the surveillance team must accomplish these procedures in a secure manner that is not detected by the Principal.

In reaction to the transition from a vehicular to foot surveillance, the surveillance effort deploys foot operators to the ground if it has sufficient assets and then establishes a box with surveillance vehicles around the Principal vehicle location. Due to the nature of a foot surveillance, with its own unique challenges, the transition from vehicle to foot surveillance is also one of the most effective for antisurveillance purposes.

If the surveillance team is unable to anticipate the Principal's actions and effect a smooth and secure transition, it will have difficulty maintaining command. The Principal will exploit these vulnerabilities for antisurveillance purposes. By planning such transitions, the Principal is able to select locations that enable him to do so quickly while limiting the surveillance team's ability to do so, such as one that allows him to park his vehicle and travel quickly into a densely trafficked pedestrian area. The possibilities are limitless but might also include traveling quickly into a public location with multiple exits or onto a mode of public transportation such as a subway train.

The surveillance team will establish a box around the Principal vehicle, particularly when he is on foot and unseen. This offers the team a measure of control, since it assumes the Principal will eventually return to his vehicle. Regardless of the boxing activity, the surveillance team's focus is still on following or finding the Principal while on foot. Surveillance vehicles support the foot operators, as necessary, both when they have command of the Principal and when they are searching for an unseen Principal. This makes the team vulnerable to antisurveillance by a quick, unexpected transition back to a vehicular surveillance.

The vehicle pick-up and follow associated with the transition from foot to vehicular surveillance involves the same vulnerabilities addressed as they apply to the foot to vehicle transition, coupled with the difficulties involved with a transition from a vehicular box to a follow. An effective chaos-inducing method is for the Principal to compel two transitions in rapid succession by executing a stop that would require the surveillance effort to transition from a vehicular to a foot status, and then forcing a transition back to vehicular surveillance while the surveillance effort is still in the process of executing the initial transition. A variation of this technique is for the Principal to park and exit the vehicle to perform a plausible activity, but one which enables him to return quickly and drive away while the surveillance has not yet established an effective box. The *Chaos Theory of Surveillance* addressed in Chapter 13 is very applicable to this rapid succession scenario.

The Principal should plan his travels in a manner that enables him to return to his vehicle while unobserved by the surveillance team or with little indication of his intentions to travel away by vehicle. Either of these circumstances requires that the surveillance team hastily transfer to the vehicular follow. If the surveillance assets are unable to discreetly move faster than the Principal in returning to the vehicles, the transition presents a risk of lost contact that the Principal can exploit for antisurveillance. This may enable the Principal to drive away along a route that is not yet boxed because the vehicles were occupied recovering operators from the foot follow, the route taken was given a low priority for coverage, or a combination of both. It may also force the surveillance team to transition to the vehicular follow before it has the opportunity to pick up its foot operators. As a result, surveillance vehicle drivers will be conducting the follow without navigators, which requires them to perform the functions of the navigator, including reading a map and transmitting information, while driving. Anytime a surveillance vehicle is forced to operate without a navigator, team effectiveness is degraded and maintaining command of the Principal becomes much more difficult. This in effect serves the purposes of antisurveillance.

Travel by public transportation (e.g. bus, taxi, train, plane) requires that a surveillance effort execute modified tactics of combined foot and vehicular surveillance. Appendix 7 (Surveillance Tactics and Surveillance Countermeasures on Public Transportation) includes antisurveillance methods applicable to public transportation.

13. ADVANCED SURVEILLANCE COUNTERMEASURES CONCEPTS AND PROCEDURES

Understanding how the surveillance threat thinks and reacts is the basis of effective surveillance countermeasures. Understanding how a surveillance effort will perceive and react to the Principal's actions, be they countermeasures or not, is vital to the effective application of specific surveillance countermeasures techniques. Surveillance countermeasures applications must be conducted with an appreciation that the surveillance effort they are directed against has a strategy, is proficient, and can react and adapt based on the situation. Individual surveillance detection and antisurveillance tactics can be readily identified as such and overcome by most capable surveillance efforts. As opposed to a reliance on individual surveillance detection and antisurveillance tactics (maneuvers) in isolation, this section presents some "master's" level concepts with a process approach that enables systematic, discreet, and comprehensive applications of surveillance countermeasures methodologies.

This process approach to surveillance countermeasures addresses the most effective surveillance detection procedure and the most effective antisurveillance procedure. *The Temporary Break in Contact* surveillance detection procedure and the *Break and Disappear* antisurveillance procedure both employ the same enabling techniques. Both are enabled by *breaking contact* with the surveillance effort, exploiting a *blind spot* to prepare for the final stages of the procedure, and then employing techniques that are unique to the objectives of each. Both procedures can also feed on the *Chaos Theory of Surveillance* — a concept with which all master level practitioners of surveillance countermeasures must be familiar.

THE CHAOS THEORY OF SURVEILLANCE

Within the surveillance professionals' community, surveillance operations are appropriately characterized as *hours of the mundane periodically interrupted by moments of chaos.*

This characterization implies that even an unwitting Principal can cause a noteworthy degree of chaos for a surveillance effort. The hallmark of a professional surveillance effort is its ability to react to and manage chaos. However, chaos that is deliberately created by a manipulative Principal can be virtually impossible for even the most capable surveillance efforts to manage. Consistent with the above characterization of a surveillance operation, the Principal can orchestrate moments of chaos to isolate, manipulate, and exploit surveillance assets — hence the term *The Chaos Theory of Surveillance.*

In mathematics and physics, Chaos Theory addresses the phenomena of how isolated events can destabilize entire systems. This theory is commonly referred to as the "ripple effect," and is probably most popularly associated with the "butterfly effect," which suggests that the flapping of a butterfly's wings might cause tiny changes in the atmosphere that ultimately cause a tornado to appear days later.

A surveillance effort employs a systematic approach that involves common tactics, techniques, and procedures. Whether the surveillance effort is a single person or multiple operators, there is basically a set system of methods that the effort applies in reaction to the Principal's movements. With multiple operators, this systematic approach becomes even more important, because each individual operator acts based on a common understanding of how all the operators can be expected to react to a given situation. This ability to understand how each operator can be expected to react is what makes a surveillance operation a system. The Chaos Theory of Surveillance, and its destabilizing effects, are as applicable to a surveillance effort as the Chaos Theory of physics is to any other systematic approach.

The psychological and physiological factors of anxiety, inertia, momentum, and friction apply to any surveillance operation. When stimulated, these factors that impact a surveillance can cause confusion, inaction, or overreaction on the part of individual surveillance assets within the larger surveillance effort (system), with destabilizing effects. When effectively applied and exploited, the Chaos Theory of Surveillance is the ultimate manipulation of a surveillance effort for isolation, detection, or evasion purposes.

The course of a standard surveillance operation generally involves the surveillance effort monitoring and recording the Principal's mundane day-to-day activities. Particularly in the case of a Principal that does not demonstrate surveillance awareness or consciousness, the surveillance effort observes the Principal's routine activities that likely remain consistent over the course of days and even weeks. This is where target pattern analysis, whether conducted as a formal process or developed repetitively over a period of time, tends to settle the surveillance effort into a sense of security and in some cases overconfidence. Over time, a surveillance effort may be drawn into a sense of complacency that can be readily exploited at the time and place of the Principal's choosing. When this sense of security is suddenly disrupted by an unanticipated maneuver on the part of the Principal, surveillance assets may become isolated and even forced to react in a manner that leaves them vulnerable to detection. In addition, this can destabilize the entire surveillance effort to facilitate effective surveillance countermeasures efforts.

When the Principal conducts an unanticipated activity that is not consistent with target pattern analysis, the surveillance effort will likely assume that the unusual activity is potentially of very high operational interest, since it deviates from established norms. This professional instinct to ensure that contact is maintained while at the same time reacting to an unanticipated event — if effectively exploited — renders the surveillance effort vulnerable to isolation and detection. As a synergistic effect, the laws of psychology and physics can be exploited to cause a situation that is chaotic for the surveillance effort, yet controlled by the Principal.

Any number of intangible factors build up over the course of a surveillance operation, but two general categories of factors that develop and can lead to poor execution in the face of uncertainty are referred to as *inertia* and *friction*. These elements, in conjunction with the generation of *momentum*, are factors of vulnerability that the Principal can manipulate against the surveillance effort.

The inertia of a situation is accentuated by destabilizing factors such as the adrenaline of the moment, fear of losing the Principal, and a drive to accomplish the objectives. In this context, inertia is action based on a general sense on the part of surveillance assets that there is a need to move and react, but an uncertainty regarding exactly what needs to be done. This movement amid confusion and without sound direction is readily exploitable for surveillance detection and antisurveillance.

There are also factors — such as an anxiety about avoiding compromise and even sleep deprivation — that can tend to generate a destabilizing friction. As a potentially debilitating counterbalance to inertia, friction is inaction or hesitation. This is a tendency of some surveillance assets to err on the side of being overcautious under uncertain circumstances. An interesting point is that, in a given situation, surveillance assets may react differently. This can result in a combination of inertia and friction that causes variations in momentum and negative momentum that can very readily desynchronize and compromise a surveillance effort.

There is a wide range of exploitable applications of this theory, and they will differ based on whether the objective is surveillance detection or antisurveillance. Given this understanding, a basic example provided for illustration purposes involves the Principal traveling to his workplace. The surveillance effort will have likely performed some target pattern analysis and will be aware of the Principal's standard route to work. As such, as the Principal progresses along the standard route to work, the surveillance effort will assume that it is a routine phase of the surveillance, with the Principal conforming to his established pattern. As the Principal is in the final approach to his work location, he can initiate the "Chaos" by continuing past the work location (or by deviating just prior to reaching it) when the surveillance effort is relaxed and fully anticipating the conclusion to another standard phase of the operation. This will immediately launch the surveillance effort into a reactive mode when it is probably poorly positioned based on the final preparation for the stop and the fact that it is now faced with uncertainty based on this new and irregular activity. At this point, any number of maneuver options are applicable to further exploit the inertia, friction, and general chaos that such a basic action can cause if properly executed.

As with the number of specific surveillance countermeasures, there are many possible applications of the Chaos Theory. In fact, if not for the serious nature of a potentially hostile surveillance effort, the Principal could "toy with" a surveillance effort using various chaos-inducing methods. Transition points such as temporary stops, transitions from vehicular to foot surveillance, and transitions from foot to vehicular surveillance also provide abundant opportunities to orchestrate chaos scenarios.

There is no professional surveillance operator with street-level experience who would dispute that such a Chaos Theory exists, although very few will have decomposed the dynamic down to this level of cause and effect. This stands as another example of the higher level of understanding needed to master the art and science of surveillance countermeasures. Once again, tactical applications are the fundamental basics, but an understanding of advanced concepts such as the Chaos Theory of Surveillance enables the Principal to enter, manipulate, and disrupt the hostile surveillance threat's decision cycle and operational process.

THE BREAK IN CONTACT

The *break in contact* is a key enabling element for both surveillance detection and antisurveillance procedures. The break in contact exploits Principal-orchestrated circumstances to manipulate the surveillance team for surveillance countermeasures purposes. As a surveillance detection application, the break in contact is executed on favorable terrain to manipulate the surveillance team and elicit a reaction that exposes surveillance assets to detection. As an antisurveillance enabler, the Principal exploits the temporary break in contact to execute a follow-on procedure that completely evades the surveillance effort.

The break in contact is normally executed by employing a variation of multiple techniques. The Principal may orchestrate a chaos-inducing scenario to affect a break in contact, or combine other techniques in a process approach to achieve a similar effect. Generally, an effective process employs a combination of *pacing, acceleration*, and *restrictive terrain* to achieve a break in contact, and to enter a *blind spot* that enables the Principal to execute follow-on maneuvers that the surveillance effort cannot observe.

The break in contact will be planned and executed in a favorable location which enables the Principal to enter a *blind spot* immediately after the break in contact. Recall that the *blind spot* is any location or situation that causes a short-term loss in contact (observation) that requires movement or action by surveillance assets in order to reestablish contact. Just as the term "break in contact" implies a loss of observation by the surveillance effort, it must be executed in a manner and location that enables the Principal to execute follow-on maneuvers that the surveillance effort cannot observe. In fact, once the Principal enters the blind spot, it will induce an immediate reaction from surveillance assets if the procedure is properly executed.

Whether the objective is surveillance detection or antisurveillance, the methods employed to affect a break in contact are basically the same. The primary difference between the two is the location and circumstances under which the break in contact is executed. The options for overt maneuvers to break contact are plentiful, but as previously discussed, these can be counterproductive if the surveillance effort perceives the activity as blatant surveillance countermeasures. If executed properly, a break in contact establishes the preconditions for effective surveillance countermeasures, based on the objectives. Again, the key components that facilitate effective break in contact efforts are pacing, acceleration, and restrictive terrain (and transition points under favorable circumstances).

An advanced understanding and application of *pacing* applies to its use as a method of manipulation to generate or reduce momentum on the part of surveillance assets that can be exploited against them. A large part of a break in contact can be summarized succinctly as *using the surveillance effort's momentum against it.* Since the surveillance effort, or individual assets thereof, accelerate and decelerate at a pace that is generally consistent with that of the Principal, the Principal is in essence dictating the pace of the surveillance effort. Although this concept may seem obvious, the effect is that this enables the Principal to control the tempo of the surveillance effort, and when appropriate, exploit the tempo against it.

By manipulating or controlling the pace or tempo of the surveillance effort, the Principal can slow the pace to generate "negative momentum" to establish the preconditions for a break in contact. The application of pacing coupled with open terrain can establish among the most suitable conditions to affect a break in contact.

In many cases, *acceleration* is a key component of any procedure involving a break in contact. This is another excellent example of how techniques used in isolation — rather than as part of a process — are less effective and in some cases counterproductive, depending on the surveillance countermeasures objectives. Employing a strategy of acceleration alone as a means to escape or break contact will likely be perceived as a surveillance countermeasure and is therefore less effective than measures combining multiple aspects. By combining the action of acceleration with a deliberate pacing effort to create "negative momentum," the end result is a more effective and discreet surveillance countermeasures effort.

By inducing (manipulating) surveillance assets into "negative momentum" and then using acceleration (ideally in conjunction with other components), the Principal can break contact while also convincing the surveillance effort that the reason for the lost contact was its own overcautiousness or poor tactical judgment. When acceleration is incorporated in a process approach, the surveillance effort will be more inclined to perceive the reason for a break in contact as a result of its own judgment regarding how to conduct the follow, and less likely to perceive it as an active surveillance countermeasures effort. The previous example of the Chaos Theory of Surveillance demonstrates how the Principal can apply this technique to create "negative momentum" accentuated by a degree of confusion (friction) to facilitate a break in contact.

Although *restrictive terrain* is readily exploited in support of surveillance detection as an isolation method in and of itself, obstacles and other types of restrictive terrain can also be exploited to affect a break in contact that in turn supports other active surveillance detection or antisurveillance measures. In fact, with a determined and aggressive surveillance effort, obstacles that physically impede movement may be the only means to facilitate evasion.

In many cases, the use of restrictive terrain to affect a break in contact is most effective when combined with the component of acceleration. The Principal should accelerate prior to entering restrictive terrain to increase distance from the surveillance effort, and accelerate out of the restrictive terrain when complete to further increase separation while the surveillance effort is still obstructed by the obstacle. Chokepoints are among the best restrictive terrain/obstacles for antisurveillance. Open terrain can also be exploited to force the surveillance effort to increase its following distance (reverse momentum), which can in turn be exploited by acceleration and evasion to achieve a break in contact.

Again, the purpose for the break in contact to facilitate either surveillance detection or antisurveillance is to enable the Principal to enter a *blind spot* where his follow-on maneuver(s) cannot be observed by the surveillance effort. There is a wide range of options available to the resourceful Principal to create exploitable blind spots.

Recall that surveillance assets conduct hand-offs to avoid mirroring and to minimize exposure to the Principal. In fact, this is a standard tactic that is executed for security when the Principal makes a turn. In virtually all cases, however, there is a varying amount of time — normally seconds — in which no asset will have contact (observation) with the Principal as the hand-off is executed. This simple factor alone can facilitate any number of variations of the blind turn (*blind corner*) method to facilitate a blind spot. While corners may be the most common options to create a temporary break in contact and blind spot situation, there are many other options that can be exploited with equal effect, and in many cases more discreetly.

THE TEMPORARY BREAK IN CONTACT SURVEILLANCE DETECTION PROCEDURE
The relationship between the Chaos Theory of Surveillance and the temporary break in contact surveillance detection procedure is tantamount to applying theory to practice. If not for the serious nature of a potentially hostile surveillance effort, the Principal could exercise elements of the Chaos Theory to "toy with" (manipulate) a surveillance effort. There is no other application that better reflects the characterization of "toy with" than the temporary break in contact surveillance detection procedure, as it can truly make the Principal a "master of puppets" in regard to potential surveillance assets. Like no other surveillance detection procedure, this one *manipulates* the surveillance effort in a manner that transforms it from the hunter to the hunted.

The *temporary break in contact* surveillance detection procedure finds its effectiveness based on the *avoid lost contact concept*. The strength of this concept is the fact that it is based on an understanding of how a surveillance effort thinks and reacts, making it among the most effective from the surveillance detection standpoint. The concept is as follows: *When placed in a situation that risks losing contact with the Principal, a surveillance effort will take aggressive, and sometimes extreme measures to retain contact with the Principal.*

For the temporary break in contact by exploiting a blind spot to be effective, there must be some type of traffic option within (or shortly after) the blind spot that would compel following surveillance assets to accelerate in an effort to regain contact. Among the more obvious reasons, a surveillance effort uses maps to look ahead and anticipate hazards prior to the Principal reaching the option. If there is a traffic option ahead of the Principal, the surveillance effort will be aware of this and react accordingly in the case of a potential lost contact situation.

The avoid lost contact concept makes the temporary break in contact surveillance detection procedure effective. Like no other concept, this is the one that truly plays on the "psyche" of a surveillance effort. Understanding that surveillance assets will react in an aggressive and potentially compromising manner to avoid a "lost contact" situation is a highly exploitable factor.

This concept most regularly applies to the risk of losing contact with the Principal when approaching a traffic option. The sense of urgency that immediately besets a surveillance effort when it loses contact with the Principal is among *the most exploitable for surveillance countermeasures* purposes. Recall that a surveillance effort executes a lost contact drill if the Principal is not observed as he reaches a traffic option or other location at which he could have taken any number of possible directions of travel. Regardless of the number of assets, for any surveillance effort the lost contact drill is a circumstance to be avoided if at all possible, because the consequences of losing contact with the Principal are significant. For instance, even if contact is regained during the course of the lost contact drill, a surveillance effort with multiple assets becomes dispersed and is at a disadvantage until it is able to reconsolidate the effort.

The *avoid lost contact* concept is a significant element of the mastery of surveillance detection tradecraft. This level of insight enables the Principal to essentially assume control of a situation by simply exploiting the psychological impact that individual instances of lost contact have on a surveillance effort. From the team (peer) perspective, an individual surveillance operator who is responsible for allowing a lost contact situation that results in a lost contact drill has essentially failed himself and his team. The psychological motivation to avoid this fate alone generates the "inertia" and "momentum" that drive surveillance assets into positions of isolation within the Principal's range of observation. Even a surveillance effort involving only one operator engenders this psychological impact of the desire to avoid failure.

Given an understanding of the dynamics of surveillance involved, the temporary break in contact surveillance detection procedure is simple. The Principal breaks contact in order to orchestrate an *avoid lost contact* situation that induces surveillance assets to react by accelerating to regain contact. The concept of pacing and the Principal's manipulation of a surveillance effort's tempo in conjunction with the blind spot is the most effective means of isolation in support of this procedure. While out of sight (blind spot) of the potential surveillance assets, the Principal then establishes, or reestablishes, a rate of travel (or stops altogether) that enables the surveillance assets to regain contact, but in a manner that enables the Principal to isolate the surveillance assets based on the fact that they bear down on him in an unnatural manner. In such a circumstance, surveillance assets may further isolate themselves for detection by visibly decreasing speed once they have regained contact. In fact, the best planned temporary break in contact maneuvers are executed in a manner in which the Principal finds a blind spot that does not allow following surveillance assets observation of the Principal until they are virtually on top of him. The desired effect is that when the surveillance asset does catch up to the Principal, its momentum either forces it to pass by the Principal in a more natural manner or to decelerate in a conspicuous and detectable manner. When placed in a situation in which an immediate decision is required, many surveillance assets will "freeze" and act conspicuously (the "friction" factor). Ideally, given the appropriate restrictive terrain, the surveillance assets' freedom of movement can be limited in a manner that gives them no option but to bear down on the Principal and decelerate in a conspicuous manner. To the opposite extreme, since momentum can rapidly devolve into *inertia* when uncertainty is introduced, an isolated asset may act conspicuously because it chooses to maintain momentum rather than stop or slow down. This may result in "action without logical purpose," which is among the most compromising positions a surveillance asset can be manipulated into.

For perspective, the time elapsed between the break in contact and the isolation of potential surveillance assets in the temporary break in contact surveillance detection procedure is generally measured in seconds. By vehicle, the execution of this technique may be a matter of less than 5-10 seconds from initiation to isolation and detection. Obviously, the time involved depends on the terrain and rate of speed, but this perspective is important to the understanding that the blind spot is more of an expedient than an elaborate set of circumstances.

Suitable terrain that facilitates speed variations to manipulate and exploit the tempo or momentum of surveillance assets enables some of the most effective applications of the temporary break in contact surveillance detection procedure. Perhaps the most common example that also has "detection" applications is that of the policeman nested away with a radar gun in a blind spot where the speeders cannot see him until they are already in range with their speeds recorded. Prime examples include areas where there are bends, crests, or dips in the road that would force a following surveillance asset to lose sight of the Principal temporarily (a blind spot). The Principal can establish negative momentum when approaching an appropriate location, accelerate into the blind spot, and then decrease speed when in or completing it. Again, there should be a traffic option within, or immediately after, the blind spot to compel the surveillance asset to accelerate into the blind spot. If successful, this results in the surveillance asset pursuing quickly into the blind spot and then bearing down on the Principal as he completes the maneuver.

By foot, the blind spot options are generally more abundant than by vehicle due to less restrictive movement options, but the temporary break in contact isolation technique applications normally take more time to orchestrate due to the slower rate of speed.

The final stage (or stages) of the temporary break in contact surveillance detection procedure is the actual surveillance detection technique that is employed against the potential surveillance effort. Recall again that the purpose of isolating surveillance assets through the temporary break in contact is to either elicit a compromising response, or execute a surveillance detection maneuver (or series of maneuvers) to elicit a compromising response from an asset after it has been isolated.

In many cases, the fact that the surveillance asset suddenly finds itself in a vulnerable position is enough to elicit a compromising reaction. This can be accomplished by simply isolating a surveillance asset in a situation where it feels compelled to react hastily to avoid detection (flight). If isolation alone does not sufficiently compromise the potential asset, it still serves to isolate the asset in order to focus the more active, overt, or aggressive detection measures. Once surveillance assets are isolated, an immediate surveillance detection maneuver will be directed against the suspected surveillance asset to elicit a compromising reaction and confirm it as such. This constitutes the "one-two punch" that normally compels even the savviest and most composed surveillance professionals to "flinch" in a detectable manner.

THE BREAK AND DISAPPEAR ANTISURVEILLANCE PROCEDURE

Recall that all antisurveillance measures are considered active and are the most difficult to conduct discreetly because they are generally more aggressive and conspicuous. To affect a permanent break in contact based on a single tactical application, the method must be singularly effective, meaning that it would be difficult, if not impossible, to execute without being perceived as an overt antisurveillance effort. Again, the consequences of this perception can range from intensification of future surveillance efforts to the immediate transition from a surveillance effort to an active pursuit. For this reason, any technique that makes the antisurveillance effort less detectable as such is to the Principal's advantage.

To this end, the most effective process is the *break and disappear* antisurveillance procedure. This procedure is based on the understanding of how a surveillance effort thinks and reacts. For antisurveillance purposes, an immediate period of *lost contact* is necessary to conduct follow-on maneuvers to confound attempts by the surveillance effort to regain contact. This is most effective as it involves orchestrating a plausible break in contact and exploiting a blind spot (as previously addressed) with the end result being that the Principal inexplicably and simply disappears.

The *break in contact* antisurveillance procedure leverages an understanding of how a surveillance effort thinks and reacts when executing the *lost contact drill*. This drill is a standard surveillance technique that involves the systematic execution of a series of maneuvers to regain observation of the Principal by searching for the Principal along all possible routes originating from the first option encountered after lost command. This basically involves the immediate prioritization of the Principal's likely routes of travel from the traffic option or other point of lost contact.

After the Principal is able to break contact and remain unobserved until reaching the first traffic option that gives him multiple possible routes of travel, he then enters the second phase of an effective antisurveillance routine which involves the actions taken to further confound and elude the surveillance effort. The key point here is that the surveillance assets will search for the Principal based on his most likely (or logical) directions of travel. Therefore, *the obvious antisurveillance approach is for the Principal to travel in the most unlikely (illogical) direction from the traffic option.*

When entering a traffic option after executing a break in contact with any potential following surveillance vehicles, the Principal takes the travel option direction that he assesses would be deemed least likely by the surveillance team when conducting the lost contact drill. An assessment of the least logical direction of travel is normally based on target pattern analysis. For example, if the surveillance effort would assume that the Principal is likely traveling to his residence when contact is lost, based on target pattern analysis, the effort prioritizes its efforts on the most likely routes of travel to his residence from the option of lost contact. Therefore, the Principal employs reverse logic and takes the most *indirect* (least likely) route in relation to his residence, and continues a pattern of travel which takes him in the opposite direction of his residence.

Figure 19 illustrates the lost contact drill executed by a surveillance team at a standard X intersection. As command surveillance vehicle (1) reaches the intersection (Point A) and informs the team that the Principal is unsighted, it checks the most logical route that the Principal would have taken — in this case straight. As surveillance vehicle (2) reaches the intersection it takes the next most logical route — in this case to the right. As surveillance vehicle (3) reaches the intersection it takes the only remaining route to the left. Any additional surveillance vehicles will reinforce the first vehicles reaching the point of lost contact in the same priority order. In this case, surveillance vehicle (4) reinforces surveillance vehicle (1) by continuing straight; surveillance vehicle (5) in turn reinforces surveillance vehicle (2) to the right; and surveillance vehicle (6) reinforces surveillance vehicle (3) to the left (See Figure 19 next page).

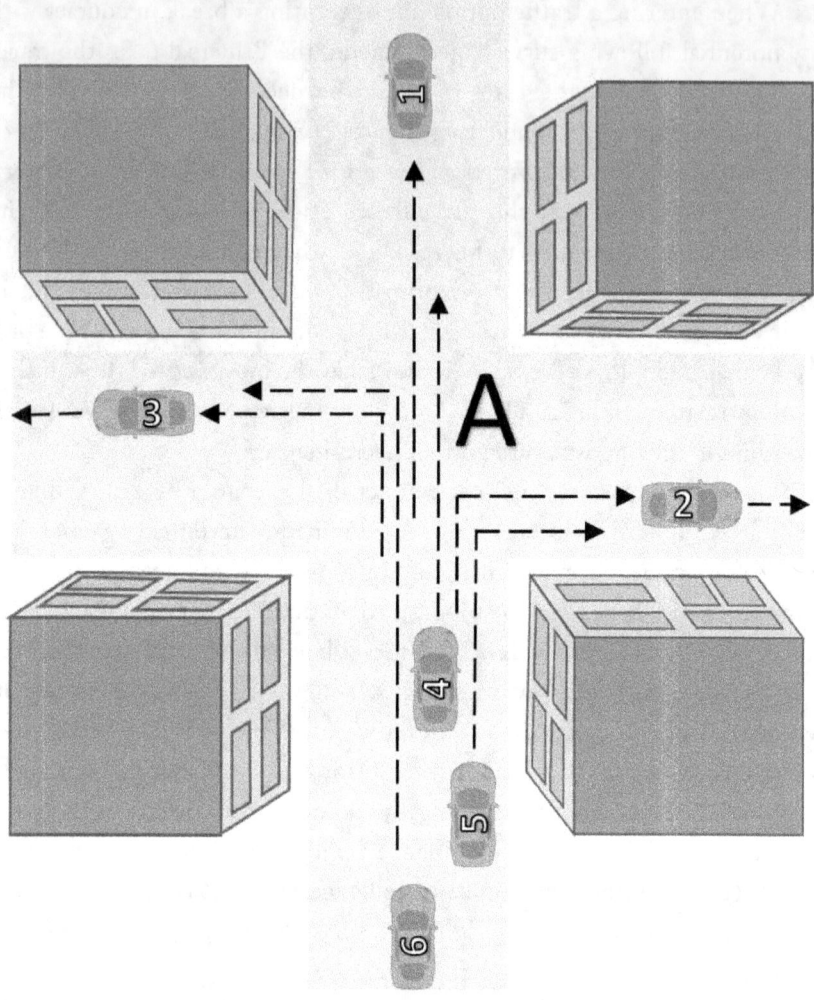

FIGURE 19

A six vehicle surveillance team initiates the lost contact drill at a standard intersection

Although the scenario in Figure 19 implies that the vehicles arriving at Point A to conduct the lost contact drill are doing so in relatively rapid succession, this would not actually be the case. In a standard surveillance operation, vehicle 2 and perhaps vehicle 3 may arrive at Point A within seconds behind vehicle 1 if not otherwise obstructed, but the other vehicles may take up to a minute or more — perhaps much more for vehicles that were out of position when the break in contact was initiated.

Having determined that traffic option A will be the location prior to which he will break contact with the surveillance team and execute the second stage of the break and disappear antisurveillance procedure, the Principal will have analyzed how a tactically-sound surveillance element will react to lost contact in a logical and systematic manner as depicted in Figure 19. After initiating the disappear stage of the antisurveillance procedure at option A, the Principal then continues with a sequential series of illogical travel patterns to further confound any follow-on (logic-based) searches by the surveillance effort. Assuming that his most logical route of travel would be to continue straight and his next most logical option would be to turn right, the Principal takes the least likely (least logical) route by turning left at Point A.

Figure 19 demonstrated that even in a surveillance consisting of a six vehicle team, only two vehicles are available to turn left at Point A and search along the Principal's least likely route of travel. As a continuation of the lost contact drill from intersection Point A, Figure 20 depicts how when surveillance vehicle (3) reaches the next traffic option (Point B), it continues straight along what would be assessed as the Principal's most likely direction of travel, and surveillance vehicle (6) turns right to search along what would be assessed as the Principal's next most likely route of travel from the intersection. Therefore, in even among the most resource intensive surveillance efforts, there is no asset available to search along the Principal's least likely route of travel (which would be to turn left at Point B). This example demonstrates the methodology that drives the reverse logic approach to the *break and disappear* antisurveillance procedure (See Figure 20 next page).

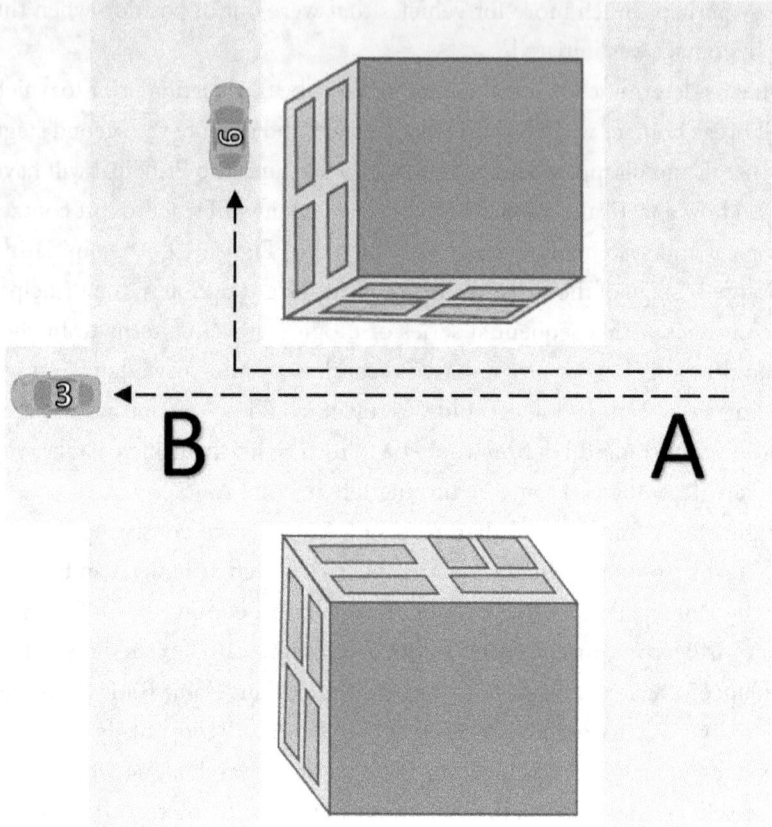

FIGURE 20

Two surveillance vehicles execute the second stage of the lost contact drill along the Principal's possible routes of travel

Figure 21 builds on the logical lost contact drill actions the surveillance team takes in Figures 19 and 20. Even assuming that the surveillance effort has at least three to six assets to cover the three possible routes of travel, as Figure 20 demonstrated, the Principal should be able to remain unsighted when reaching Point B, because the route he is on was given the lowest priority and was not taken until the third surveillance asset reached Point A. Figure 21 depicts the finishing maneuvers of this antisurveillance procedure. At Point B, the Principal again takes the least likely (least logical) route, which in this case is left toward Point C. At Point C, the Principal should not turn back toward his original route but should continue to take traffic options that are in the opposite direction of which it is assessed the surveillance effort would prioritize its search (in this case right at Point C and left at Point D). The Principal then continues a pattern of sequential right and left turns taking him out of the area of lost contact, traveling in the general direction of Point E, which again, is opposite of what the surveillance effort would assess as his most likely/logical route of travel.

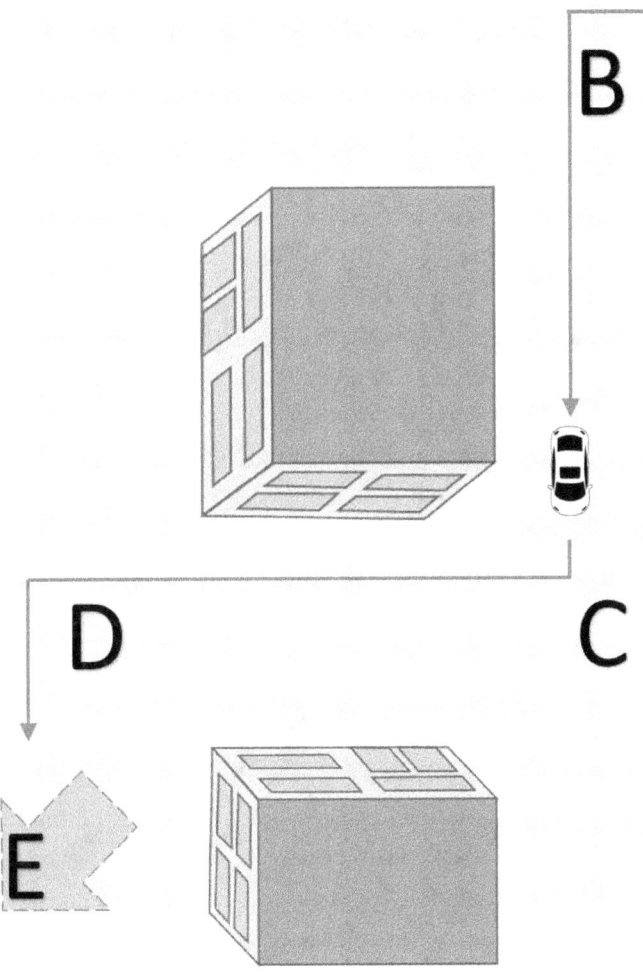

Figure 21
The Principal continues to travel in the least likely (least logical) route away from the point where the lost contact drill was initiated

For perspective, it is interesting to understand the metrics of how rapidly the *break and disappear* antisurveillance procedure degrades a surveillance effort's capability. With this simple example, every option through which the Principal remains unsighted would require multiples of three in available surveillance assets to conduct an optimally effective search. For instance, to conduct a minimally effective lost contact drill at the first option (Point A) the surveillance effort would require a minimum of three assets. Any fewer than this, and the Principal will evade surveillance without contest, again assuming that the surveillance effort searches in the Principal's most likely routes of travel. When the Principal remains unsighted at the next option, it requires that the surveillance effort have a minimum of nine surveillance assets to conduct a minimally effective lost contact drill at Point B, which would require three assets to have been available to search toward the option assessed as the Principal's least likely direction of travel. Therefore, by remaining unsighted through Point B, the Principal will have exhausted the capability of even the most resourceful surveillance efforts. To further make the point, by remaining unsighted through Point C, a minimally effective lost contact drill would require 27 surveillance assets, which exceeds virtually all possible feasibilities. This example demonstrates how the number of required surveillance assets increases by multiples of three at each option — from three to nine to 27 . . .

It is important to note that whenever a surveillance effort loses contact with the Principal, it will rarely stop attempting to regain contact until all options have been exhausted. Even in the situation when a surveillance effort breaks contact for security to avoid being isolated in a compromising situation, it is important to understand that in most cases, contact is only relinquished to avoid a single instance of compromise, but every effort will be made to attempt and regain contact after the potentially compromising situation has subsided. Anytime the Principal achieves a break in contact for antisurveillance purposes, it must be immediately followed by a series of evasive maneuvers conducted to confound any follow-on efforts to regain contact.

Although a sophisticated surveillance effort with the resources to conduct a *floating box* is generally uncommon, the purpose of employing advanced surveillance techniques such as these is to posture for instances of lost contact as detailed in the practical application above. When the Principal does have reason to believe that the adversarial surveillance effort (suspected or detected) may possess such capabilities, then a variation of the *break and disappear* antisurveillance procedure may be executed in a location that would restrict the surveillance effort's freedom of movement (such as channelized terrain) to employ advanced surveillance techniques.

Accordingly, Principals (to include security details) that operate on a "worst-case" basis would plan to execute this procedure in an area with appropriate restrictive terrain as a standard practice. Among the many examples of leveraging channelized or other appropriate terrain to restrict the effectiveness of advanced surveillance methods such as the floating box, is for the Principal to travel on a one-way road with the parallel routes being one-way roads in the opposite direction. The employment of this or any number of other such restrictive measures would likely require some variation to the practical application provided above, but this should require only minor adjustments based on the best available alternatives for the application of reverse logic.

By foot, the Principal has a wide variety of options to perform the break and disappear procedure leveraging the appropriate locations, to include public locations, and incorporating the appropriate restrictive terrain to combine for an effective antisurveillance outcome.

APPENDIX 1:

TECHNICAL SURVEILLANCE COUNTERMEASURES AND THE LIMITATIONS OF TECHNICAL SURVEILLANCE

Surveillance professionals regularly employ technical surveillance techniques/ capabilities to enable the accomplishment of the overall objectives of the surveillance operation. However, there are operational and practical considerations that limit the effectiveness of technical surveillance capabilities. Therefore, this section focuses less on the employment, detection, and defeat of technical surveillance capabilities — which would be broad and highly variable — and more so on the pragmatic technical surveillance considerations and limitations that the professional surveillance countermeasures practitioner must understand.

A fundamental principle involving technical surveillance is that any surveillance effort that relies primarily on technical surveillance capabilities is not a truly sophisticated/effective surveillance effort; and any surveillance countermeasures effort that focuses primarily on countering technical surveillance capabilities is ignorant of the real threat and exposes itself as highly vulnerable to the truly sophisticated/effective surveillance efforts.

Technical surveillance countermeasures is a broad, and obviously, technical discipline. Therefore, employing technical capabilities/solutions/expertise to counter the technical surveillance threat is for most an imprecise, uncertain, and often impracticable countermeasures approach. As will be detailed, a Principal who concentrates on a technical approach to surveillance countermeasures may be wasting resources and priorities on a threat that could be tantamount to a "needle in a haystack," or one that may not exist due to motivations which mitigate against a surveillance effort employing technical surveillance capabilities, which will also be explained.

The effectiveness of most technical surveillance means (e.g. audio, video, motion monitoring) is reliant on the Principal not recognizing the risks and not taking some very basic countermeasures. Therefore, basic technical surveillance threat awareness and vulnerability mitigation measures are the best defense against this broad threat. By implementing some basic anti-technical surveillance measures to negate the effectiveness of technical surveillance capabilities, the Principal actually facilitates the overall surveillance countermeasures effort by compelling the surveillance element to revert and rely solely on conducting physical surveillance, which exposes operators and vehicles to the most effective surveillance detection and antisurveillance methods.

TECHNICAL SURVEILLANCE CAPABILITIES

Technical surveillance alone can meet the information needs of some limited-scope surveillance operations, but in most cases, technical methods are employed as enabling capabilities to augment a full-spectrum surveillance operation. In addition, technical surveillance capabilities are employed when possible to develop information while avoiding unnecessary exposure of operators to the Principal.

The application of surveillance capabilities primarily consists of stand-off audio and video monitoring capabilities. Such capabilities may include close access technical monitoring such as denied area (residence, work place) stand-off technical monitoring (audio, visual), mobile device monitoring (conversational, data, locational), and vehicle tracking capabilities. Other capabilities more directly augment the effectiveness of a physical surveillance operation with personnel or vehicle movement tracking capabilities, or deployable audio and video capabilities, such as directional microphones and concealed/mobile video applications.

The range of technical surveillance technical capabilities is rapidly expanding. Cyber surveillance is prevalent and can assist a surveillance effort in developing information on a target individual — to include monitoring movement and locations. Every major city has comprehensive video monitoring capabilities that can be leveraged by federal/local law enforcement officials, or compromised and leveraged by capable non-state threats, for specific surveillance purposes. Drone and autonomous vehicle capabilities are significantly expanding the reach of surveillance capabilities, and the next tech frontiers, to include artificial intelligence, are rapidly emerging. In fact, the risk of discussing technological advances in a work like this is that information becomes rapidly dated due to the dynamic and highly variable nature of technology development.

TECHNICAL SURVEILLANCE LIMITATIONS

There is a continuous cycle of technological advances to enable, augment, and even supplant many aspects of a sophisticated, adversarial surveillance effort. A common misconception, however, is that many of these highly variable capabilities represent operationally-expedient panaceas which justify ignoring the non-technical aspects of the trade. The reality of this cycle is that as soon as a cutting-edge technical surveillance-enhancing capability is introduced, an equally effective countermeasure is developed by those who might otherwise be impacted by the emergent capability. This dynamic is continuous; regardless of who may be on the "right" or "wrong" side.

In contrast to pop culture perceptions regarding surveillance capabilities, the real-world shadow warriors avoid an over-reliance on technical surveillance capabilities based on valid operational lessons learned in the "school of hard knocks." In fact, the overriding irony of the technology misconception is that the time-proven techniques developed to ensure absolute security from adversarial elements, which this manual emphasizes, have actually been developed to be *technologically agnostic* — meaning they were intended to apply across the continuum of operations regardless of how sophisticated opposing technical capabilities may become. In fact, the unstable and unreliable "cat and mouse" games of technology/counter-technology are ones that the true professionals have learned to only engage in with great caution, or avoid altogether.

Even in today's age of enhanced technical enablers, there are significant operational considerations that mitigate against a heavy reliance on such capabilities for surveillance purposes. In virtually all cases, technical surveillance alone will not meet the overall objectives of the surveillance operation. Therefore, there is a trade-off analysis that the surveillance effort must always conduct in the determination to employ technical surveillance capabilities, which is the assessment of whether the potential benefits of their use justify the risks that they invariably present. The reality is that technical surveillance will rarely develop the level of information needed to meet significant objectives, while likely exposing vulnerabilities that are outside the control of the surveillance effort.

In most cases, the surveillance effort only employs technical capabilities in a measured and judicious manner, and will rarely allow the success of an operation to hinge on an over-reliance on technical surveillance. This measured approach is ingrained in the psyche of organizations that survive and thrive in the underground.

Surveillance efforts, as with most covert elements, exercise a highly risk averse mentality. This intrinsic and "zero-tolerance" predisposition of covert operational entities to avoid unknown/uncontrolled risks dictates against an over-reliance on technical capabilities. As an example of the well-earned paranoia of technology, covert elements tend to operate in compartmentalized "cells" to limit information, and only use physical "cut-outs" to communicate among operationally dependent/supportive cells. This mentality pervades in covert surveillance operations as the objectives of the overall operation may outweigh the risk of the detection of a technical surveillance capability. For elements such as these, the risk of detection has implications ranging from compromise and failure of the surveillance operation itself, to the risk of detection by third parties (such as law enforcement) that would not only compromise the operation, but may have even more extreme consequences for surveillance operators and the sponsoring entity.

In many cases, the employment of technical surveillance capabilities imposes unacceptable risks on an operation, because the surveillance effort loses (at least a degree of) control of the operation due to the risk of physical detection and technical signature vulnerabilities they impose on the operation. For example, the point at which the surveillance effort emplaces a listening device (bug) in the Principal's residence or emplaces a tracking device on his vehicle, they have lost a degree of control because the Principal then has the capability to detect the technical surveillance device(s) without the surveillance effort's knowledge. In addition to "physical" detection vulnerabilities, a further example is that a remotely monitored listening device will likely emit a "technical signature" that could be detected/intercepted by the Principal or third parties, which would compromise the existence of the technical surveillance effort.

Compounding the risk of the Principal detecting the employment of technical capabilities is the threat posed by witting and unwitting third-parties. In addition to the risk of compromise to the Principal inherent in the employment of technical surveillance capabilities, a sophisticated surveillance effort is ever-cognizant regarding the risks of compromise to third-party entities; and may be even more vigilant regarding these vulnerabilities than they are regarding the threat of detection from a witting or unwitting Principal. In fact, most surveillance efforts operate under the assumption that the Principal is not the only (and probably not the greatest) risk of technical surveillance capability detection and compromise. Therefore, many surveillance efforts are unwilling to rely heavily on technical surveillance means — not because of the risk of detection by the Principal — but because of the sophistication of technical detection capabilities employed by national, regional, and local intelligence and law enforcement agencies. This game within the game becomes a tangled web as law enforcement agencies are vigilant in detecting criminal and even other law enforcement agencies invading their turf, and government agencies are always sensitive to opposing national covert efforts operating in their jurisdictions or areas of interest, and generally have the ability to detect and exploit virtually any technical signature if given a high enough priority. Due to these highly capable and pervasive risks of detection and compromise, covert elements (to include surveillance efforts) that do not have official government status/protection would assume an omni-present risk of technical surveillance capability detection, and may very likely consider the employment of such capabilities as risk prohibitive. Even those with official authority to do so may opt not to employ technical surveillance capabilities due to the risk of compromise by well-intentioned but unwitting fellow-government agencies, or by agencies with overlapping jurisdictions or competing agendas.

TECHNICAL SURVEILLANCE DETECTION

Although there are methods to detect technical surveillance at its source such as the detection of listening devices or concealed cameras, this is a time-consuming effort and requires an extreme degree of technical expertise to conduct these activities in a comprehensive and effective manner — and in a manner that does not provide the surveillance effort with confirmation of surveillance consciousness on the part of the Principal. There is a wide range of commercially available equipment, such as energy source detectors and frequency spectrum analyzers, that can be employed to detect technical surveillance equipment. However, these enablers range in effectiveness and may be ineffective and lead to false security conclusions when operated by individuals without the requisite technical skills.

Capable government intelligence and security agencies have highly specialized teams to emplace and monitor technical surveillance capabilities, and counterpart teams to detect the presence of technical surveillance capabilities. There is an increasing number of well-resourced non-government organizations capable of employing this same level of sophistication. Short of the highly specialized skills resident on such teams of expert technicians, the ability to detect the presence of a technical surveillance effort with any level of confidence is negligible. As previously addressed in regard to covert elements, such elements only employ/emplace technical capabilities in areas (such as denied areas) where they concede control if the risk of detection by the Principal or third parties is extremely low. Therefore, they will be activated in a highly discreet and effective manner making the likelihood of detection by the Principal low to infeasible. In addition, even in the event of the deliberate or fortuitous detection of one technical surveillance capability, this does not negate the overall threat, so these efforts may be counterproductive based on various criteria.

In many cases and assuming a somewhat technically proficient threat, the best detection measure may be to determine that an area that would be the likely target of technical surveillance has been compromised, as opposed to detecting the actual "needle in a haystack" inside that potential target area. A basic detection measure is to stage "triggers" that would indicate that a denied location such as a residence or workplace has been covertly entered. A common trigger is scotch tape on doors and drawers, but this is readily detectable by a professional surveillance effort. Other more discreet examples are to place items that may need to be moved to access likely locations for technical surveillance in a very specific manner that only the Principal would recognize if the item(s) had been moved. Again, however, any such activities risk the projection of surveillance consciousness on the part of the Principal, as such triggers may be readily detectable or bypassed by a professional surveillance effort, who will take great efforts to ensure that there are absolutely no signs that a location has been compromised, even in the case of well-placed triggers.

The detection of technical surveillance capabilities by deliberate inspection efforts or other means will obviously disclose/confirm that the Principal is in fact under surveillance. However, the discovery of one technical surveillance means should not lead to a conclusion that the threat is defeated. Rather, the detection of one device/capability is likely indicative of a much broader threat — so the Principal must continue to operate as though he is constantly under the threat of technical surveillance. Therefore, the most effective countermeasure to the technical threat is a persistent anti-technical surveillance mindset.

Cyber threats potentially associated with technical surveillance are readily detectable, but they are rarely discernible. An adage that applies to this concept is that "a spy swims in a school of criminals." Espionage elements and other covert actors can operate aggressively in the cyber domain because if their activities are detected, there is rarely any direct attribution, and they know that their actions will likely be attributed to the prolific amount of criminal/malicious activity on the internet. Therefore, the detection of activity that can be attributed to a surveillance effort in differentiation from other malicious and intrusive activity can be relatively impossible, particularly if executed by a capable cyber threat actor. So again, an antisurveillance mindset is most effective in countering technical surveillance efforts targeting technical communications and information processing devices.

ANTI-TECHNICAL SURVEILLANCE

Given the difficulties and other consequences associated with the detection of technical surveillance capabilities, the most effective technical surveillance countermeasures approach is a deliberate plan to avoid (antisurveillance) vulnerabilities to these capabilities, if present. Therefore, the key fundamental is that an aware Principal can readily take measures to negate the effectiveness of technical surveillance capabilities and force the surveillance effort to employ non-technical techniques. Although the range of available technical capabilities is prolific, they all generally rely on the Principal performing activities which makes himself vulnerable to these capabilities. A security conscious Principal who employs the basic security techniques to mitigate or eliminate the vulnerabilities to these technical threats will essentially force the surveillance effort "to ground" to develop the information, which then levels the playing field and renders surveillance operatives vulnerable to the techniques detailed in this work. An appropriate analogy is that the Air Force may be able to bomb a country with highly technical, precision-guided stand-off capabilities with relatively little threat of interdiction, but the Army will eventually have to put "boots on the ground" to go in and win the war. The same stands true for surveillance operations — eventually the surveillance effort must conduct physical surveillance of the Principal to meet the fundamental/final objectives of virtually any operation.

The employment of technical surveillance is based largely on target pattern analysis and where the Principal is assessed to be most vulnerable to these capabilities. Static locations such as the Principal's residence and work place are the most common as they are predictable locations that target pattern analysis will tell the surveillance effort that the Principal is likely to spend a large part of his time. The simple anti-technical surveillance approach is to not talk about or conduct any activities that might meet the objectives of a surveillance in these and any other locations that the effort might select for technical surveillance. This simple measure negates the effectiveness of the world's most sophisticated technical collection capabilities.

When mobile, technical surveillance capabilities will either be located with the Principal or his vehicle. Assuming a persistent threat of monitoring associated with the vehicle, the Principal will simply refrain from discussing or conducting any activities that might meet the objectives of the surveillance in his vehicle. Borrowing or renting a vehicle is an effective, although perhaps overt, anti-technical surveillance method. A resourceful Principal could even use a vehicle that is assumed to be technically monitored as a decoy in some circumstances. Other than the vehicle, the other mobile technical surveillance capabilities are those which can be emplaced or carried on the Principal's body. Mobile devices such as phones are the more obvious targets/vulnerabilities. Commonly worn/carried items such as briefcases, purses, wallets, or watches are other common targets for technical capability emplacement. The basic anti-technical surveillance method is for the Principal to "sterilize" himself of such items when conducting activities that might meet the objectives of an adversarial surveillance.

Effective anti-technical surveillance actually facilitates the effectiveness of the overall surveillance countermeasures effort. As addressed, there are many considerations that influence a surveillance effort to balance the employment of technical capabilities or avoid their use altogether. In any case, a sophisticated surveillance effort understands that it must rely largely, or exclusively, on the time-tested physical techniques that involve human operators who can think, react, and terminate surveillance rather than compromise the operation. Any fully capable surveillance effort intent on ensuring that it meets mission objectives will ensure that its physical surveillance capability is intact, even when technical surveillance is a key aspect of the overall surveillance plan. A sophisticated and determined surveillance effort will not prioritize technical surveillance over the ability to employ assets (vehicles and operators) who can track the Principal where technical capabilities cannot. This is based on the limitations of technical capabilities and the strong possibility that the Principal will not conform to the technical surveillance plan. Therefore, the most effective anti-technical surveillance approach is for the Principal to confound any potential technical surveillance plan in place. This in effect serves to "level the playing field" by forcing the surveillance effort "to ground," which exposes operators and vehicles to the most effective surveillance detection and antisurveillance methods, as detailed throughout this manual.

APPENDIX 2:
OBSERVATION

Observation is a critical aspect of surveillance detection. It also supports antisurveillance, particularly in identifying the need to elude surveillance by detecting it. The Principal's perceptive ability to observe and retain specifics regarding the surrounding environment enables him to identify indications of surveillance and subsequently confirm them through repeated observations of surveillance operators or vehicles.

A sophisticated surveillance team rarely commits tactical errors that allow the Principal to identify its presence during an isolated incident. Although there are specific surveillance detection maneuvers that are designed to expose surveillance immediately, most depend on the Principal's ability to observe his surroundings and confirm any suspicions at subsequent times and locations.

OBSERVATION PRINCIPLES

Observation is the act of seeing or fixing the mind upon something for the purpose of recognizing and retaining some fact or occurrence. It is conducted through the body's senses of perception. Perception is an individual's awareness of the elements of environment, gained through physical sensation in reaction to sensory stimulus. Sensory stimulus is perceived by the body's senses, which consist of sight, hearing, touch, smell, and taste. For surveillance detection purposes, observation relies primarily on the sense of sight, but it can be enhanced by hearing and, to a much lesser degree, smell.

Effective observation requires a conscious and continuous effort. This consists of a keen awareness of surrounding activity to observe and retain the images of specific individuals, objects, and occurrences. This includes the perception of shape, size, and features; colors, shades, and lighting; and speed, time, and distance. The process of observation consists of three sub-processes: attention, perception, and retention. Attention is the aspect of observation that is most critical to surveillance detection, because without attention, perception and retention are impossible. Attention is the awareness of surroundings that provide the sensory stimulus on which perception is based. People normally apply voluntary attention to the activity they are undertaking. An item or occurrence that does not fit within an individual's frame of reference for what is the status quo normally draws involuntary attention. For example, someone may walk through a crowd of faceless people until a person with a limp immediately draws his involuntary attention. People who are particularly large or small have this same effect, as do bright colors and loud or sharp sounds.

As mentioned, an individual's attention is normally focused on the activity he is undertaking at the time. His attention is limited to items and occurrences that have a direct impact on that activity, unless it is seized by an unusually large, loud, or relatively unanticipated item or occurrence. An individual driving down the road normally focuses his attention on those factors which impact that activity — primarily the traffic and road ahead. The Principal practicing surveillance detection, on the other hand, must expand his attention to include the entire surroundings.

The skill of observation requires a knowledge of the principles of perception and an understanding of how they are employed. The most basic detractor one must overcome in attempting to enhance perceptive skills is the tendency to perceive and retain only those items or occurrences that fall within his range of interests or understanding. Everyone has a unique range of interests and understanding based on mental capacity, education, and background. Personal interests are conditioned throughout a lifetime, and to expand observation beyond those requires a conscious and focused effort. Perception is also limited by an individual's base of knowledge. The mind tends to subconsciously filter out items and occurrences for which there is no frame of reference by which to describe them in known terms, and will therefore not retain such items or occurrences for subsequent retrieval. The Principal must be constantly aware of these tendencies in order to overcome their impact on observation.

Every individual perceives his surroundings uniquely. In the context of observation for the purposes of surveillance detection, the Principal's frame of reference for how people and vehicles are observed must be expanded through concentration and training. The unassuming individual may view all individuals equally — or ignore them equally. A person who holds prejudices immediately averts his attention to those who do not conform to his standard of "normal," whereas those who do conform will pass unnoticed. For example, a person who has been the victim of a violent crime at the hands of an individual of a particular category of persons (e.g. race, ethnicity) will display vigilance in directing his attention to those who meet this profile in comparison to other individuals around him. Another common example of how attention is programmed is that attractive individuals of the opposite sex normally seize people's attention. This brief psychological synopsis illustrates the impact an individual's frame of reference has on his attention.

Again, perception and retention are only possible after attention is applied. Most people's perception of what a surveillance operator looks like comes from Hollywood interpretations and spy novels. This frame of reference only serves to filter out the actual surveillance operators because, contrary to popular perceptions, they will be among the most unassuming individuals on the streets. This perception must be overcome for surveillance detection purposes to ensure that the Principal's attention is not focused on misconceived indicators.

Appendix 8 (Disguise and Deception) provides additional insights regarding observation.

Observation And Surveillance Detection

A basic understanding of the principles of observation is a critical aspect of surveillance detection. Much of surveillance detection depends on observing possible or suspected surveillance operators or vehicles, retaining their images or key aspects thereof, and confirming that they are surveillance operators or vehicles through subsequent observation. Once again, perception and retention are contingent on attention. The Principal's voluntary attention must transcend the frame of reference that has developed over his lifetime and he must apply attention to all surrounding activity to the greatest degree possible. Then, through a keen knowledge of surveillance tactics and an ability to detect indicators of surveillance, he can eliminate those individuals and vehicles that are not indicative or suspicious and key on those that are.

Any sophisticated surveillance effort operates based on a keen understanding of the principles of observation. A surveillance effort conforms to what most people see as the status quo or norm with respect to the surrounding environment. This minimizes or negates the degree to which it draws the involuntary attention of the Principal. Although the Principal cannot discount unique individuals and vehicles immediately, those which stand out are rarely representative of a sophisticated surveillance effort because of the attention they attract. In professional surveillance circles, the ideal is for an operator to be "the gray man," meaning that he is so plain that no one would notice him.

For the purposes of surveillance detection, the primary objective of observation of surrounding individuals is to retain their characteristics — consisting of features, form, dress, and mannerisms — for later recognition. It is not feasible to retain all of these observations for each individual observed. The Principal must attempt to key on those characteristics that are the most dominant and difficult to alter, and not those that are easily altered and possibly of no subsequent value. By doing so, he can concentrate on retaining specific characteristics of a number of surrounding individuals in a short period of time.

OBSERVATION OF FEATURES

Body features consist primarily of face, head, and hair. Three factors that directly impact these are gender, race, and age, though these are not considered features in and of themselves because none can stand alone as an identifying characteristic for surveillance detection purposes. Body features are the most accurate characteristics by which to identify individuals. With the exception of hair, these are generally the most difficult and time-consuming to alter. Body features, however, are the most difficult to observe because they require that the Principal be close to the individual under scrutiny. The tactically sound surveillance operator rarely places himself in a position that allows this degree of observation.

Facial features consist primarily of the eyebrows, eyes, nose, mouth, lips, chin, and ears. They can also include wrinkles, scars, dimples, birthmarks, moles, complexion, or other such markings as applicable. With many individuals, these variables can be the most distinguishable for observation

186

purposes. Generally, however, the primary features are the ones used for retention. The most effective method of observing an individual's facial features for retention is to first develop an overall image of the face and then key on the most distinguishable feature or features.

The head is normally distinguished by its shape. Although this could also qualify as a characteristic of form, it is included in the category of body features because of its impact on facial features and the overall development of a facial image. Additionally, the shape of the head includes the shape of the face. The shape of the head is generally differentiated as being round, high in the crown, bulging at the back, flat at the back, or keel (egg)-shaped. The shape of the face is distinguished by its height and breadth. Although oval is the most prominent facial shape, faces can also be round, square, broad, fat, thin, or long. Body fat, or the lack thereof, may have a significant impact on the shape of a face.

Hair is a significant aspect of an individual's appearance. It can be a very deceiving feature, however, when one is operating against a sophisticated surveillance effort. As will be discussed in a subsequent section, hair is the surveillance operator's quickest and most effective method of altering his appearance without resorting to elaborate disguise techniques. Hair is generally distinguished by color, length, texture, body, and style. The lack of head hair is a particularly prevalent feature. Facial hair, which is primarily distinguished by color, texture, and style, is yet another prevalent feature. Additionally, body hair such as arm and leg hair can assist detection observation.

Body art (tattoo) is a type of "feature" that violates the "gray man" rule, unless an operator can effectively obscure such a feature throughout the course of a surveillance operation. Visually significant and distinguishable body art is a disqualifier for a sophisticated surveillance element. Individuals wearing unseasonably long sleeves or pants during periods of warm weather may be indicative of a surveillance operator attempting to hide body art.

The observation of surrounding vehicles for surveillance detection purposes also depends on the perception of features. Whereas each individual's appearance is unique in many ways, there is much more duplication among vehicles with regard to makes, models, and colors. For this reason, the ability to observe features that may distinguish one vehicle from like models is critical to surveillance detection. Unique features such as dents, scratches, tires, hubcaps, designs, and distinguishable license plates are examples of those the

Principal must concentrate on in order to isolate a possible surveillance vehicle from others on the road. At night, features such as a unique headlight appearance are useful for surveillance detection.

OBSERVATION OF FORM

Form consists of shape, build, and size. The overall body shape is formed by the neck, shoulders, trunk, stomach, buttocks, hips, legs, feet, arms, and hands. Distinguishable aspects of any portion of the body can be isolated for observation purposes. Body shape is directly affected by body fat and muscularity. The fit of clothing must be considered, as it may distort perception in the observation of body shape. Build is generally categorized as heavy, stocky, medium, slender, and thin. This, too, is directly affected by body fat and muscularity and can also be distorted by clothing. Size is a relative characteristic based on individual perceptions. It is generally described in terms of height, width, and breadth. In assessing an individual's size, one must factor in the distortion to perception caused by distance.

Height is categorized as short, medium, and tall, but it should be estimated specifically by feet and inches. In assessing an individual's height, the observer must factor in the distortion to perception that may occur when he and the individual under observation are situated at different levels. Additionally, height can be altered by thick soles or heels on the shoes.

Body width and breadth are particularly subjective and relative to the perception of the individual making the observation. For example, some individuals may be heavy or stocky in build but relatively small in overall size, whereas others are simply big without necessarily being fat or muscular. Again, width and breadth can be distorted by clothing. Finally, posture can have a significant effect on overall form, but this is normally considered a characteristic of mannerisms.

Form is also applicable to the detection of surveillance vehicles. From a distance, a vehicle's form is more readily distinguishable than its features. At night, the form projected by the silhouettes of following vehicles is one of the few aspects which can be discerned for surveillance detection purposes. This same silhouette characteristic also applies to forms inside a vehicle, such as those of the occupants.

OBSERVATION OF MANNERISMS

Mannerisms are those characteristics or idiosyncrasies that are unique to an individual. They are peculiarities in action or bearing, including posture, stride, pace of motion, and voice quality. The number of examples is unlimited. Mannerisms that stand out or appear awkward can be effectively exploited for surveillance detection.

An individual's demeanor and bearing are established through myriad mannerisms. These are actions which are either programmed over a lifetime or result from physical characteristics. Those that develop through the years become subconscious actions and therefore can only be controlled by a conscious effort. Mannerisms that result from physical characteristics are much more difficult to alter because the mind cannot control and conceal what the body is unable to. For these reasons, the observation of unique mannerisms in surrounding individuals is an important aspect of surveillance detection. Whereas a surveillance operator can effectively alter appearance through disguise, most mannerisms require a continuous conscious effort to conceal or alter, and many are physically impossible to conceal.

Physical mannerisms such as stride and posture are the easiest to observe. Unique physical mannerisms such as limps and nervous twitches are particularly conducive to surveillance detection. In addition to representing themselves through physical mannerisms, people do so through their outward manner or demeanor. Demeanor generally consists of attitude, disposition, and temperament. These factors significantly influence how people carry themselves. For example, extroverted individuals normally display a more outgoing, positive, or aggressive demeanor. Regardless of his degree of extroversion or introversion, every individual exudes unique characteristics of demeanor that require a conscious effort to alter or conceal.

Some of the most difficult mannerisms to control are those associated with nervousness and anticipation. Although surveillance operators attempt to maintain an inconspicuous demeanor at all times, there is a natural tendency to become driven by the increase in adrenaline brought about by a surveillance operation. This can result in conspicuous actions or mannerisms such as pacing, focused staring, and continuously checking a watch or a phone.

Other mannerisms that are unique to surveillance operators and may be exploited in surveillance detection observation are those associated with wearing body communications equipment. Many sophisticated surveillance teams equip surveillance operators with concealed body communications equipment for enhanced operational effectiveness. As a result, operators develop distinctive idiosyncrasies such as adjusting upper-body equipment, talking into their chests, fidgeting with their hands in their pockets, and checking their ears with a finger.

OBSERVATION OF DRESS

Habits of dress are characteristics an individual develops over a lifetime. They are influenced by factors such as background, heritage, status, profession, and lifestyle. Some individuals are meticulous in the selection and maintenance of their clothing while others give this aspect of their outward appearance little concern. A person's position along this spectrum of dress dictates the fashion in which he feels natural, comfortable, and confident.

This is an important factor from the perspective of surveillance detection because individuals have a tendency to appear unnatural when dressing in a manner that does not conform to their standard of fashion. A surveillance operator may be required to dress in a manner that is not natural for him in order to blend in with a particular situation and surrounding. The appearance of dress and mannerisms associated with discomfort or unfamiliarity may be detected by the Principal.

Dress is an aspect of appearance that is more readily observed from a distance than many others, such as body features. Unless someone is making an active effort to observe the dress of surrounding individuals, attention is normally drawn only to clothing that does not conform to his standards. Unique, striking, or colorful clothing usually draws involuntary attention. Although clothing is an important criterion for the observation of surrounding individuals for detection purposes, a sophisticated surveillance team will minimize the impact that dress might have on the compromise of surveillance operators. They will therefore dress in a manner that conforms to the standards of the surrounding populace. Furthermore, the surveillance effort will likely capitalize on the ease with which appearance can be altered by changing clothing in order to degrade the effectiveness of surveillance detection.

Dress also includes jewelry. A sophisticated surveillance effort will generally forego wearing jewelry because the purpose of wearing such items is to attract attention — which, of course, the surveillance effort is actively attempting to avoid. There are, however, some cases in which wearing jewelry lends itself to surveillance detection. Most basically, there are some minor items of jewelry, such as wedding bands and watches, which surveillance operators may continue to wear despite the risk. A watch is an extremely important piece of equipment to surveillance operators. Since they will rarely own enough watches to match the number of times they are required to change clothing, they will generally accept the risk of wearing the same watch. Rings may leave identifiable marks such as tan lines on the fingers. When a surveillance operator changes clothing, he may opt to continue wearing a ring if there is no replacement, because any identifiable marks may appear even more conspicuous to the Principal practicing surveillance detection.

The discussion of jewelry touches on a key point as it applies to the observation and detection of a surveillance operator based on dress. Anytime a surveillance operator changes dress in an effort to alter appearance, it should be complete. As a rule, when a surveillance operator alters one aspect of appearance he should make an effort to alter all aspects. This is where the fatal flaw of the favorite watch applies. Another related consideration is shoes, which are often the most distinguishable items of clothing that individuals wear. Surveillance operators appreciate shoes that are practical and comfortable, and therefore tend to make them an exception to the rule, which may be to the observant Principal's advantage.

OBSERVATION OF DISGUISE

The fact that a sophisticated surveillance effort employs disguise to minimize the probability of detection is an aspect of surveillance detection that can make observation difficult. The initial exposure of a surveillance operator to the Principal is not critical, but all subsequent instances of exposure disproportionately increase the probability of detection. The use of disguise allows a surveillance team to project the appearance of different individuals, making it much more difficult for the Principal to isolate a single surveillance operator for detection.

Recall that for the purposes of surveillance detection, observation involves concentrating on features, form, dress, and mannerisms. Surveillance operators use disguise to alter each of these aspects of appearance and thereby deceive the Principal. Many characteristics of appearance are easy to alter, while others are difficult if not impossible. Most features require extensive disguising techniques to conceal or alter. The primary exception to this is hair, which is the single most effective means of altering appearance. By cutting, dying, or restyling hair, or shaving facial hair, a surveillance operator can drastically alter his appearance.

Form is altered primarily by clothing. Surveillance operators use clothing to alter appearance by simply changing clothing from one portion of a surveillance operation to another. Changing to or from loose-fitting clothing can project the illusion of a different form. Deceptive devices such as shoulder pads or girth expanding pillows may also be used to alter form. Height can only be altered by thick-soled or heeled shoes, which are readily detectable through observation. Changing posture can also alter form. Altering mannerisms is more difficult because it requires constant concentration on the part of a surveillance operator. Some mannerisms are physically impossible to alter or conceal.

Although disguise makes surveillance detection much more difficult, there are techniques that can be used to minimize its effectiveness. The first critical factor to understand is that if a disguise is not complete, it actually increases the surveillance operator's vulnerability to detection by an actively observant Principal. Normally, the degree of disguise that a surveillance operator employs is proportional to the degree to which he has been exposed to the Principal. This is a subjective judgment that is also influenced by an assessment of how observant the Principal may be. A total disguise is reserved for circumstances in which the surveillance operator was forced relatively close to, or received a degree of scrutiny from, the Principal. In many cases, however, the surveillance operator will employ only a partial disguise as a standard security precaution after a period of minimal exposure to the Principal. This can be exploited in surveillance detection.

The Principal should practice observation in a manner that is natural and unalarming. This serves to deceive surveillance operators into employing partial disguise as opposed to total disguise. One of the most effective methods of surveillance detection is to confirm that a surveillance operator is using disguise. By using a partial disguise, a surveillance operator may alter some characteristics of appearance while leaving others unaltered. For example, the surveillance operator may shave his mustache, restyle his hair, and change clothes, but leave on the same pair of shoes, the same watch, and walk with the same stride. This can completely reverse the effects of disguise by confirming to the observant Principal that surveillance is present.

APPENDIX 3:
COUNTERSURVEILLANCE

Like other methods of surveillance detection, countersurveillance is employed to identify specific indications of surveillance of the Principal; but more specifically, it is employed to identify the same surveillance operator(s) in two or more separate locations that are unrelated or non-coincidental. (*Note*: Although this tutorial is focused on the practice of identifying specific surveillance operators at multiple locations, when the term (surveillance) *operator* or *operators* is used, in many cases, it could equally apply to a surveillance *vehicle* or *vehicles*)

Countersurveillance differs significantly from other methods of physical surveillance detection in that it consists of actions taken by a third party — consisting of one or more persons — to detect the presence of surveillance on the Principal. The term third party simply separates countersurveillance operators from the first person (the Principal) and the secondary surveillance operators. The Principal may use trusted associates as third parties to provide countersurveillance coverage. Due to the expertise and discipline required, it is best to employ professional surveillance operators from private investigative agencies or other organizations that maintain a capable surveillance team.

Countersurveillance is the most sophisticated and effective method of physical surveillance detection. All methods of surveillance detection addressed to this point involve the Principal observing his surroundings to identify the presence of surveillance.

Countersurveillance allows the Principal to travel in a more natural manner since he does not have to concentrate on observing for surveillance coverage. Countersurveillance assets position themselves in locations that provide a field of observation the Principal would not be able to achieve himself.

Countersurveillance is very characteristic of intelligence and law enforcement agency activities. When intelligence operatives meet with their agents, they commonly employ the support of countersurveillance to ensure that their activities are not compromised, or that their contact is not a double agent. Intelligence agencies also employ countersurveillance when they suspect that an agent is under surveillance. Law enforcement agencies commonly employ countersurveillance to ensure the security of their agents during undercover operations such as meetings with confidential informants or narcotics buys.

Countersurveillance is normally employed as a final confirmation measure after the Principal has found specific indicators of surveillance through other detection measures.

COUNTERSURVEILLANCE PLANNING

As with all methods of surveillance detection, countersurveillance is conducted in a systematic manner based on target pattern analysis. Countersurveillance requires more thorough planning because the Principal must synchronize his travel and movements with the countersurveillance coverage. The countersurveillance plan may comprise nothing more than observing the Principal's standard travels, or it may incorporate surveillance detection maneuvers as addressed in the previous chapters.

Countersurveillance is most effectively employed at designated locations that are suitable for the isolation and identification of surveillance operators. This enables countersurveillance operators to establish static positions with appropriate cover, concealment, and observation. Countersurveillance coverage that moves with the Principal is much less effective and also makes countersurveillance operators vulnerable to detection by the surveillance team.

The countersurveillance plan is normally developed around a surveillance detection route (SDR). The SDR developed for countersurveillance is normally established around surveillance detection points (SDPs), which are designated locations where countersurveillance operators can isolate and detect surveillance coverage. An effective SDR incorporates at least five SDPs. Recall that surveillance operators are most vulnerable to detection when they are forced into confined or static positions that provide limited cover. SDPs give countersurveillance operators opportunities to exploit these vulnerabilities.

The SDR developed for countersurveillance must appear logical to a surveillance team, if present, but not be logical for others to travel along the same route. To facilitate this, the SDR will normally have a *theme*. As an example, the Principal might travel to any number of hardware stores as though shopping for or pricing particular items. This establishes a logical reason for traveling an otherwise illogical route, while providing SDPs (the hardware stores themselves) for countersurveillance operators to concentrate on. Any individual other than the Principal who is observed at two or more of these locations is indicative of surveillance coverage.

The resources necessary to conduct countersurveillance can be extensive or relatively minimal. Although it may seem as though manning up to five separate SDPs would be manpower-intensive, this is not necessarily the case. In fact, there are advantages to the same countersurveillance operator or operators rotating to each SDP, because this makes it easier to confirm surveillance by negating the guesswork involved with comparing descriptions or images of the possible surveillance operators observed by different countersurveillance operators.

Another disadvantage in having different countersurveillance operators man separate SDPs is that it is often difficult to isolate possible surveillance operators at a single location. A well-trained and disciplined surveillance team can operate with a level of proficiency that makes it difficult for even a concentrated countersurveillance effort to detect operators at a given location. When the same countersurveillance operators man each SDP, they can virtually confirm surveillance by observing the same individual in unrelated locations. This is much more conclusive than relying upon the detection of isolated incidents that are indicative of surveillance. If different countersurveillance operators are employed at separate SDPs, they should employ some means of image capture (photo, video) to record possible surveillance operators when practical.

The difficulty involved in moving countersurveillance operators to the various SDPs is easily overcome through planning. As will be discussed later, it is essential that countersurveillance operators be positioned at SDPs prior to the Principal's arrival. To facilitate this, the SDR can incorporate actions that give countersurveillance operators time to reposition. Another option is to develop a plan wherein countersurveillance operators depart the SDP before the Principal does. This can be coordinated by timing, specified activities of the Principal, or a discreet signal provided by the countersurveillance team to the Principal.

A primary concern for any countersurveillance operation is security. A surveillance team's detection of countersurveillance involves the same consequences associated with its identification of any surveillance detection practice. With the exception of the coordination required to move the same countersurveillance operators between separate SDPs, the only disadvantage to this method of manning SDPs is the operators' inherent vulnerability to detection. Just as the objective of the countersurveillance coverage is to identify the same individuals at separate, unrelated locations, surveillance operators can confirm surveillance detection by identifying countersurveillance operators at these non-coincidental locations.

Prior to any countersurveillance operation, countersurveillance operators must conduct reconnaissance of proposed SDPs. The Principal should not be involved in this because of the obvious threat of actual surveillance. The reconnaissance should evaluate possible SDPs for cover, concealment, and observation. An understanding of how a surveillance team operates in a specific situation provides the basis for the positioning of countersurveillance operators to maximize the probability of surveillance detection. The need to establish well-concealed countersurveillance locations applies during all countersurveillance activities, but it is significantly greater when employing the same operators at separate SDPs. This concealment must be achieved while still establishing an effective observation position. In planning for countersurveillance operations, each SDP must be evaluated to ensure that it satisfies these criteria.

As is the case with surveillance operators, countersurveillance operators must determine the cover for actions that they will employ during the operation. This cover should be determined based on the worst-case assumption that the countersurveillance operator will undergo the scrutiny of surveillance operators. Even when a countersurveillance position is identified as offering a unique degree of concealment that deems the probability of compromise low, countersurveillance operators must still maintain effective cover for action to avoid arousing the suspicions of other individuals such as security personnel, who may take actions that compromise the operation.

In formalizing the countersurveillance plan, countersurveillance operators will inform the Principal of where they will be located at each SDP so that he will avoid moving too close in or having an unplanned contact with one of them. Given this information, the Principal must practice discipline in overcoming the natural tendency to look in their direction during the operation.

It may be necessary for countersurveillance operators to depart an SDP before the Principal in order to ensure that they are positioned at the next SDP prior to his arrival. A disadvantage of this is that it precludes their observing for surveillance as the Principal transitions from a static to mobile portion of the SDR. When possible, the SDR should be developed to provide countersurveillance operators time to observe this transition and still move to the next SDP ahead of the Principal. This can be arranged by the Principal taking a longer yet still logical route or making a short stop along the way to the SDP.

When the plan involves the same countersurveillance operators manning multiple SDPs, a plan for their disguise is also required. A professional surveillance team is well practiced in the principles of observation and operates under the assumption that countersurveillance coverage is always possible. If at any point during the course of a countersurveillance operation an operator assesses that there is the slightest possibility of scrutiny from a surveillance operator, he must execute an effective appearance change prior to continuing in the operation, or terminate participation.

The principles of disguise addressed in Appendix 2 and Appendix 8 apply to countersurveillance operators as well. In most cases, it is more effective for a countersurveillance operator to use a disguise at the beginning of the operation, because it is easier and faster to take off a disguise than to apply one. When necessary, a countersurveillance operator should forgo the coverage of an SDP in order to take the time to apply an effective disguise.

If at any point in the countersurveillance operation an operator believes that he may have been observed, even in the slightest, by a surveillance operator, he must determine the feasibility of continuing. This should be based on whether he can employ a disguise or man positions at subsequent SDPs that ensure with absolute certainty that he will not be detected. If he has any doubt, he should terminate his involvement in the operation. The countersurveillance plan must also incorporate emergency contact procedures or signals that a countersurveillance operator can use to instruct other operators to terminate the operation when he has assessed that the surveillance team may suspect countersurveillance.

Concealed body communications equipment assists coordination during a countersurveillance operation, but for security reasons, the Principal should not wear any such equipment. The countersurveillance plan may include discreet signals from the Principal to countersurveillance operators to inform them to move to the next SDP, or for other purposes such as to signal them to terminate the operation. Any signal employed should be a natural action that would not draw the suspicion of surveillance operators. It should not be a quick movement such as scratching the head or checking the watch, because countersurveillance operators' attention will be focused primarily on activities taking place around the Principal, and only periodically on the Principal himself. Any signals used should be longer-term, such as placing a newspaper under the arm, sitting at a bench, or taking off a hat.

Countersurveillance operators should rarely be required to signal the Principal during the course of an operation. In fact, requiring the Principal to observe a countersurveillance operator in order to receive a signal is an extremely poor security practice, as it may direct surveillance operators' attention to the countersurveillance operators and compromise the operation.

There are unique situations in which the nature of the surveillance threat or the purpose of the countersurveillance operation dictates that the Principal be informed at the first indication of surveillance. An example might be when the Principal is concerned with the possibility of an attack or when the purpose of countersurveillance coverage is to ensure that surveillance is not present in order to allow the Principal to conduct protected activity. Under such circumstances, the plan should incorporate a signal that does not require direct interface between the Principal and countersurveillance operators, such as a beverage can placed in a specified location that the Principal will walk by.

THE COUNTERSURVEILLANCE OPERATION

The SDR for a countersurveillance operation should begin at a stakeout location. Recall that the stakeout is a phase in which a surveillance team is particularly vulnerable to detection because it must remain in static positions for extended periods of time. A team may tend to be less vigilant in its security measures when it is certain that the Principal is inside the stakeout location. This facilitates discreet countersurveillance observation of the possible stakeout area to detect surveillance operators or vehicles.

Given an understanding of how a surveillance team transitions from the stakeout phase into the pick-up and follow, countersurveillance operators observe for these indicators as the Principal departs the stakeout location. They will position themselves based on the Principal's preplanned direction of travel from the stakeout location. In this application, countersurveillance can be very effective in identifying vehicles or individuals moving from a static to mobile status as the Principal departs the stakeout location, and noting these as possible surveillance assets.

Recall that there should be no mobile countersurveillance coverage during the mobile phase of the operation due to the security risks of countersurveillance operators mirroring the Principal's travels. A primary rule for the manning of SDPs is that countersurveillance operators must be in position at the SDP before the Principal arrives. One reason for this is that it gives them an opportunity to establish their positions with cover and concealment before the surveillance effort arrives, precluding the possibility of observation by surveillance operators who arrive with the Principal.

Although SDPs normally involve a static location for the reasons previously addressed, in some circumstances terrain may facilitate the positioning of an SDP along a mobile portion of the SDR. Recall that channelized terrain and choke points are very effective in making surveillance assets vulnerable to detection. This applies to an even greater degree to countersurveillance operations, due to the enhanced observation and detection capability involved. Countersurveillance operators will man static positions (SDPs) along a route where they can exploit these surveillance vulnerabilities.

When SDPs are positioned along mobile routes, the terrain must provide adequate concealment to countersurveillance operators and restrict the rate of movement through the area so that countersurveillance operators have time to observe and note all following foot and vehicular traffic. One example of exploiting channelized terrain in a secure manner is the use of pedestrian overpasses. Countersurveillance operators can establish secure positions from which to observe for individuals who enter the overpass after the Principal. This provides an opportunity to use vision enhancement devices or image/video capture capabilities to observe or record all individuals moving through the channelized terrain. In this particular example, countersurveillance operators should also observe individuals who opt not to use the overpass and instead travel by a less safe or less convenient route.

Operational effectiveness is the primary reason for countersurveillance operators to man their SDPs prior to the Principal's arrival. All SDPs require that the surveillance team transition from a mobile follow to a surveillance box, similar to a stakeout box. Some require that the surveillance team transition from a vehicular follow to a foot follow and then to a surveillance box. It is during all such transitions that a surveillance team is particularly vulnerable to detection, because they are periods of anxious uncertainty for the team. During such transitions, the surveillance team may compromise secure tactical discipline when outside the observation range of the Principal to ensure it maintains command of the Principal. Obviously, countersurveillance coverage is most effective when the surveillance team assumes the risk that third-party observation is not present, and acts with less tactical discipline.

An additional aspect making surveillance operators potentially vulnerable to countersurveillance coverage is communications practices. A disciplined surveillance operator rarely transmits information via concealed body communications equipment when it might be detectable by the Principal. However, countersurveillance is more effective in detecting this vulnerability because surveillance operators tend to be more careless in transmitting information when they are certain their actions are undetectable by the Principal.

A surveillance team's use of visual communications signals is particularly vulnerable to countersurveillance. Countersurveillance operators should have a field of observation that enables them to observe how signals are used and how the surveillance team interacts. All such surveillance team communications, while rarely observable by the Principal himself, are vulnerabilities that countersurveillance can capitalize on. Visual signals by a suspected surveillance operator also reduce the search area for countersurveillance operators to observe for other surveillance operators who may be receiving and reacting to these signals.

Recall that public locations are effective in drawing surveillance operators into a confining area that is suitable for surveillance detection. Public locations are equally effective for countersurveillance, provided that countersurveillance operators can ensure an appropriate degree of cover and concealment. Incorporating a public location as an SDP can be a very effective surveillance detection measure, as it forces surveillance operators into unfamiliar terrain that offers only limited options for developing cover for action. Public locations with only one entrance (chokepoint) can be used effectively as SDPs, as they channelize all following individuals through a single point, allowing for the observation of possible surveillance operators.

The number of public locations that are suitable for countersurveillance is unlimited. A restaurant is an example of one that is particularly effective.

Countersurveillance coverage of a Principal dining in a restaurant provides a degree of observation that is difficult for a lone Principal to achieve. Countersurveillance operators can observe as individual patrons enter the establishment and coordinate their seating arrangements, noting those who appear interested in the activities of the Principal while dining.

An effective tactic that can be incorporated into the countersurveillance plan involving a restaurant is to set up a dinner meeting between the Principal and another individual. In such a situation, a surveillance team will be particularly interested in placing an operator in a location that facilitates overhearing any conversation between the two. This offers unique opportunities for countersurveillance operators to observe how other patrons react to the activities of the Principal. Of particular value to surveillance detection effort is the reaction of surrounding individuals as the Principal departs the restaurant. Countersurveillance operators will observe for individuals who display particular interest, appear to communicate by a concealed communication means, or make a phone call at this same time. Countersurveillance operators should remain in the restaurant after the Principal has departed to observe for individuals who conclude their meals unnaturally and leave.

The countersurveillance plan can incorporate surveillance detection enablers based on an understanding of how a surveillance effort will react to potential covert/protected activities. A surveillance effort intent on observing protected activities conducted by the Principal will be keenly interested in activities indicative of covertly transferring material or communicating information to another individual (contact) employing a "dead drop" methodology. Common techniques to perform either of these activities are to drop an item that would appear to be trash, to place such an item into a trash container, or to stop for a period and then leave an item behind such as a paper cup at a park table or a newspaper at a street side bench. In reaction to any such circumstance, a sophisticated surveillance element will dedicate at least one surveillance asset to watch the potential "drop" location in anticipation that a contact of the Principal's will eventually "service" the drop – essentially confirming the conduct of protected activities. By incorporating such an activity into the countersurveillance plan and SDR, countersurveillance operators may be able to observe this dynamic in reaction to the Principal-orchestrated scenario. A less sophisticated (or poorly disciplined) surveillance effort may send an operator to physically examine the potential drop after the Principal has departed the area, which essentially confirms surveillance to the countersurveillance effort.

Another related activity that may be incorporated into the countersurveillance plan is based on the likelihood that a surveillance effort will take great interest in the Principal's use of a random, public mail box. Covert elements and individuals conducting protected activities will continue to communicate through the traditional postal system due to the significant security vulnerabilities of electronic mail and other web-enabled communications methods. Traditional mail can be delivered with no attributable information other than the general location from where it is marked as posted; and is therefore an effective means of communicating information that cannot not be attributed to the source once entering the delivery system. A sophisticated surveillance effort that is prepared to react to this type of potential protected activity and intent on gaining eventual access to a letter dropped by the Principal will drop a large envelope (normally manila) in the box as soon after the Principal's drop as possible. This traditional counterespionage tradecraft is employed to mark the location of the letter and segregate it from letters subsequently dropped. This method is employed as an alternative means to isolate the letter when access to the box contents is attained, assuming that any covert correspondence will have no attributable information such as a return address to assist in discovery. The observation of an individual dropping a large and readily distinguishable envelope in the box directly after the Principal delivers his letter is readily detectable by countersurveillance operators and highly indicative of surveillance.

An extension of countersurveillance coverage that is extremely sophisticated and complex is the transition from countersurveillance to an active surveillance of an identified surveillance operator. This is the epitome of reducing the hunter to the hunted, which involves employing countersurveillance to isolate a suspected surveillance operator and then following that individual to confirm surveillance and determine his identity. This is an aggressive measure to detect surveillance at its source. Obviously, it requires that countersurveillance operators be tactically capable surveillance operators as well, and that there be pre-established criteria for the termination of countersurveillance and the transition to a surveillance operation.

One final caution — and it may seem fantastic to some who have not been deep in the game — but there is also the threat/risk of counter-countersurveillance...

APPENDIX 4:

FIXED AND PROGRESSIVE SURVEILLANCE OPERATIONS

FIXED SURVEILLANCE

Fixed Surveillance consists of observing the Principal's activities at a specified location from a static position. Such operations only satisfy specific objectives because they provide limited insight into the Principal's overall activities. They are normally employed when it is suspected that the Principal will conduct *protected activities* at a specific location, such as his residence, his workplace, an associate's residence, or any other location identified as significant based on previous surveillance. Fixed positions are normally manned by surveillance operators or monitored through a remote technical means. A surveillance team may use any number of fixed positions during a fixed surveillance operation. Long-term fixed surveillance operations may use an established observation post (see Appendix 5) that enables surveillance operators to maintain constant, discreet observation of the specified location.

PROGRESSIVE SURVEILLANCE

A specific variation of the mobile surveillance is *progressive surveillance*. Progressive surveillance is the phased coverage of a Principal to determine specific travel patterns or specific routes of travel. The most notorious practitioners of progressive surveillance are terrorists and "hit men," because such coverage allows them to determine a specific travel pattern of a potential victim securely, and to identify a point along that route that is routine and vulnerable to attack. Progressive operations can only satisfy the very limited objective of determining the route or routes of travel that a Principal takes from a common point of origin. They are normally used when limited resources such as personnel or communications equipment restrict the surveillance team from conducting extended foot, vehicular, or combined operations. Progressive operations are also used when security is the highest priority, as they are the most secure method of physical surveillance because the team's degree of exposure to the Principal is limited.

The basic concept of the progressive surveillance is to follow the Principal or observe his travel from a point of origin until he reaches a particular location, at which point the surveillance is terminated. The next phase of the operation is based from the location where the previous one was terminated, and this process is repeated over time until the operational objective is satisfied.

The most secure method of progressive surveillance is one that incorporates *fixed surveillance* techniques. In such cases, the surveillance effort will establish fixed surveillance assets — normally at major travel options along the anticipated route — to incrementally develop information regarding the Principal's route(s) of travel. This method further reduces the risk of detection by negating the vulnerabilities associated with the surveillance effort traveling behind the Principal in (even a limited) a mobile follow.

APPENDIX 5:

OBSERVATION POST DETECTION AND ANTISURVEILLANCE

An observation post serves a very important purpose in support of the stakeout because it provides a secure position from which to observe a location without having to expose a surveillance vehicle or operator. It enables the surveillance team to persistently observe a location without requiring that the entire team remain on stakeout during hours of limited activity, such as at night. Whether the observation post serves the purpose of a fixed surveillance or it is used in support of a stakeout, it consists of the same general characteristics.

The primary locations for the employment of an observation post are the Principal's residence, workplace, or another location at which the Principal spends considerable time when not mobile. The fact that the observation post will be based to observe the exterior of a denied area is a major factor the Principal exploits in detection. Be it a residence, a workplace, or a similar location, the Principal will have free access to the interior of the denied area while the surveillance team is generally restricted from observing inside.

Through analysis, the Principal determines which locations a surveillance team may target through the use of an observation post. The Principal first determines the specific location around the area which the surveillance team would prioritize focus. Normally, the primary objective of an observation post around a residence is to observe the Principal enter his vehicle and drive away. Therefore, it is logical to assume that an observation post would be in position to observe the vehicle or the garage door, and possibly the primary exit the Principal is expected to use when departing the location. Observation posts may also be positioned so surveillance operators can observe activities inside location windows where possible.

In residential areas it is relatively easy to isolate possible observation post locations through the process of elimination. Although law enforcement or national investigative agencies may commission the cooperation of a neighbor to set up an observation post in the residence, this is only practiced when absolutely necessary. In a residential area where the Principal knows the neighbors, or is at least aware of who resides at specific residences, it is easy to eliminate locations as possible observation posts. In apartment complexes or commercial areas, the Principal should be able to identify a number of possible locations for observation posts. When he has done so, the Principal begins to observe the observers.

The Principal identifies a location from which he can observe the suspected observation post. An attic that affords outside observation is normally best for this purpose. Whatever location is chosen, it should be one that would not be a primary focus of surveillance observation. Assume that the surveillance team knows the layout of the location and is aware of which areas within should be the most active. The Principal analyzes the surveillance team's likely interests and positions himself in a location that is not consistent with that focus. The area should be void of any light that provides a silhouette to observers. Windows to the location should be concealed by heavy fabric or double-layered curtains to deter observation by image-enhancing optical equipment. The Principal should use a slight divide in the center of the curtains at the base of the window or one in either side of the window frame for outside observation. This process can be lengthy and most often frustrating, requiring much patience. However, a less tedious approach when employed in a discreet manner is to fix a video capture capability on the suspected location and periodically screen the recorded video.

An observation post shares many of the same principles of concealment mentioned in the previous paragraph. Surveillance operators manning an observation post will remain concealed inside the location to avoid any exposure to the Principal. Therefore, the Principal may detect such locations based on their conspicuous inactivity. Any rooms of a possible observation post that are illuminated at night can be eliminated. The Principal should observe for specific rooms that remain concealed during the day. By eliminating some rooms and identifying others as possible observation post locations in this way, the Principal can then narrow the focus of follow-on detection efforts.

The same surveillance operators cannot remain inside an observation post indefinitely. Eventually observation post teams will exchange duties, leaving themselves vulnerable to detection. This exchange normally takes place in the middle of the night, even when it may seem more likely that this would occur during the day when the Principal is away. The reason for this is that the surveillance team is not only trying to avoid drawing the attention of the Principal, but also that of neighbors who may become suspicious of unusual activity.

More aggressive active measures to be employed in the detection of observation posts include the use of infrared-detecting equipment to determine whether the opposition is using infrared devices. Another active measure is to have an anonymous package delivered to a suspected location with instructions to leave it at the door if there is no answer. This action may draw a surveillance operator to the door for observation, but it is likely that surveillance operators will leave the package in place and remain concealed. The Principal will then continue constant observation of the package because a surveillance operator will eventually emerge, probably under the concealment of darkness, and remove the package to restore a more natural appearance to the observation post location.

Even more aggressive measures include reporting an emergency, such as a civil disturbance, at the suspected observation post location. The Principal should ensure that the distress call cannot be traced to its origin. While emergency personnel respond, the Principal observes to identify individuals occupying the location. Regardless of the result, the surveillance effort will consider its observation post compromised and depart. This departure will be done without panic, in a manner which would draw no attention, and again, it will probably take place under the concealment of darkness. If there are no signs of law enforcement personnel responding to the report, then it is likely a law enforcement, or other government agency, asset (observation post).

Mobile surveillance systems may be used as observation posts when there are no fixed structures available to provide sufficient cover. Mobile observation posts normally take the form of a passenger van similar to others common to the area. Observation post vans may also have an official designation or commercial wording on the exterior to provide a plausible reason for their being in a particular area. Vans with distinctive wording can only serve a limited purpose, however, because their extended presence will eventually appear suspicious.

Mobile observation posts may also be established out of campers or trucks. A standard vehicle with remotely monitored video equipment can also be positioned as an observation post. A mobile observation post must be able to observe a specified location while not appearing conspicuous. In areas where there is a concentration of vehicles parked on the street, it is easy to blend in. In sparsely trafficked or residential areas, remaining inconspicuous is more difficult.

A fully integrated mobile system is equipped with observation, video, and photographic equipment. The equipment is installed in a manner to enable surveillance operators inside to monitor surrounding activity without physically observing out of the vehicle. Many systems have a periscope built out of the top to appear as a sun roof extension, a ventilator unit, or another standard item. The vehicle is also constructed in a manner that precludes any outside observation of the interior. The front will be completely segregated from the rear portion to prevent anyone from seeing into the rear through the windshield or front windows. The rear portion of the vehicle will either be void of windows or have windows covered by curtains, tinting, or reflective lining. To the unwitting pedestrian, this will not appear suspicious, but to the observant Principal, such characteristics are strong indicators of an observation post vehicle.

Primary considerations for the Principal in detecting an observation post vehicle, or any surveillance vehicle for that matter, are familiarity with the vehicles that are normally in the area of the possible stakeout location and an ability to identify those that are alien. Familiarity with the indigenous vehicles facilitates initial efforts to isolate possible observation post vehicles. The Principal determines locations that are appropriate for the employment of an observation post vehicle. In observing for such a vehicle, he attempts to identify those characteristics previously addressed. He focuses on any vehicle that remains in place for an extended period of time, or perhaps in the area but in a different parking location. In order to maintain a natural appearance, a surveillance operator will park the observation post vehicle and then depart, leaving it with surveillance operators who are manning the rear portion. A poorly disciplined surveillance team may park the observation vehicle and man it with the driver. If the Principal is fortunate enough to observe a driver parking a vehicle without ever departing, he has confirmed surveillance.

In areas where parking space is at a premium, the surveillance team will park the vehicle at a time of day that affords the best selection of parking spots in order to position it in an appropriate location for observation. In many areas this will be early in the morning, so the Principal should observe for vehicles that appear in the area overnight. In urban residential areas, parking is most available during the day when most residents are at work, so the Principal should take the opportunity to look for potential observation post vehicles being positioned during this timeframe. The surveillance team may park the vehicle in a location that it subsequently determines does not provide optimum observation. Although this is a poor security practice, the team may choose to move it to another location with a better vantage point. Unless the surveillance operators are extremely cavalier, they will only do so when they are certain that the Principal is not in the area to observe them. Regardless of the security practices the team employs, the Principal should be able to identify vehicles that remain in the area but not necessarily in the same location for extended periods.

The Principal should continually observe any vehicle he suspects is an observation post. Eventually a surveillance operator will return to the vehicle to move it. Additionally, surveillance operators cannot remain in an observation post vehicle for extended periods — for sanitary reasons, if nothing else. An observation post vehicle that is parked in a good location will remain while operators are rotated out. As with the observation post, the surveillance team rarely rotates operators during the day when the Principal is away from the area because this will appear suspicious to anyone else who may be observing. The team normally rotates operators only at night, when the possibility of detection is at a minimum. Thus, by maintaining constant observation of a suspected observation post vehicle, the Principal may confirm surveillance by observing operators exchanging duties.

A more aggressive detection measure to be employed is to report a suspected vehicle to law enforcement authorities. The call should be made so it cannot be traced to the Principal. The Principal will observe as police officers approach the vehicle, possibly forcing out the surveillance operators. If the vehicle is in fact a surveillance asset but passes the scrutiny of the police inquiry, the team will nevertheless consider the vehicle compromised and move it at the first secure opportunity. If the vehicle moves without ever being approached — or at least driven past by police officers — the Principal has virtually confirmed that it was a law enforcement agency observation post vehicle.

APPENDIX 6:

SURVEILLANCE AND SURVEILLANCE COUNTERMEASURES AT NIGHT

The basic surveillance and surveillance countermeasures tactics are generally the same for night operations as they are for operations wherein observation is less restricted. However, darkness does impose many additional considerations that must be anticipated and prepared for. In addition to advanced night observation techniques, the Principal must understand the nuances associated with vehicular and foot surveillance countermeasures practices at night.

OBSERVATION AT NIGHT

Observation is significantly limited at night due the obvious physiological limitations of the eyes. Visual illusions are also common when observing at night. An understanding of the principles of darkness adaptation assists in the effectiveness of night observation.

Darkness adaptation is the process by which the human eye increases in sensitivity to low levels of light. Since vision is made possible by reflected light, effective observation is directly proportional to the degree of light available. Although individuals vary in degrees and rates of dark adaptation, eye sensitivity generally increases about 10,000 times during the first 30 minutes in the dark. After that point eye sensitivity increases very little. Therefore, an individual's natural night vision reaches its highest clarity 30 minutes after beginning low-light observation. Visual sharpness at night is about one-seventh of what it is during the day, significantly reducing visual acuity. This dictates that object identification at night is generally limited to silhouettes and forms. Depth and color perception are also affected. At night, color perception is generally limited to distinguishing between light and dark colors, and even this is dependent on the intensity of reflected light.

Adaptation is adversely affected by exposure to bright lights such as matches and headlights. In order to maintain darkness adaptation, the eyes should be covered to avoid the effects of such lights. Recall that initial adaptation takes up to 30 minutes, but recovery from exposure to bright lights can take up to 45 minutes.

Adaptation to darkness is adversely affected by the use of night vision devices. If full adaptation is made before using night vision devices, however, it can be regained within two minutes after their use. The use of night vision devices decreases the senses of hearing and smell due to the concentration required for effective sight.

There are two methods of observation that can be used to enhance visual effectiveness in darkness. Both are based on the fact that central viewing, or looking directly at an object, is ineffective at night due to the night blind spot that exists during low illumination. At night, it is essential to avoid looking directly at a faintly visible object because of this night blind spot.

Scanning is a method which enables the Principal to overcome many of the physiological limitations of the eyes as well as reducing confusing visual illusions in darkness. This method consists of scanning from left to right, or right to left, using a slow, standardized eye movement. Figure 22 depicts two typical scanning patterns to enhance night observation of a target object (T) (See Figure 22 next page).

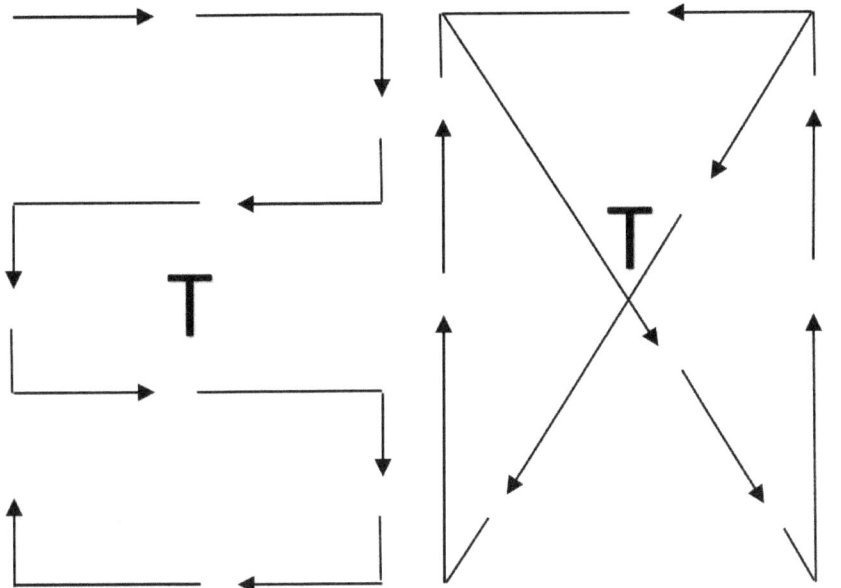

FIGURE 22

Two typical scanning patterns to enhance night observation

Off-center viewing is another way to avoid the limitations of central viewing at night. This technique consists of viewing an object by looking slightly above, below, or to either side rather than directly at it. Figure 23 depicts points of observation (circles) around the target object (T). Even when off-center viewing is used, the image of an object becomes a solid, bleached-out tone when viewed for longer than three to five seconds. For this reason, it is important to shift the eyes regularly from one off-center point to another to maintain an uninterrupted peripheral field of vision (See Figure 23 next page).

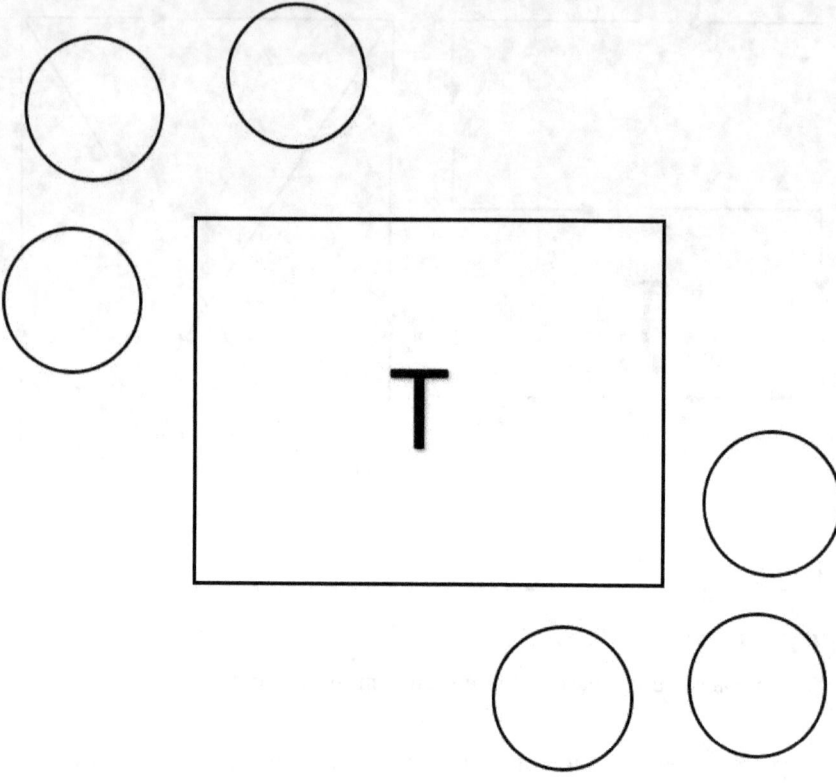

FIGURE 23

Points of observation around the target object for use in off-center viewing

VEHICULAR SURVEILLANCE DETECTION AND ANTISURVEILLANCE AT NIGHT

Vehicular surveillance detection at night can be a challenge for the Principal, unless he draws the surveillance effort into an open and lightly trafficked area that is optimal for detection. In such circumstances, it is nearly impossible for surveillance vehicles to remain anonymous, even if they are adept at operating without vehicle lights projecting. However, the orchestration of these circumstances may be perceived as surveillance detection, and any security conscious effort would likely terminate coverage under these conditions.

In dense traffic the lights of surrounding vehicles can make the surveillance team virtually invisible to the Principal. In these conditions, surveillance vehicles are likely compelled to follow very closely behind the Principal unless the Principal vehicle has a very distinguishable rear light signature. As the hour gets later and the traffic density decreases, the surveillance vehicle's lights make it virtually impossible for it to remain discreet, but following surveillance vehicles should be able to securely increase following distance in these conditions. In open areas or when traffic is so light that vehicle lights can be seen at a substantial distance, a surveillance becomes more detectable by actions such as *mirroring* and *convoying*.

Darkness gives the Principal traveling by vehicle a significant advantage over a possible surveillance team. A primary consideration to facilitate *antisurveillance* at night is to drive a vehicle that does not have a unique or readily distinguishable rear light signature. At night, a surveillance team must rely on this feature for recognition, so by projecting a signature that blends in with those of other vehicles on the road, the Principal is more capable of effective antisurveillance. In dense traffic, it is difficult for a surveillance team to maintain command of the Principal if he does not have a unique rear light profile. The Principal can maneuver through dense traffic to make it impossible for the team to distinguish his rear light signature from that of other vehicles on the road. The tactics associated with accelerating when entering and breaking out of dense traffic are equally effective at night.

In open or desolate areas, the Principal should exploit the restrictions imposed on a surveillance team. The open terrain, which makes following surveillance vehicles detectable from a greater distance by the projection of their headlights, forces them to increase their following distance. This increases the Principal's antisurveillance options. The previously addressed tactic of accelerating after entering a blind bend or hill in the road becomes even more effective with the increased following distance night surveillance dictates. An overt tactic the Principal can employ in this situation is to kill the vehicle lights after eluding the line of sight observation of all following vehicles. Through previous planning, the Principal will have identified an appropriate location to turn into that is undetectable to following vehicles. To negate the effectiveness of a surveillance box along the previously established route, the Principal should depart the area by another route.

FOOT SURVEILLANCE DETECTION AND ANTISURVEILLANCE AT NIGHT

The conduct of *foot surveillance detection* at night incorporates specific factors that are characteristic of darkness. Observation is significantly limited at night, which affects both the Principal and the surveillance effort, but the Principal can employ darkness adaptation and observation techniques to minimize the physiological effects of darkness. Although surveillance detection is limited somewhat under such circumstances, the Principal can exploit the limitations that darkness also imposes on the surveillance team.

Illumination from the moon varies based on the moon phase of the illumination cycle. Depending on the moon phase, illumination can range from very bright (full moon) to zero (pitch-dark). Based on surveillance detection objectives, the Principal may choose to conduct surveillance detection when the moon phase is appropriate to meet the desired objectives.

Despite the enhanced degree of concealment that darkness provides the surveillance team, the hours of darkness are almost exclusively characterized by less pedestrian traffic, unless the Principal chooses to conduct surveillance detection in an area that remains active at night. The decreased traffic decreases the degree of cover available, which in effect enables the Principal to isolate surveillance operators for detection in the appropriate circumstances. Additionally, the enhanced concealment provided by darkness may give a following foot surveillance operator an increased sense of security, which the Principal can exploit when applicable.

Observation is not limited to the sense of sight. Due to physiological factors, when one or more of the body's senses are impaired, perception of the other senses is intensified to compensate for the ones being degraded. In darkness, an enhanced sense of hearing facilitates observation because sight is obstructed while hearing is enhanced due to a generally quieter environment. Due to the physiological factors noted, the sense of smell may also enhance observation at night.

A surveillance team may employ night observation devices to overcome the effects of darkness. Night observation devices either magnify existing illumination for enhanced vision or generate their own light source through an infrared beam. Many night vision devices emit light at the source through the eyepiece unless measures are taken for concealment. In creating their own light source, infrared night vision devices emit a red beam that is almost undetectable, but a dull red light does appear when shone directly into the eyes of an individual. The Principal can detect the use of an active night vision capability under these circumstances.

Limited visibility at night generally dictates that surveillance operators follow in a manner that minimizes the possibility of losing sight of the Principal, once attained, even momentarily. A surveillance operator who is proficient in the principles of darkness adaptation and observation understands the importance of maintaining constant command at night. Night observation techniques such as scanning and off-center viewing (addressed previously) are much more effective for observing an already identified object than for finding an object in darkness. This generally dictates closer coverage unless moonlight or other illumination mitigates darkness.

The enhanced degree of concealment and decreased visual acuity are factors the Principal exploits in conducting *active surveillance detection* at night. Distance perception is degraded at night, which enables the Principal to fluctuate his speed in order to bring a surveillance operator closer or force him to hasten his pace. A significant increase in speed has the same effect as accelerating into a blind turn. To maintain or reestablish observation in darkness, a surveillance operator may bear down on the Principal blindly and react in a suspicious manner when he finds himself uncomfortably close. Additionally, the more aggressive pace of a surveillance operator attempting to close distance on the Principal may be audibly detectable.

At night, the Principal can use the characteristics of darkness to employ the concepts of a blind turn in many more locations, so the tactic becomes much more flexible. Surveillance operators may react more aggressively to any circumstance of lost visibility at night, due to previously addressed factors. The number of specific examples in which the Principal can use darkness to drastically decrease his rate of speed or stop in a location that is undetectable to surveillance operator for surveillance detection purposes is relatively unlimited.

Dusk and darkness provide natural concealment that enables *antisurveillance* by foot. Unless a surveillance effort employs state-of-the-art night vision capabilities in a discreet and effective manner, the hours of darkness provide the best opportunities for foot antisurveillance for a determined Principal. Although the cloak of darkness provides a wide variety of antisurveillance options to the resourceful Principal, there are some fundamental factors that further enhance the effort.

By traveling through poorly lit areas, the Principal can readily escape by any number of options. The Principal may choose to conduct antisurveillance when the moon phase provides low illumination when appropriate to meet the desired objectives.

Scanning vision techniques for increased darkness acuity are most effective with an already established and relatively static object. Therefore, movement is an antisurveillance enabler at night. The sense of sound is enhanced at night so the Principal should ensure that clothing (e.g. shoes), jewelry, or other items do not project audible/distinguishable sounds.

If the Principal does identify the source of a potential night vision devise, the projection of a bright light toward the source will "wash" the devise and render it temporarily ineffective.

APPENDIX 7:

SURVEILLANCE TACTICS AND SURVEILLANCE COUNTERMEASURES ON PUBLIC TRANSPORTATION

Travel by public transportation (e.g. bus, taxi, train, plane) requires that a surveillance effort execute modified tactics of combined foot and vehicular surveillance. This is necessary because foot surveillance always precedes or resumes when the Principal either enters or exits public transportation. With the exception of taxi and long distance bus travel, a standard vehicular surveillance cannot be conducted on public transportation systems due to their unique methods of movement. When modes of transportation follow an established route and schedule, the surveillance team will use this information to anticipate the Principal's travels.

The surveillance of *city buses* involves a completely unique surveillance methodology. Due to the generally slow movement and frequent stopping of most buses, a surveillance team will attempt to position itself ahead of the Principal's bus route because it is virtually impossible to discreetly maintain a vehicular follow from the rear. The surveillance team will match the bus number to city route maps to determine destinations and stop locations. The team will attempt to place a surveillance operator on the bus with the Principal but will avoid doing so at the stop where the Principal boards. An operator will board at a stop further along the route, or if there is time, at one prior to the Principal's. The vehicular surveillance team will then position itself at stops along the route before the scheduled arrival of the bus in anticipation of the Principal's eventual exit.

As the Principal waits at a bus stop with the intention of boarding a bus, he should observe people who reach the bus stop after he has. Although they may be surveillance operators, a tactically sound surveillance team will attempt to either have an operator board the bus prior to the Principal or at one of the stops after his, making the appearance of a surveillance operator less suspicious. One overt method of surveillance detection involving public buses is for the Principal to remain at a bus stop and not enter the bus as other individuals at the stop do. Obviously, anyone who does the same should be regarded as a possible surveillance operator. At stops that service multiple bus routes, the Principal must be aware of the various routes in order to determine which individuals have remained at the stop after all possible buses have passed.

As the Principal enters the bus he should observe the passengers — particularly those seated to the rear. He should also observe people who board at subsequent stops. When conducting surveillance on a bus, a surveillance operator will attempt to sit to the rear of the bus in order to observe the Principal, thus preventing observation by the Principal, who is likely facing forward when seated. To counter this, the Principal should sit as far to the rear of the bus as possible to observe individuals who board at subsequent stops. If a surveillance operator is already sitting to the rear as the Principal selects a seat in the same proximity, this will certainly make the operator uncomfortable and may make him act in an unnatural manner or exit the bus quickly to avoid exposure. If the Principal is already at the rear when a surveillance operator enters the bus, the operator will be forced to sit closer to the front to avoid getting too close to the Principal. As passengers enter the bus, the Principal should observe for anyone who begins moving toward the rear but stops suddenly to sit when noticing that the Principal is sitting at the rear of the bus. Sitting at the rear of the bus also better enables the Principal to observe for the possibility of a poorly disciplined effort that follows the bus with a surveillance vehicle that parks somewhere behind the bus at each stop and then again follows the bus between stops. Alternatively, the Principal could opt to sit near the front of the bus and observe for individuals who select seats in the rear while foregoing more convenient available seats.

By establishing a vantage point from the rear of the vehicle, the Principal can conduct overt surveillance detection by determining if any passengers remain on the bus beyond a point along the route at which a given individual's continued presence becomes illogical and suspicious. The most overt such method of surveillance detection is for the Principal to stay on the bus through the last stop and identify anyone who has also followed this illogical pattern. A surveillance operator who is not familiar with the bus route may be easily exposed by this tactic. To ensure the effectiveness of this tactic, the Principal must be familiar with the route and observe all individuals who enter the bus after him.

There are unique tactics involved with the vehicular surveillance of a bus when the Principal is a passenger because a standard vehicular surveillance follow is not secure due to the bus's frequent stops. Based on a knowledge of the bus's route, the surveillance team will concentrate on the forward positioning of surveillance vehicles to have surveillance operators available to take to the ground for a foot follow immediately upon the Principal's exit. This requires that surveillance vehicles maneuver ahead of the bus to establish their positions. When there are few surveillance vehicles involved or there are too many bus stops to be covered, surveillance vehicles may be forced to pass the bus more than once during the course of the route. The Principal should therefore be observant of vehicles that meet this profile.

Generally, a surveillance operator will remain on the bus until after the Principal has exited if there are other surveillance assets in support. For this reason, anyone who exits the bus at stops prior to the Principal's can be eliminated as possible surveillance operators. The exception to this rule is when the Principal is traveling to the last stop on the specified route. In this situation, the surveillance operator may exit the bus at the next to last stop to avoid getting off the bus at the last stop with the Principal, so the Principal should be particularly observant of passengers who exit at the next to last stop. Obviously, the Principal should also be observant of those who exit the bus at the same stop as he does.

As the Principal exits the bus he should observe for indications of a foot stakeout or the transition to a foot surveillance follow. When the Principal takes a bus to a specific location, it is a logical assumption that he will return to the same bus stop for the return trip after the purpose of his travel is concluded. The surveillance team will operate under this assumption while the Principal is on the ground, particularly if it loses sight of the Principal during the conduct of the foot surveillance. For this reason, the Principal should observe for indications of a stakeout box when returning to the bus stop.

Surveillance on *mass transit systems* such as subways or metros presents challenges which are among the most difficult for a surveillance effort to mitigate tactically. In many cases, the impediments caused by underground stations and travel lines on a surveillance team's communications capabilities are antisurveillance enablers. Even when surveillance operators have radio communications equipment they may be unable to communicate from the station to the team outside, which may require that an operator moving above ground relay information. Mobile phones may also have degraded communication while underground. Even when the foot team inside the station is able to inform them which train the Principal enters, the vehicular team outside must attempt to deduce which stops along the route may be the Principal's destination. Multiple subway train exchanges virtually destroy team integrity. For this reason, the foot surveillance team will attempt to place as many operators on the subway train with the Principal as possible, entering with him and exiting behind him, to maintain integrity and a surveillance capability at his destination.

Surveillance detection on subways and commuter trains employs many of the same concepts addressed with public bus travel. Generally, the density of traffic associated with subway travel makes detection more difficult than with buses. One advantage in surveillance detection on the subway is that a surveillance team will attempt to place multiple operators on the Principal's train, although not all operators will be within observation range of the Principal. Surveillance operators on the train will invariably disembark at the same location as the Principal. The well-documented Hollywood tactics of surveillance detection involving jumping off a subway train to detect a surveillance operator who mirrors this activity are overt and only marginally effective against a sophisticated surveillance effort. However, any Principal who meets the criteria of an overt target, as addressed in Chapter 2, can certainly use public transportation as an effective means of active surveillance detection. During high travel times (rush hours), the Principal can move in a manner contrary to (against) the natural flow of movement to identify individuals who mirror this irregular movement or to evade surveillance in dense pedestrian traffic.

Subway stations provide a high concentration of people, choke points, and channelized terrain. These locations give the Principal an opportunity to blend with the populace while moving to high-speed avenues of escape (antisurveillance) on the subway trains. Subway stations impose unique restrictions on a surveillance team because it is virtually impossible to maintain team integrity in such an environment if the Principal executes multiple interchanges. Although an overt antisurveillance tactic in design, multiple changes between subway trains further degrades the team's integrity and eventually make continued surveillance impossible without detection.

A primary tenet the Principal must appreciate is that when the surveillance team loses the Principal when he is traveling by commuter public transportation (bus or subway), it will normally return to the location of lost command in anticipation that he will eventually return via the same route. In order to avoid this standard lost command stakeout tactic, the Principal should return via an alternate route, unless it is appropriate for him to pick-up surveillance again to decrease the team's suspicion of antisurveillance tactics (for example, after conducting unobserved *protected activities*).

Many passive surveillance detection tactics are similar for *plane travel*, ticketed (long-distance) *bus travel*, and ticketed (long-distance) *train travel*. In these cases, a surveillance team will likely make an effort to determine in advance the Principal's travel itinerary. When he makes his travel arrangements at the station just prior to travel, a surveillance operator will need to be close enough to the ticket window or kiosk to overhear/observe the transaction as the Principal purchases his ticket. For this reason, the Principal should note and commit to memory any individual who may be, explicably or not, within observation range of the transaction. This concept is also applicable to airplane travel when the Principal is either purchasing a ticket or checking in his luggage.

When traveling on a plane, train, or bus, the Principal should observe all individuals for subsequent recognition. Many trains are compartmented, which assists in the isolation of potential surveillance operators, but possible operators on the train are not limited to those traveling within observation range of the Principal. Longer rides provide the Principal more opportunities to identify individuals who may be giving him more attention than is warranted or appear conspicuous in some other way.

Although possible by other means of public transportation, due to the relative length of passenger bus, train, and plane travel which facilitates plausible opportunities for personal interaction, there is a relatively higher potential that a surveillance effort may opt to place a surveillance operator "up against" the Principal in order to elicit information or establish a relationship (See Chapter 5).

One antisurveillance technique by train or bus is for the Principal to telegraph what his destination is, or provide other indicators of where his intended destination is, and then exit the train/bus at a stop prior to this destination. Very remote stations provide excellent opportunities to observe for potential surveillance operators also departing the train or bus.

If the Principal is flying and his flight plans were not previously disclosed, it will be virtually impossible to have a vehicular surveillance capability at his destination unless another surveillance element can be contacted for support. Under such circumstances, if the team intends to continue the follow at the destination, it must place as many operators on the plane as possible. For train and bus travel, the route may be one which allows the surveillance team to send vehicles to the destination to either meet or catch up to the foot team. Again, the team will attempt to place as many operators on the train or bus as possible, unless the exact destination is known with a high degree of certainty and it is assessed as unlikely that the Principal would conduct *protected activities* while traveling. At the destination of either a plane, train, or bus, if the team has transported communications equipment, operators can rent vehicles for a limited vehicular surveillance capability. As the Principal disembarks the plane, train, or bus, he should observe for indications of a surveillance box and the subsequent pick-up.

When it is feasible that the surveillance effort may have a vehicular follow capability at the point of destination, the Principal my rent a vehicle and conduct surveillance detection and antisurveillance measures as appropriate. Alternatively, leveraging a taxi to facilitate surveillance countermeasures is another available option.

The surveillance of a *taxi* is basically the same as standard vehicular surveillance if the surveillance team has vehicles to perform the surveillance follow. If the team does not have its own vehicles, the only available option may be to have one or more taxis following the taxi in which the Principal is traveling. This tactic is relatively risky in that most taxi drivers will be alerted to a following taxi and may alert the passenger (Principal) regarding this suspicious occurrence.

Traveling by taxi does not preclude active surveillance detection. Passive observation is difficult because the Principal does not have the range of mirrors normally available. He has little to lose, however, by asking the taxi driver to observe for indications of surveillance. He simply tells the taxi driver that he suspects surveillance and that assistance in detection will be rewarded. Taxi drivers are generally good sources for observation because they are familiar with standard traffic patterns and can readily identify anything that appears suspicious. If the Principal is particularly concerned with the possibility of surveillance, he can instruct the taxi driver in surveillance detection maneuvers. This also provides a somewhat plausible reason for the use of overt tactics, because the surveillance team will likely attribute aggressive maneuvers to the erratic driving typical of many taxi drivers. He can also commission a taxi driver to conduct antisurveillance maneuvers, as detailed in Chapter 12.

APPENDIX 8:

DISGUISE AND DECEPTION

Disguise and deception can enhance antisurveillance because a surveillance team must recognize the Principal in order to follow him. The Principal can manipulate the concepts of recognition that a surveillance team relies on to maintain observation to elude surveillance. Surveillance operators establish a mental picture of the Principal, based primarily on previous observations, which they come to rely upon for identification during the surveillance operation. The Principal can deceive the surveillance effort by establishing an appearance that is not consistent with this frame of reference. The Principal leverages an understanding of the concepts of observation, as detailed in Appendix 2, to facilitate disguise and deception for antisurveillance purposes.

A surveillance team relies primarily on features, form, dress, and other mannerisms for recognition. It is difficult for operators to rely on features exclusively because this requires that they get too close to the Principal. Mannerisms are the most easily overlooked aspect of changing appearance. A surveillance team uses mannerisms such as bearing, pace of motion, posture, and form for recognition because these are unique to the Principal, remain consistent without a conscious effort to alter them, and can be observed from a distance. For this reason, it is essential that the Principal alter mannerisms to complement and make any other method of disguise effective. Recognition of form and mannerisms develops as the surveillance team has more opportunities to observe the Principal. Dress is a variable, but most people maintain a standard style of dress that makes them somewhat distinguishable. Many people also wear certain items such as coats, hats, and shoes with more regularity than others.

The Principal can employ any number of appearance alterations and disguise methods. Baggy or loose-fitting clothes can alter the form, and filling them out with materials to appear larger or bulkier enhances this effect even further. Mannerisms can be altered by such methods as changing posture and pace of motion. Altering features is more complex and time-consuming. The simplest methods are to dye, cut, or restyle hair. This includes shaving any facial hair that might alter appearance significantly. Wigs offer another way to disguise hair. More complicated methods of altering features primarily involve applying facial makeup, which is available at any theatrical supply store.

Disguise is a very aggressive method of antisurveillance. The Principal must ensure that the use of disguise is complete, because if the surveillance team detects it, antisurveillance is confirmed. This dictates that if the Principal alters one aspect of his appearance, he should make an effort to alter all aspects. For example, it serves little purpose to alter facial appearance but wear clothing or jewelry that the surveillance team would readily identify.

Perhaps the most effective form of deception is the employment of a decoy vehicle as an antisurveillance method to elude the vehicle stakeout box. Deception is an option for avoiding stakeout detection when the stakeout is based around a location with a parking area that the surveillance team cannot observe, such as a residence with an enclosed garage, a large business parking garage, or a secured compound facility. A surveillance team depends significantly on the Principal's vehicle for identification of the Principal himself. It is normally difficult to observe each vehicle leaving a denied location and identify whether the Principal is the driver or a passenger. In fact, in many circumstances, although operators are unable to confirm that the Principal is driving his vehicle, they will pick-up and follow it when initially observed without hesitation, assuming he is inside as usual. Given this likelihood, the Principal can elude surveillance by driving out of the denied location in a different vehicle than the one he used to enter. The use of disguise makes this virtually undefeatable. Another option is for a third party to drive the Principal out of the denied area in a vehicle that is not known to the surveillance team. Again, the use of disguise makes this tactic virtually undefeatable, and if the Principal conceals himself by hiding in the trunk or ducking down in the seats, it will be absolutely effective. And as a final variation, a third party could depart the location driving the Principal's vehicle, and then the Principal can depart the location directly after the surveillance team would have picked up the decoy vehicle and began the follow.

About the Author

Aden C. Magee is an internationally renowned expert on full-spectrum threats to our way of life. He has performed as an expert advisor to senior officials at the highest echelons of the U.S. government, where he has been recognized as the preeminent expert on full-spectrum threats to many priority U.S. national security interests, to include threats to the national critical infrastructure protection and nuclear weapons security programs.

Mr. Magee is a career Counterintelligence Agent who served on the front lines in the closing years of the Cold War, and then shaped clandestine tradecraft to meet the challenges of the new age. As a shadow warrior, Mr. Magee directed surveillance and neutralization efforts against the most sophisticated foreign espionage and terrorist organizations, and has executed covert operations in denied areas that required the detection and evasion/neutralization of hostile operators.

Mr. Magee is a widely published author of threat analysis studies and other security-related think-pieces, but his most widely read works are his three previous books produced under his subsidiary ACMIV Security Services.

Aden C. Magee is a retired U.S. Army Officer and a veteran of foreign wars.

www.ingramcontent.com/pod-product-compliance
Lightning Source LLC
Chambersburg PA
CBHW070638290526
45790CB00001B/127